Working with Sexual Attraction in Psychotherapy Practice and Supervision

Working with Sexual Attraction in Psychotherapy Practice and Supervision addresses some of the challenges associated with sexual attraction in psychotherapy practice and supervision, as well as within services, and helps therapists, supervisors, and managers to navigate them with openness and self-reflection.

The book focuses on practical and applied issues, using a relational humanistic-integrative theoretical approach as a backdrop for understanding. Split into three parts, it deals with issues related to clinical practice, supervision, and ethical issues. Chapters support in-depth exploration in all three arenas of practice and are completed by editors providing a reflective summary.

Enriched with case examples and research written by senior relational practitioners, the book will be beneficial to therapists, supervisors, and service managers in the field of psychotherapy.

Biljana van Rijn is a psychotherapist, supervisor, and author. She works at Metanoia Institute in London, where she heads a Faculty for Research Strategy and Innovation, and teaches. She also practices as a Transactional Analysis Psychotherapist and supervisor, and a Counselling Psychologist. Biljana has established a long-standing research clinic at Metanoia Institute with an emphasis on routine outcomes evaluation of humanistic and integrative psychotherapies.

Jasenka Lukac-Greenwood is a Chartered Psychologist and an Integrative Psychotherapist, working in a variety of self-employed roles: as a therapist in private practice, as a visiting lecturer, and as an organisational consultant and coach. She has a particular interest in understanding and working with gender dynamics at work, which instigated her doctoral research and inspired this book.

Working with Sexual Attraction in Psychotherapy Practice and Supervision

A Humanistic-Relational Approach

Edited by
Biljana van Rijn
and Jasenka Lukac-Greenwood

LONDON AND NEW YORK

First published 2021
by Routledge
2 Park Square, Milton Park, Abingdon, Oxon OX14 4RN

and by Routledge
52 Vanderbilt Avenue, New York, NY 10017

Routledge is an imprint of the Taylor & Francis Group, an informa business

© 2021 selection and editorial matter, Biljana van Rijn and Jasenka Lukac-Greenwood individual chapters, the contributors

The right of Biljana van Rijn and Jasenka Lukac-Greenwood to be identified as the authors of the editorial material, and of the authors for their individual chapters, has been asserted in accordance with sections 77 and 78 of the Copyright, Designs and Patents Act 1988.

All rights reserved. No part of this book may be reprinted or reproduced or utilised in any form or by any electronic, mechanical, or other means, now known or hereafter invented, including photocopying and recording, or in any information storage or retrieval system, without permission in writing from the publishers.

Trademark notice: Product or corporate names may be trademarks or registered trademarks, and are used only for identification and explanation without intent to infringe.

British Library Cataloguing-in-Publication Data
A catalogue record for this book is available from the British Library

Library of Congress Cataloging-in-Publication Data
Names: Rijn, Biljana van, editor. | Lukac-Greenwood, Jasenka, editor.
Title: Working with sexual attraction in psychotherapy practice and
supervision: a humanistic-relational approach / edited by Biljana van Rijn and
Jasenka Lukac-Greenwood.
Description: Abingdon, Oxon; New York, NY: Routledge, 2020. |
Includes bibliographical references and index. |
Summary: "Working with Sexual Attraction in Psychotherapy Practice and Supervision addresses some of the challenges associated with sexual attraction in psychotherapy practice and supervision, as well as within services, and helps therapists, supervisors and managers to navigate them with openness and self-reflection. The book focuses on practical and applied issues, using a relational humanistic - integrative theoretical approach as a backdrop for understanding. Split into three parts, it deals with issues related to clinical practice, supervision and ethical issues. Chapters support in-depth exploration in all three arenas of practice and are completed by editors providing a reflective summary.
Enriched with case examples and research written by senior relational practitioners, the book will be beneficial to therapists, supervisors, and service managers in the field of psychotherapy"— Provided by publisher.
Identifiers: LCCN 2020014114 (print) | LCCN 2020014115 (ebook) |
ISBN 9780367250720 (hardback) | ISBN 9780367250768 (paperback) |
ISBN 9780429285851 (ebook)
Subjects: MESH: Psychotherapy—methods | Humanism | Psychotherapy—ethics |
Sexual Behavior—ethics | Professional-Patient Relations—ethics
Classification: LCC RC480.5 (print) | LCC RC480.5 (ebook) |
NLM WM 420 | DDC 616.89/14—dc23
LC record available at https://lccn.loc.gov/2020014114
LC ebook record available at https://lccn.loc.gov/2020014115

ISBN: 978-0-367-25072-0 (hbk)
ISBN: 978-0-367-25076-8 (pbk)
ISBN: 978-0-429-28585-1 (ebk)

Typeset in Times New Roman
by codeMantra

Contents

List of contributors — vii

Editors' Introduction — 1

PART 1
Clinical practice: sexual attraction in the therapy room — 17

1.1 Let's talk about sex: female therapists' experiences of working with male clients who are sexually attracted to them — 19
JASENKA LUKAC-GREENWOOD

1.2 Mapping the 'erotic' in the therapeutic relationship — 39
PAUL HITCHINGS

1.3 The meaning of the asking — 55
JAMES AGAR AND BRIAN FENTON

1.4 Gender identity and sexual attraction in the therapeutic encounter — 76
MICHELLE BRIDGMAN

1.5 Editor's summary and reflection of the themes related to practice issues — 89
JASENKA LUKAC-GREENWOOD

PART 2
Sexual attraction and sexual identity in supervision — 97

2.1 The supervisory dimension — 99
JILL HUNT AND CHARLOTTE SILLS

2.2 The disturbance and comfort of forbidden conversations (sexuality and erotic forces in relational psychotherapy supervision) 115
CAROLE SHADBOLT

2.3 Sexual orientation in the supervisory relationship: exploring fears and fantasies when different sexual orientations are present in the client/therapist and/or supervisory dyad 134
DI HODGSON

2.4 Editor's Summary and reflection on sexual attraction and orientation in supervision 152
BILJANA VAN RIJN

PART 3
Ethics: preventing and dealing with transgressions 159

3.1 Sexual transgressions and transgressing gender and sexuality 161
STEVEN B. SMITH

3.2 Firefighting: managing sexual ruptures and transgressions within counselling and psychotherapy services 177
BILJANA VAN RIJN

3.3 An ethical container for erotic confusion 195
SUE EUSDEN

3.4 Editor's Summary and reflection on ethical practice and prevention of transgressions 216
BILJANA VAN RIJN

Index 223

Contributors

James Agar, MSc, STA(P), MBACP Snr. Accred. Supervisor, is a United Kingdom Council for Psychotherapy (UKCP) registered psychotherapist and clinical supervisor who works in full-time private practice in the South-West of England. He has also practiced as a counsellor, psychotherapist, and supervisor since 1988 with organisations in higher education, social services, residential addiction rehab, trauma services, and eating disorders. He has a keen interest in the centrality of shame in human experience and the value of earned and learned secure attachment and wisdom across the life span.

jamie@agarward.myzen.co.uk

Michelle Bridgman, MSc, is a UKCP registered psychotherapist, registered Clinical Hypnotherapist, and experienced Gestalt Psychotherapist with over 25 years of experience in private practice and hospital settings. Working with clients from diverse cultural and social-economic backgrounds has provided her with a firm base from which to work in the most demanding fields. She has been working with clients presenting with Gender Dysphoria for over 20 years, particularly with young people and their families. Michelle is a regular commentator on trans issues in the media and frequently speaks at conferences and seminars. She is married with two daughters and a granddaughter.

shelleybridgman@gmail.com

Sue Eusden, MA, TSTA-P, is a UKCP-registered psychotherapist. She maintains a private practice in the Cotswolds and a supervision practice in Edinburgh. She is a member of Faculty for Psychotherapy and Counselling at Metanoia Institute in London and teaches at other establishments across Europe. Sue has just completed her doctorate research on the experience of asking for help. She has delivered several keynote speeches and training workshops exploring how therapists use supervision and seek the help they need, particularly in difficult times. Sue is a founding member of the International Association of Relational Transactional

Analysis and the author of several journal articles and book chapters. In 2019 she was awarded the European Association for Transactional Analysis Gold Medal.

Sue.Eusden@metanoia.ac.uk

Brian Fenton, Psych BSc (Hons), MSc Psychotherapy, Post Grad Dip in Clinical Supervision, is a UKCP registered psychotherapist and supervisor. He has a particular interest in the development of Relational Transactional Analysis and has published works on both relational psychotherapy and relational supervision. Brian has gained extensive experience through working in private practice and in the public sector. He has worked in Primary Care as a GP counsellor for five years, specialising in addiction concerns, and in Secondary Care as a highly specialist psychotherapist, where he provided one-to-one and group psychotherapy for 12 years. He also worked for 15 years as a psychotherapist for young people placed within the care system. He currently has a private psychotherapy and supervision practice based in Whitstable in Kent, and provides training and supervision to psychotherapists, counsellors, and clinical and counselling psychologists.

brianjfenton@yahoo.co.uk

Paul Hitchings M.Sc., B.Sc., PGCE, Chartered Psychologist (British Psychological Society), Registered Psychologist (Health Care Professions Council – UK), Registered Euro Psychologist, and Integrative Psychotherapist (MIAHIP). Paul has worked as a practitioner and educator in the field of Counselling Psychology for over three decades. He is a past Chair of the BPS Division of Counselling Psychology. During the last twenty years, he has been primary tutor on various Masters and Doctoral level programs at Metanoia Institute in West London and was Chief Assessor, for the British Psychological Society Qualification in Counselling Psychology. Paul relocated from London to Dublin in 2015 where he works as a private practitioner with individuals and couples. He also provides consultation (Clinical supervision) to other practitioners in the field and has published in this area.

paulhitchings@me.com

Di Hodgson is a psychotherapist, supervisor, and trainer with 30 years of experience. She is the Head of the MSc in Gestalt psychotherapy at the Metanoia Institute, UK. Di is a member of the editorial team of the British Gestalt Journal. She is a regular facilitator of workshops at National and International Conferences, and is a visiting trainer and examiner at several institutes across Europe. For many years she also worked as an organisational consultant and coach. She has been a member and chair of several committees on equality and diversity. She is the author of several book chapters and articles.

Diane.Hodgson@metanoia.ac.uk

Jill Hunt, MSc, is a Teaching and Supervising Transactional Analyst, UKCP Registered Psychotherapist, and BACP Accredited supervisor. Although Jill has recently retired from clinical practice, she worked for many years in West Sussex and London as a psychotherapist, counsellor, and clinical supervisor. Jill has extensive experience as a supervisor and a tutor, and has worked at both Metanoia Institute and Cascade Associates. She specialised in clinical supervision and devised and taught a supervision course for Transactional Analysts at Metanoia Institute. Jill has an interest in the process and the use of the supervisory relationship in the development of psychotherapy. She also has a long-standing interest in the importance of the erotic and sexual attraction in the therapeutic relationship.

jillshunt@starfire.org.uk

Jasenka Lukac-Greenwood is a Chartered Psychologist and an Integrative Psychotherapist, working in a variety of self-employed roles: as a therapist in private practice, as a visiting lecturer, and as an organisational consultant and coach. She has a particular interest in understanding and working with gender dynamics at work, which instigated her Doctoral research and inspired this book.

jlukacgreenwood@gmail.com

Carole Shadbolt, MSc (psych), CTA, TSTA (psychotherapy), Dip. Supervision (Metanoia), CQSW, Dip. App. Soc. Sci., lives and practises in the United Kingdom. In a career of over 30 years, she originally trained as a social worker and worked both as a generic social worker and later as a psychiatric social worker at the Maudsley Hospital in South London. She went on to train as a Transactional Analyst and qualified as a UKCP-registered practitioner. A relational psychotherapist by instinct, Carole is a published author and a founder member of the International Association of Relational Transactional Analysis. She can be reached at: Hawthorne, Horseshoe Lane, Chadlington, OX7 3NB, United Kingdom.

caroleshadbolt45@gmail.com

Charlotte Sills is a psychotherapist, supervisor, trainer, and consultant in private practice in West London. She is also a member of Faculty at Metanoia Institute, London, where for many years she was Head of the Transactional Analysis (TA) Department and now contributes as visiting tutor to the MSc programmes in TA, Humanistic, and Gestalt psychotherapies. As Professor of Coaching at Ashridge Business School, UK, she also teaches on the Master's in Executive Coaching and the Organisational Supervision Programmes. She is the author or co-author of a number of publications in the field, including *Skills in Gestalt* with Phil Joyce (Sage 4th ed. 2018), *An Introduction to Transactional Analysis* with Phil Lapworth (Sage 2011), *Transactional Analysis – a Relational Perspective* by Hargaden and Sills (Routledge 2002), and *Coaching Relationships* with Erik de Haan (Eds) (Libri 2012).

contact@charlottesills.co.uk

Steven B. Smith is a UKCP Registered Integrative Psychotherapist and is currently Programme Leader for the MSc in Integrative Psychotherapy with Metanoia Institute. Steven holds several academic and clinical qualifications, including: BA (Hons) Applied Social Sciences (Coventry Lanchester Polytechnic), BA (Hons) Christian Theology and World Faiths (Leeds University), Diploma and MSc Integrative Psychotherapy (Metanoia Institute and Middlesex University), Certificate in Integrative and Transpersonal Supervision (The Psychosynthesis Education Trust), and MA in Jungian and Post-Jungian Studies (Centre for Psychoanalytic Studies, Essex University). In 2018, he received his PhD in transpersonal psychology, exploring the relationship between sexual and spiritual ecstasy, from Liverpool John Moores University. Steven endeavours to integrate developmental psychoanalysis, humanistic and psychoanalytic notions of relationality, and Jungian concepts to honour the client's multiple and unique ways of being, experiencing, and relating. This supports him to identify and work with the client's developmental deficits and traumas, current relational struggles, and spiritual issues as these emerge as figure and ground within the therapeutic relationship.

steven.smith@metanoia.ac.uk

Biljana van Rijn is a psychotherapist, supervisor, and author. She works at Metanoia Institute in London, where she heads a Faculty for Research Strategy and Innovation and teaches. She also practices as a Transactional Analysis psychotherapist and supervisor, and a counselling psychologist. Biljana has established a long-standing research clinic at Metanoia Institute with an emphasis on routine outcomes evaluation of humanistic and integrative psychotherapies. Her professional interests are in psychotherapy assessment and formulation, with an emphasis on reflective, relational practice. She has published books and papers in these areas.

Biljana.Vanrijn@metanoia.ac.uk

Editors' Introduction

Despite the commonly agreed premise that sexuality and sexual attraction are normal relational processes, they are complex to attend to in clinical practice, supervision, and counselling/psychotherapy organisations. The experience of sexual attraction within an intimate and boundaried space of psychotherapy is also impacted by the wider cultural issues and has a potential to evoke shame and avoidance and lead to transgressions with far-reaching consequences for therapists and clients. The aim of this book is to support therapists and their supervisors to navigate these issues with openness and self-reflection, by bringing them into the professional forum. In order to achieve this aim, the book will bring to focus clinical and ethical issues related to working with sexual attraction in both clinical practice and in supervision. In order to support and model self-reflection, the authors also explore these themes from the standpoint of sexual orientation and gender and provide a reflexive exploration of their conceptualisation and practice.

Our approach to this subject is rooted within a relational humanistic-integrative therapeutic perspective, embracing co-creation and intersubjectivity to explore the emergence and the development of sexual dynamics in the therapeutic encounter.

The rationale for the book emerged from doctoral research by one of the editors (Lukac-Greenwood, 2019) which showed that working with sexual attraction is still a difficult area for female therapists working with male clients, raising questions related to power, authority, and role confusion, which when not understood, could pose a risk in relation to the client's and therapist's wellbeing or the therapeutic relationship. Her findings in addition to the general paucity of literature and training on the subject raised questions about the experience and effectiveness of working with sexuality and sexual attraction for different types of therapeutic dyads.

As editors, we did not aim to give explicit directions for practice. We wanted to avoid oversimplification as well as make the book accessible to novices, but also of interest to experienced therapists, supervisors, and clinical mangers. To achieve this aim, and consistent with relational psychotherapy, authors have offered case examples, professional and personal reflection, new theoretical understanding and research.

Our theoretical perspective

Our aim in this book was to think about sexuality from the relational humanistic-integrative theoretical approach. This approach, drawing on two-person psychology, focusses on how therapists and their clients co-create experiences and meanings during the process of psychotherapy. In psychoanalytic writing, this is referred to as intersubjectivity (Orange et al., 1997), a process where subjectivities of the therapist and the client intersect to create a unique field of meaning and experience. Within the humanistic psychotherapies (Fowlie and Sills, 2011; Summers and Tudor, 2000, 2014) this relational practice entails emphasis on the centrality of the therapeutic relationship with active engagement by the therapist, focus on both conscious and unconscious relating and subjective meanings. This requires therapist's sensitivity and willingness to critically reflect and engage with their own experience, as well as that of the client, and allow uncertainty.

Background to the subject

Different conceptualisations of sexual feelings in the therapeutic relationship

'Erotic transference' as a resistance to treatment

The phenomenon of the erotic transference within the therapeutic relationship was first described by Freud (1915), who described it as an inevitable process of a female patient falling in love with her doctor. He saw it as a form of resistance, regularly occurring precisely at a point of time when the client is having to admit or remember some particularly distressing and heavily repressed piece of her history. It is seen as a reflection of the patient's endeavour to destroy the doctor's authority by bringing him down to the level of a lover.

Freud's way of dealing with it was to withhold any response to it. He saw the craving for love as having its roots in infancy because of which the patient needed to be led through the primal period of her mental development to allow her to acquire the extra piece of mental freedom which would distinguish her conscious mental activity from unconscious.

The relational turn in psychoanalysis

Since Freud, the thinking about sexuality and the nature of the erotic feelings in therapy has expanded. Contemporary psychoanalysts have come to see it as located in an interactive, relational field, as an expression of relational configurations and early object relations (Gabbard, 2001; Gerrard, 1996; Mann, 1997; Mitchell, 1988). Consequently, they have moved away from seeing erotic dynamics in therapy as simply a re-enactment of a patient's early years and now see it as a multifaceted phenomenon with the variety of meanings dependent upon a complex interplay of patients' and therapists' transference-countertransference interactions (Flax and White, 1998).

In order to account for some of the complexity of the phenomena, some authors have made a distinction between erotic and eroticised transference and countertransference (e.g., Bolognini, 1994; Gabbard, 1994; Schaverien, 1995). Whilst erotic transference is viewed as a natural phase of the therapeutic process, eroticised transference is seen as a delusional form of transference, characterised by a more sexualised form of relating in which capacity for symbolisation is thwarted and transference is experienced as something real. The client may start to demand gratification, which destroys the therapeutic alliance and ruins the potential for growth (Schaverien, 1995).

Another aspect of the thinking that has changed since Freud is acceptance that erotic feelings are not necessarily only a resistance to the treatment but also have the potential to be a positive element of the therapeutic process. For example, drawing on Ferenczi's ideas, Gerrard (1996) claims that it is only when a patient arouses our deepest loving feelings (not empathy) that we can hope for a truly positive outcome of the therapy.

However, it is sometimes said that one of the effects of this emphasis on an early, mother-infant relatedness and the view of sexuality as a manifestation of other, earlier relational needs is de-sexualisation of the therapeutic relationship (Renn, 2013; Target, 2007). One of the results is the split between the meaning and the bodily experience of the erotic phenomenon, for me best illustrated by Mann's (1997) description of the erotic as 'psychological experience independent of sexual reproduction and the desire for children' (Mann, 1997, p. 5).

Contemporary views on sexual dynamics in therapy

In recent years, thinking about sexual dynamics within psychotherapy has shifted again. As mentioned above, writers from theoretical traditions not previously concerned with sexual aspects of the therapeutic relationship have started to engage in the debate.

Considering Cognitive Behavioural Therapy (CBT)'s view on the phenomenon of sexual attraction within therapy, Worrell (2014) suggests ways in which CBT's traditional focus on technical interventions may need to be expanded. Drawing on evidence which suggests that 'core beliefs' and 'schemas' are inherently interpersonal (Safran and Muran, 2000), he suggests an integration of some of the existential-phenomenological concepts into CBT, including that human existence is always embodied and sexual, thus expanding CBT's 'character' to encompass qualities of 'spontaneity', 'chaos', and 'passion' (Worrell, 2014).

The existentialist's approach to sexuality is particularly challenging of the view that takes our biology as an explanation. Overall, although this approach is by no means unified, their theoretical stance situates the focus of the therapeutic work with sexual dynamics within the notions of 'isolation' and 'personal meaning'. Sexuality and sexual attractiveness are conceived as an attempt to moderate our core existential anxieties, overcome existential isolation and derive a sense of meaning from life (Berry, 2014). Consequently, existential writers emphasise the complexity and fluidity of individual experience and warn against normative or reductionist thinking which categorises, judges, or simplifies the experience (Milton, 2014).

Whilst the contemporary writing points to a greater integration of bodily and affective responses to the understanding of the sexual aspects of the therapeutic relationship and starts to consider both in potentially positive terms (Nuttall, 2014), there still exists a split between a more acceptable category of 'loving' and a less acceptable category of 'sexual' feelings in psychotherapy. Although there are writers who have been very open in describing their sexual feelings within therapeutic work (Bridges, 1994; Celenza, 2010; Flax and White, 1998; Hargaden, 2001; Maroda, 1998, 2010), it is still quite rare to find a very explicit *positive* account of therapeutic work with sexual feeling. I was most struck by Cornell's (2001) writing in this respect. He incorporated sexual feelings into a theoretical framework by arguing that in addition to what is sometimes referred as the "secure base" (the need for establishment of stabilising, predictable relationships in one's life), there is also a role for something he called the 'vitality base', which includes the need for challenging unpredictable and lively relationships.

Consequently, one of the outstanding questions left unclear to me is the extent to which we have really progressed in our thinking about the impact of sexual attraction (rather than love) on the therapeutic relationship.

Sexual attraction as a 'transferential' versus 'real' phenomenon

An additional aspect of current psychoanalytic theoretical thinking is the concept of 'real' versus 'transferential' therapeutic relationship, when it comes to sexual attraction. Notwithstanding the reports of a paradigm shift based on the notions of 'mutuality' and 'co-construction' (Mitchell, 1988; Renn, 2013; Stolorow et al., 2002), the notion of a 'real' relationship is still not uniformly embraced or discussed.

For example, Rodgers (2011) found that all of her participants, irrespective of their theoretical orientation, used the terms 'erotic transference' and 'sexual/loving feelings in the relationship' interchangeably. In addition, as Bodenheimer (2010) points out, although discussion on the nature of the 'transferential' and 'real' aspects of the therapeutic relationship is currently being embraced in the literature, the notion of having a 'real' and potentially loving (let alone sexually charged) relationship with the client still causes terror in young clinicians.

From reading psychoanalytic literature (Bridges, 1994; Flax and White, 1998), it appears that co-construction is something which is considered part of authors' thinking and supervision but tends to be considered from the vantage point of the past. How to think about the 'real'/'present' in the relationship is not discussed, leaving us to wonder whether there is an unspoken assumption that once the dynamic between the client and the therapist can be located in the therapist's and client's past, the present affect will dissipate.

Furthermore, whilst some authors look for ways in which they can bring their own sexual feelings towards the patients to the fore (Maroda, 2010; Renn, 2013), overall, therapist's self-disclosure, particularly when it comes to sexual feelings, is discouraged (Bridges, 1994). The clearest message related to the actual work was one of prohibition, warning therapists about potential acting out and therefore advising against disclosure. Bridges (1994) raised the concept of a 'real' attraction in the therapeutic room but dismissed its importance given the unethical nature of behaviour stemming from it which in any case she felt was dealt with by legislation. It therefore appears that the meaning and the use of the notion of 'co-construction' when it comes to sexuality, is still limited.

Interestingly, existential accounts of working with sexual attraction do not concern themselves with this question, presumably because they do not work with the concept of transference. As put by Smith-Pickard (2014), the notion of transference is seen as the disavowal of the therapist's body because the therapist is accepting the sexual feelings of the patient while at the same time attempting to deny their impact on him/herself.

The existentialists' emphasis on co-creation and mutuality as well as freedom of the therapist's self-disclosure seems particularly refreshing, clear, and direct. For example, Berry (2014) suggests that therapists often avoid discussing sexual issues not out of interest for the client's well-being or the effectiveness of the therapy, but rather due to the therapists' own discomfort, fear, or embarrassment. This, he suggests, is ethically dubious because, for existential psychotherapists to refuse to address sexual attraction in the consulting room would mean to evade personal responsibility and act inauthentically. Therefore, drawing on the use of the existential concept of 'authenticity', he urges clinicians to attend to the sexual attraction and disclose the impact it has on them whilst making use of the concept of 'meaning', to help them interpret the experience of sexual attraction itself. Thus, exploration of the key existential themes provides avenues for exploration of the meaning of sexual attraction making the meaning much more important than the attraction itself.

A case for therapists' self-disclosure of sexual attraction is also made by Giovazolias and Davis (2001), who reported that most of their respondents (87.5%) believed that disclosure had a positive impact on the therapy. Similarly, Marshall and Milton's (2014) research suggested that disclosure played a part in fostering honesty in the therapeutic relationship and had a beneficial effect on the therapy. Given the fact that the question of disclosure in this study was discussed in situations when the sexual attraction was felt to be mutual, there is a question whether therapists' thoughts about disclosure would be the same if they were not sexually attracted towards their clients. Nonetheless, this research raises a very important point which needs greater attention – of what it means to work relationally with sexual attraction in the therapy.

One of the questions that this literature raises is about ways of holding onto all different aspects of the therapeutic relationship when working with sexual attraction (e.g., 'transferential', 'real', 'mutual', and 'unequal') and avoiding using any one for defensive purposes. Nuttall (2014) attempts this by showing the potential ways of seeing sexual aspects of the therapeutic relationship as present in each of Clarkson's (2003) five modalities of therapeutic relationship, whilst Cornell (2001) does it by emphasising the role of future in therapy, something which can sometimes be overlooked. By linking the present in the therapy and the future in the outside world (as opposed to the past in the outside world) Cornell (2001) presented us with one way of thinking about how present dynamics between the therapist and the client can have legitimacy and still serve therapeutic purposes. As he puts it, the emphasis on the therapeutic relationship, not as an end in itself but rather as a means for the client's ability to develop real life and relationships outside the therapy room, can help contextualise clients' and/or therapists' sexual (as well as any other) feelings less as a threat to the therapeutic relationship and more as a source of stimulation and a manifestation of their ability to live and feel intensely.

Our professional and personal perspectives on the subject

Biljana's story

As editors we come from different professional backgrounds. I am a Transactional Analysis psychotherapist and a Counselling Psychologist. I have worked as a practitioner, academic and service manager for many years. In all of these positions I have experienced working with sexual attraction, and recognise the need for further literature, research and professional discussion on the topic, in all areas of therapeutic practice.

Personally, I come from a big city background from a country now broken up by the civil war (Yugoslavia). My experience of growing up in the (then peaceful, Belgrade), was the ease with which sexuality was talked about and sexual attraction expressed. I left Yugoslavia as a young woman, before I was established either professionally or personally and I assumed that the sense of sexual equality between the genders that I experienced in my environment was universal, even though it didn't involve the full domestic equality. The subsequent civil war and the atrocities which involved sexual violence, made me question my experience and wonder how much of the tolerance and ease I experienced were limited to a relatively narrow, educated urban environment I grew up in. This became even more obvious in the discussions with Jasenka during the process of developing this book. Even though we share the broad cultural background our cultural experiences differed. This highlighted that subcultures in Yugoslavia, as elsewhere, were stratified, leading to different individual experiences and expectations. This shows that cultural generalisations are likely to oversimplify our understanding of any cultural and political dimensions, including expressions of sexuality and sexual attraction.

Jasenka's story

The idea of this book was created as a result of my and Biljana's (my research supervisor) work on my Doctoral research study in which I explored the female therapists' experience of working with male clients who are sexually attracted to them. As I outline in detail in Chapter 1, this was one of the most complex clinical experiences I encountered during my psychotherapy training years, which I wished to explore to a greater extent. In particular, given my own negative associations with being an object of male sexual desire, I was curious about other female therapists' experiences of it.

Socio-historically, it could be said that I am a product of two different cultural streams coming together, the stream of modernisation as well as tradition. I was born in 1974, in Yugoslavia, in a part which is currently recognised as an independent country, Bosnia and Herzegovina. Yugoslavia was a progressive country which took modernisation as its task. Possibly, as a consequence of its communist ideals and possibly as a consequence of its 'youth', the new country created a sense of possibility, progress, and change. With its secularisation, the religion ceased to define people's identities and with it, social practices. I grew up with the sense of equality amongst sexes, in terms of women's rights and practices. In retrospect, I can see that this particularly applied to women's place within the employment market, with equal rates of employment between sexes, 'female engineers' and aspiring female students. However, inside people's homes, situation was different. There, the division of labour was done on the basis of gender roles (despite women working and earning) with women still predominantly doing household chores and being primary child carers. Despite the modernisation, the definitions of feminine and masculine remained deeply traditional. So therefore, although I grew up with the sense of possibility and choice as a woman, fiercely fighting and winning against 'my place in the kitchen', I now realise that my place in the bedroom was an aspect of that fight which I never fully articulated to myself or others. This is an aspect which played itself out in my therapeutic work with male clients who found me sexually attractive.

Knowing this about myself, I was curious in the experiences of other women, spurring me on to do the research into this area. However, as would be expected, upon the completion of my study, I was left with more questions than I had at the outset.

One of the key questions which directly came out of my study was the female to female sexual attraction. All but one of my participants directly asked if I was *only* interested in the sexual desire of *male* clients or whether I was also interested in the sexual attraction of their female clients. Although I wondered about my participants' questions about my focus as a potential manifestation of their discomfort in talking about the specific dynamic of male sexual desire which can sometimes be overlooked or subsumed by a more general theme of 'erotic transference' or 'love', equally I was made to think that my focus might have been too narrow. I also wondered about the possibility that it was unconsciously motivated by my desire to 'design myself out' of the research process. Huysamen (2018) talked about her own difficulty of being made into a sexual object as a constraint in her research with men who paid for sex. Similarly, for myself, allowing discussion on female-to-female sexual attraction might have risked me being implicated in the sexual dynamics with my participants – something which I am not sure I was ready to do [see Gabbard (1994) for the discussion of a similar dynamic within therapy]. This was the first of the questions which I came to wish to know more about, leading me to wonder about experiences of the other types of client – therapist dyads with different sexual orientations, different cultural background as well as different theoretical orientations. This book is a step in the step towards findings some of those answers. The aim of it was to bring together as many varied experiences of working therapeutically with sexual attraction, leaving it open to the contributors to decide what within it is of the most importance to them.

Structure of the book

The ultimate collection of essays in this book does not aim to give a definitive view of the subject. We are well aware that this topic is somewhat a taboo (Celenza, 2010; Luca, 2014) and that it takes courage to open oneself to the vulnerability that it exposes, especially, as we wished it to be considered from the applied, practitioner, rather than theoretical point of view. We are very grateful to all of our contributors for that.

The book will be split into three sections, dealing with issues related to (1) clinical practice, (2) supervision, and (3) ethical issues. Each section will contain chapters in order to support in-depth exploration in all three arenas of practice.

In order to aid systematisation and avoid repetition, each section of the book will be completed by editors providing a reflective summary of the chapters in the section. Although the aim of the book is to inform and support practitioners, it will not offer direct guidelines, but will instead outline good practice and pose reflective questions.

Introduction 9

Chapter outline

Part 1 – Clinical practice: sexual attraction in the therapy room

This section offers four chapters written from different perspectives. The four chapters will present research (Lukac-Greenwood), theory (Hitchings), and experiences from clinical practice (Agar & Fenton; Bridgeman).

1.1 JASENKA LUKAC-GREENWOOD: LET'S TALK ABOUT SEX: FEMALE THERAPISTS' EXPERIENCES OF WORKING WITH MALE CLIENTS WHO ARE SEXUALLY ATTRACTED TO THEM

This chapter outlines the results of a research project which looked at the experiences of female therapists working with male clients who were sexually attracted to them. Participants described it as a changing dynamic, the nature of which was dependent on the context and the interaction of experiences that the therapist and the client brought into the relationship. The research, therefore, suggested that working with being at the receiving end of the client's sexual desire is not a unified or concrete phenomenon to be 'mastered' and 'learned' but instead should be explored reflectively and reflexively.

The type of challenge to be reflected on and worked with appeared to be somewhat different depending on whether therapists had reciprocal feelings towards their client or not. In situations in which therapists' feeling were not reciprocal, issues related to therapist's safety and power were predominant. In situations when therapists' and clients' feelings were reciprocal, one of the themes included therapists reporting a sense of their different roles (societal and therapeutic) clashing and negatively impacting the therapeutic relationship, whilst the other one included the sense of 'mutuality and love' which had a positive and deepening effect on the therapeutic work. The chapter focusses on the implication of these results for the clinical work.

1.2 PAUL HITCHINGS: MAPPING THE 'EROTIC' IN THE THERAPEUTIC RELATIONSHIP

This chapter examines the 'erotic' (or embodiedness of two people in a relationship) in the form of a matrix map which utilises a continuum from the 'real' to the 'transference' relationship and further considers this across a dimension from the 'ordinarily embodied' to the 'genital sexual'.

It is envisioned that this matrix will offer a broader map than the frequent discussed and more narrow focus in the literature, that of the 'erotic transference'. The map places the 'erotic' into a broader **embodied** map, places sensuality and sexuality into the therapeutic encounter, and invites non-shaming reflexivity. It is likely to be of use as a reflexive aid to clinicians, supervisors, educators, and those currently in training.

As a conceptual tool this map invites reflection of the wholeness of two people engaging in an 'embodied' relationship within a humanistic-integrative paradigm.

The chapter focusses on each of the four dimensions – whilst always acknowledging that there is a continuum involved. Issues for clinical work will be considered across this model, illuminated with case vignettes.

1.3 JAMES AGAR AND BRIAN FENTON: THE MEANING OF THE ASKING

In this chapter, we explore the impact of therapist and patient affective processes such as desire, disgust, and sexual attraction as they are felt and/or enacted within the consulting room. These processes will be considered in relation to theories and cultural forces which underpin notions of good sex and bad sex.

We will present our work as a dialogue between the two of us as qualified and experienced colleagues who have undertaken many years of personal therapy and who have attended an established supervision group together for ten or more years. This group has been a rich and stable resource for us over the years and is a place where we have the trust of our supervisor and the membership to *lean into* clinical issues which may interest or trouble us.

We are both privileged as white, heterosexual male psychotherapists in private practice. We have also both been supported in dealing with complaints while working in statutory or voluntary agency settings in the past. We are interested in the contrast between this multidisciplinary work and the privacy, intensity, and potential isolation of private practice, where issues of vulnerability and power emerge in the asymmetrical relationship between therapist and patient. Our ultimate ethical consideration is for the well-being of our patients.

We will describe past transgressive experiences and offer some reflection on what we consider with hindsight to be missed opportunities. We will also offer reflections on conditions that support atmosphere where clients can express and make meaning of what is in their minds and hearts.

1.4 MICHELLE BRIDGEMAN: GENDER IDENTITY AND SEXUAL ATTRACTION IN THE THERAPEUTIC ENCOUNTER – A TRANSGENDER PERSPECTIVE

This chapter explores some of the challenges encountered by Trans therapists when sexual attraction becomes figural in the therapeutic relationship. I look at the interplay between sexuality and gender and how it impacts on the trans therapist and the client. A trans therapist may have experienced their sexuality as heterosexual when they were in the gender role as assigned at birth. Conversely, they may experience themselves as Gay when previously they had lived a heterosexual experience.

The impact of male privilege from two perspectives, that is, Transmen and Transwomen, also impacts on how sexual attraction may be experienced.

This, in turn, leads us to the impact of shame and how the Trans therapist may be using energy to remain in stealth. I will share my personal experience as a psychotherapist who is also a Transwoman and how I have experienced sexual attraction in the therapeutic relationship.

1.5 JASENKA LUKAC-GREENWOOD: SUMMARY AND REFLECTION OF THE THEMES RELATED TO PRACTICE ISSUES

This brief chapter brings together themes emerging from the previous writing, such as the personal and the professional, shame, and power, and reflects on principles of good practice in terms of boundary violations and therapeutic work.

Part 2 – Sexual attraction and sexual identity in supervision

This section focusses on sexual attraction and sexual identity and in supervision, both from the perspectives of supervising a therapist who is dealing with these issues in their practice, and addressing the dynamic between the supervisor and their supervisee.

2.1 JILL HUNT AND CHARLOTTE SILLS: THE SUPERVISORY DIMENSION

This chapter focusses on using supervision to support therapists in dealing with issues of sexuality and sexual attraction in their therapeutic practice.

The emergence of sexuality in the therapy room can evoke some of the most disturbing and difficult experiences, feelings and sensations that practitioners can encounter in their work with clients. The role of the supervisor is to facilitate the practitioner to contain these strong sensations, in order to begin to reveal the understandings and meanings in the longings and desire being expressed consciously or unconsciously. The aim of the chapter is to explore ways of enabling the practitioner and the client to survive ruptures and disappointments in the therapeutic relationship.

In this chapter, we draw on our own experiences of being supervisors of practitioners encountering these disturbing feelings and, using case material, explore how supervision helped us to find understanding and ways forward to further the therapeutic process.

2.2 CAROLE SHADBOLT: THE DISTURBANCE AND COMFORT OF FORBIDDEN CONVERSATIONS (SEXUALITY AND EROTIC FORCES IN RELATIONAL PSYCHOTHERAPY SUPERVISION)

In this chapter Carole Shadbolt addresses aspects of the supervisory relationship when sexuality and the erotic are present. The chapter is written in an "auto-ethnographic", that is, personal, voice, and through the medium of a long case study and a number of other illustrative case examples Carole reflects on the issues and dilemmas involved in what is portrayed as multilayered, complex and nuanced area of the supervisory encounter. Using relational, feminist philosophical ethical principles as a containing foundation she names relevant underpinning concepts and theories which elaborate and deepen an understanding of the dilemmas presented in the supervisory encounter when the forces of sexuality and the erotic are present. In what might be seen as a two person approach to the supervisory encounter she discusses ethical principles, considerations of risk, power dynamics, and gendered political processes between the working pair, paralleling processes, co-transference and embodied phenomena, dissociative process, intersubjectivity, and enactments. She introduces into the Psychotherapy Supervision practice discourse two "clinical" concepts, the "Transgressive Edge" and the "Liminal Space", and shows how she used them as a useful means to approach and address and potentially resolve the supervisory issues described.

2.3 SEXUAL ORIENTATION IN THE SUPERVISORY RELATIONSHIP: EXPLORING FEARS AND FANTASIES WHEN DIFFERENT SEXUAL ORIENTATIONS ARE PRESENT IN THE CLIENT/THERAPIST AND/OR SUPERVISORY DYAD

This chapter will explore how the supervisor's capacity and willingness to explore their own attitudes towards sexual orientation influences the work with clients. I explore the influence of the changing field or context. Using examples, I will explore how the supervisor's actual and perceived receptivity and evident "diversity lens", affects what is brought to supervision. I consider the issue of sexual identity and how often the person in the minority group (supervisor or supervisee) finds themselves in the position of educator, and the differing implications depending on who is in the more powerful position. I include considerations of disclosure and how it is handled in supervision. I discuss the co-created supervisor/supervisee relationship and the parallel processes within the client work, and how the potential for shame is acknowledged and worked with. I consider the responsibilities and receptivity of the supervisor and the need for courageous conversations.

2.4 BILJANA VAN RIJN: EDITOR'S SUMMARY AND REFLECTION ON SEXUAL ATTRACTION AND ORIENTATION IN SUPERVISION

The summary and reflection by the editors will bring together the themes emerging from all chapters and identify principles of good practice and remaining questions.

Part 3 – Ethics: preventing and dealing with transgressions

This section focusses on working ethically with issues of sexual attraction and sexuality in psychotherapy, from different working environments and different perspectives.

3.1 STEVEN B. SMITH: SEXUAL TRANSGRESSIONS AND TRANSGRESSING GENDER AND SEXUALITY

This chapter will explore the ethical and relational challenges that can emerge when working with our clients, so-called, 'sexual transgressions'. When our clients disclose their sexual fantasies or reveal the sexual acts that they engage in with other consenting adult(s), we need to be vigilant and non-defensive as to how these issues might impinge upon our own values and ethical principles. We need, therefore, to be aware of our own sexual preferences, which ultimately involve 'permissions' and 'taboos', *and* hold fast to our ethical obligations to be a cause for good (beneficence) and harm (maleficence) as we wrestle with such complex and delicate material. Consequently, due care and attention is called for as we sensitively explore these challenges within the relational frame between therapist and client; and in the parallel process between client, therapist, and supervisor.

Three case examples are used to illustrate the importance of fostering a humane stance to manage the ethical, professional, and relational challenges that relate to working with 'sexual transgression'.

3.2 BILJANA VAN RIJN: FIREFIGHTING. MANAGING SEXUAL RUPTURES AND TRANSGRESSIONS WITHIN COUNSELLING AND PSYCHOTHERAPY SERVICES

This chapter explores sexual boundary infringements and transgressions in counselling and psychotherapy from a perspective of a manager of clinical services. As a clinician, I recognise sexuality and sexual attraction within the therapeutic relationship as a natural and widespread experience, which I endeavour to normalise and address in clinical supervision and personal therapy. However, the service perspective differs to that of an individual practitioner and the hidden and shameful nature of sexual transgressions makes them difficult to recognise and to prevent harm.

In order to illustrate the multifaceted nature of transgressions and their impact, I have given an overview of the literature in psychotherapy and the related mental health professions, showing the extent of the reported transgressions and their meaning, some personal and organisational predisposing factors, and highlighted the harmful impact on the clients. I have offered reflections on the subject from my experience as a manager of a large community counselling service within a training institution and given experience-based case vignettes to invite the reader into reflection on their own experiences. Finally, I offer a discussion with some suggestions and guidance on recognising and addressing these issues from the perspectives of the counselling and psychotherapy services, as well as training institutions.

3.3 SUE EUSDEN: AN ETHICAL CONTAINER FOR EROTIC CONFUSION

This chapter considers the ethical issues relating to sex and sexuality inside the psychotherapy profession. Often these areas evoke strong countertransferences and potentially shame in therapists. Ethics can be used reactively and defensively at such time *or* creatively and constructively.

Eusden reflects on the history and tensions of sexual transgressions and focusses on the inevitability of collisions and collusions of two subjects in the therapeutic encounter and how to navigate the ethical tensions between daring and caring in relation to sex and sexuality in the support of transformation for the client.

She discusses three conceptual frameworks that can be used to support transformative practice; exploratory contracts, issues of consent, and the ethical compass. Together these frames can keep the therapeutic/supervisory space open to offer an ethical container for erotic confusion, where two subjects can learn through experiences of objectification, excitement, and opportunity with mutual respect and professional integrity.

3.4 BILJANA VAN RIJN: EDITOR'S SUMMARY AND REFLECTION ON ETHICAL PRACTICE AND PREVENTION OF TRANSGRESSIONS

The summary and reflection by the editors will bring together the themes emerging from all chapters and identify principles of good practice and remaining questions.

References

Berry, M. D. (2014) Existential psychotherapy and sexual attraction: Meaning and authenticity in the therapeutic encounter. In: Luca, M. (ed.) *Sexual Attraction in Therapy, Clinical Perspectives on Moving Beyond the Taboo, A Guide for Training and Practice*. West Sussex: John Wiley & Sons Ltd, pp. 38–53.

Bodenheimer, D. (2010) An examination of the historical and current perceptions of love in the psychotherapeutic dyad. *Clinical Social Work Journal*, Published online: 10 September 2010, Springer Science + Business Media LLC 2010. https://philadelphiatherapy.net/wp-content/uploads/2015/03/examination-of-love.pdf

Bolognini, S. (1994) Transference: Eroticised, erotic, loving, affectionate. *International Journal of Psycho-Analysis.* 75, 73–86.

Bridges, N. (1994) Meaning and management of attraction: Neglected areas of psychotherapy training and practice. *Psychotherapy.* 31(3), Fall, 424–433.

Celenza, A. (2010) The guilty pleasure of erotic countertransference: Searching for radial true. *Studies in Gender and Sexuality.* 11(4), 175–183.

Clarkson, P. (2003) *The Therapeutic Relationship* (2nd ed.). London: Whurr.

Cornell, W. F. (2001) There ain't no cure without sex: The provision of a "vital" base. *Transactional Analysis Journal.* 31(4), 233–239.

Flax, M. and White, J. (1998) The erotic spell: Women analysts working with male patients. *Gender and Psychoanalysis.* 3, 5–31.

Fowlie, H. and Sills, C. (Eds.) (2011) *Relational Transactional Analysis. Principles in Practice*. London: Karnac Books Ltd.

Freud, S. (1915) Observations on transference-love, *Standard Edition of Complete Psychological Works of Sigmund Freud*, Volume XII (1911–1913): The Case of Schreber, Papers on Technique and Other Works, 157–171.

Gabbard, G. (1994) Sexual excitement and countertransference love in the analyst. *Journal of the American Psychoanalytic Association.* 42, 1083–1106.

Gabbard, G. (2001) A contemporary psychoanalytic model of countertransference. *Psychotherapy in Practice.* 57(8), 983–991.

Gerrard, J. (1996) Love in the time of psychotherapy. *British Journal of Psychotherapy.* 13(2), 163–173.

Giovazolias, T. and Davis, P. (2001) How common is sexual attraction towards clients? The experiences of sexual attraction of counselling psychologists towards their clients and its impact on the therapeutic process. *Counselling Psychology Quarterly.* 14(4), 281–286.

Hargaden, H. (2001) There ain't no cure for love: The psychotherapy of an erotic transference. *Transactional Analysis Journal.* 31(4), 213–239.

Huysamen, M. (2018) Reflecting on the interview as an erotic encounter. *Sexualities.* 23 (3) 376–392.

Luca, M. (ed.) (2014) *Sexual Attraction in Therapy, Clinical Perspectives on Moving Beyond the Taboo, A Guide for Training and Practice.* West Sussex: John Wiley & Sons Ltd.

Lukac-Greenwood, J. (2019) *Let's Talk About Sex: Female Therapists Experience of Working with Male Clients Who Are Sexually Attracted to Them.* Doctorate theses available from Middlesex University's Research Repository: https://eprints.mdx.ac.uk/id/eprint/27296

Mann, D. (1997) *Psychotherapy: An Erotic Relationship Transference and Countertransference Passions.* London: Routledge.

Maroda, K. (1998) Enactment: When the patient's and analyst's pasts converge. *Psychoanalytic Psychology.* 15, 517–535.

Maroda, K. J. (2010) *Psychodynamic Techniques, Working with Emotion in the Therapeutic Relationship.* London: Guilford Press.

Marshall, A. and Milton, M. (2014) Therapists' disclosures and their sexual feelings to their clients: The importance of honesty – An interpretative phenomenological approach. In: Luca, M. (ed.) *Sexual Attraction in Therapy, Clinical Perspectives on Moving Beyond the Taboo, A Guide for Training and Practice.* West Sussex: John Wiley & Sons Ltd, pp. 209–226.

Milton, M. (ed.) (2014) *Sexuality, Existential Perspectives.* Monmouth: PCCS Books Ltd.

Mitchell, S. A. (1988) *Relational Concepts in Psychoanalysis, An Integration.* Cambridge, MA: Harvard University Press.

Nuttall, J. (2014) Sexual attraction in the therapeutic relationship: An integrative perspective. In: Luca, M. (ed.) *Sexual Attraction in Therapy, Clinical Perspectives on Moving Beyond the Taboo, A Guide for Training and Practice.* West Sussex: John Wiley & Sons Ltd, pp. 22–38.

Orange, D., Atwood, G. E., and Stolorow, R. D. (1997) *Working Intersubjectively: Contextualism in Psychoanalytic Practice.* Mahwah, NJ: The Analytic Press.

Renn, P. (2013) Moments of meeting: The Relational Challenges of Sexuality in the Consulting Room. *British Journal of Psychotherapy.* 29(2), 135–153.

Rodgers, N. (2011) Intimate boundaries: Therapists' perception and experience of erotic transference within therapeutic relationship. *Counselling and Psychotherapy Research: Linking Research with Practice.* 11(4), 266–274.

Safran, J. D. and Muran, J. C. (2000) *Negotiating the Therapeutic Alliance: A Relational Treatment Guide.* New York: The Guilford Press.

Schaverien, J. (1995) *Desire and the Female Therapist, Engendered Gazes in Psychotherapy and Art Therapy*. London: Routledge.

Smith-Pickard, P. (2014) The role of psychological proximity and sexual feelings in negotiating relatedness in the consulting room: A phenomenological perspective. In: Luca, M. (ed.) *Sexual Attraction in Therapy, Clinical Perspectives on Moving Beyond the Taboo, A Guide for Training and Practice*. West Sussex: John Wiley & Sons Ltd, pp. 67–80.

Summers, G. and Tudor, K. (2000) Cocreative transactional analysis. *Transactional Analysis Journal*, 30(1), 24–40.

Summers, G. and Tudor, K. (2014) Co-creative transactional analysis. In: Summers, G. and Tudor, K. (eds.) *Co-creative Transactional Analysis: Papers, Responses, Dialogues, and Developments*. London: Karnac Books, pp. 1–28.

Stolorow, R. D., Atwood, G. E., and Orange, D. M. (2002) *Worlds of Experience*. New York: Basic Books.

Target, M. (2007) Is our sexuality our own? A developmental model of sexuality based on early affect mirroring. *British Journal of Psychotherapy*. 23, 517–530.

Worrell, M. (2014) 'Hot cognition in sexual attraction': Clarifying, using and defusing the dionysian in cognitive behavioural psychotherapies. In Luca, M. (ed.) *Sexual Attraction in Therapy, Clinical Perspectives on Moving Beyond the Taboo, A Guide for Training and Practice*. West Sussex: John Wiley & Sons Ltd, pp. 3–22.

Part 1
Clinical practice
Sexual attraction in the therapy room

Part 1

1.1 Let's talk about sex

Female therapists' experiences of working with male clients who are sexually attracted to them

Jasenka Lukac-Greenwood

Context of the research study and this chapter

The chapter of this book is based on the research I conducted as a part of my professional training as a counselling psychologist and a psychotherapist which was inspired by my desire to delve deeper into an area of clinical work which I felt was particularly complex.

In my personal experience, my response to a male client's sexual attraction was the least understood or discussed area of my work. My tendency was to feel either maternal or ashamed and I was curious to explore the extent to which some of those feelings might be embedded within the wider socio-cultural context as well as belonging to my individual, psychological background.

The most difficult aspect of the therapeutic relationship with this client was associated with a period of work when he implicitly or explicitly communicated his sexual feelings towards me whilst paying me directly in cash. For me, the situation had strong connotations of prostitution which made me feel dirty, non-professional, and unskilled. Although this was not a persistent aspect of our work, it was the one I made no use of. I mentioned it in supervision, but I made light of it, laughing and not giving it proper weight.

Later on, when I separated the context of payment, and as such the image of prostitution, I managed to address the issue of sexual attraction with the client, but I did it with the sense of 'being done to', as if the client was a 'perpetrator', and I was the 'victim'. Under the protection of being a passive recipient of sexual attraction, I started to enjoy the situation. I found this even more difficult to admit to myself, discuss in supervision, or make use of in the work. The difficulty was associated with what it means to be enjoying being an object of sexual desire – 'the slut', by my own and society's standards of behaviour for married, professional women. Therefore, fear of embodying the prostitute in different ways, either by being paid for services which (although not directly) were linked with the client's sexual arousal, or by enjoying the feeling of being a sexual object, was detrimental in exploring the nature of our relationship. At other times, on the other hand, I also remember having tender, motherly feelings towards the client. In retrospect, it is difficult to know whether my motherly response was a defence against more difficult feelings of being a 'slut' or whether my different responses were a reflection of different aspects and phases of our work. However, what is very clear is my difficulty in using and working with the more sexualised feelings.

Although, my experience was shame and embarrassment (as well as enjoyment at a later stage), I did not want to make a presumption that all female therapists would experience the same feelings. Instead, I wished to explore the experiences of other therapists and the extent to which they were able to use it in their work with clients. This was the starting point for my investigation which I share here, hoping that other practitioners might also find it of interest and use.

Brief outline of the study

In this research, I explored female therapists' experience and ways of working with male clients who are sexually attracted to them. I used Hollway and Jefferson's (2008) hybrid method 'Free association narrative interview' which provided me with a way of integrating my psychotherapeutic and research skills. Most importantly, it enabled me to work with the notions of 'unconscious' and 'embodied' knowledge and to include my and participants' personal and interpersonal reflections as part of data with which I worked.

The process of research involved open-ended interviews with five psychotherapists, three of whom I interviewed twice and two of whom I interviewed three times. The follow-up interviews helped with building rapport and trust, aided reflection, and enabled more collaborative meaning making between participants and me.

One of my participants refused information on age and ethnicity. Other participants were all older than 50 years of age and had extensive experience of working as psychoanalytic or TA psychotherapists. The names given to them in this chapter are not real.

Key findings

As a result of analysis of the interviews, I produced detailed reports on the work within and between participants' accounts. However, in this chapter I will focus on three key themes which stood out for me and which I believe would be of most interest to practitioners. First, in relation to the question of the nature of experience, participants reported that experience differs depending on the client. More specifically, my study suggests that experience differs depending on whether therapists felt reciprocally sexually attracted towards the client or not.

Secondly, the research question about the extent to which therapists used the experience in the work with clients appears to be related to the extent to which therapists feel the conflict between personal and professional selves. And thirdly, in relation to the most personal question of whether other therapists had similar experience of feeling like a prostitute, my study suggests that I was the only one feeling like that! I will explore each of these themes and their implications in detail below.

What was the experience of female therapists?

As mentioned above, in response to my first research question, all participants reported that it is not something that is possible to describe in a generalised way because experience varies with each client. They described it as a changing dynamic dependent on the context and the interaction of experiences of sexuality that the therapist and the client bring into the relationship.

Although in retrospect this sounds obvious, in fact, this is not something which particularly stood out for me either from reading the literature or from my experience of working therapeutically.

In terms of the literature, from the theoretical point of view, this is a far cry from some of the classic writing on the subject which considered erotic phenomena as an inevitable process of the therapeutic process, a transference from the earlier childhood relations onto the therapist (Freud, 1915). This view of the sexual attraction is more in line with more recent relational thinking in psychotherapy which emphasises the importance of the therapists' and patients' intersubjectivity (Gabbard, 2001; Gerrard, 1996, 2010; Mitchell, 1988), rendering it complex phenomena, difficult to predict or master.

However, even the most recent literature betrays a certain degree of tension between the theoretical thinking on the subject and its application in the consulting room. For example, whilst there is a widespread agreement about the importance of the co-construction of the therapeutic relationship (Maroda, 2010; Stolorow et al., 2002), the issue of a 'real' relationship and its related notion of 'the present' in the consulting room is not something which is uniformly discussed or appears to be agreed upon. With the exception of the most recent literature in the existentialist tradition in relation to therapists' self-disclosure (Berry, 2014; Marshall and Milton, 2014), the most prevalent way of considering the work with sexual dynamics involves linking them with our own or our client's early history without much being said about how to deal with the feelings evoked in the present moment.

This made me wonder whether it might be assumed that once understood as originating in the past, the feelings in the present would cease to have a grip on an individual. However, based on my experience of talking to therapists, I was left wondering whether this really is the case and whether to help therapists contain some of the difficult feelings associated with sexual attraction, more than an understanding of the transferential aspects of it might be required. Consequently, I have come to see my study's finding that therapists experience varies with each client as a further prompt indicating the need for further theoretical conceptualisation of the 'present' in psychotherapy and ways in which this can be worked with.

Additionally, from a more practical point of view, one of the key implications of this finding relates to the provision of training and clinical supervision. Although participants noted the relative lack of teaching on the subject, echoing similar views expressed in the literature (Bodenheimer, 2010; Rodgers, 2011) ultimately, this research suggests that rather than being taught, the real learning on the subject comes from having spaces where the dynamic can be explored reflectively and reflexively. Participants reported that this was most commonly done in their personal therapy and clinical supervision, something which is also highlighted in the previously published literature as well as numerous chapters in this book (Smith-Pickard, 2014a; Worrell, 2014). On the whole, participants described a positive role of supervision in terms of it helping them recognise the dynamic, finding ways of verbalising it, recognising ways in which they might be implicated in it (i.e., by being seductive) and ultimately in helping them be less defensive so that the dynamic becomes more available for examination and work with the client.

Who hits on whom? Experience differs depending on reciprocity of the sexual feelings between therapists and clients

Again, although this may seem very obvious, in retrospect, it wasn't something which for me clearly stood out from the literature I read so far. However, as Agar and Fenton (Chapter 1.3) or Hitchings (Chapter 1.2) write, 'who hits on whom' makes all the difference.

When therapists do not experience the reciprocal sexual attraction, my study suggests, it is power dynamics that get activated between them. On the contrary, in the situation when there is a reciprocal sexual attraction felt by therapists, they reported the sense of mutuality, love, and fears of boundary transgressions.

Lack of reciprocity in sexual feelings and resultant power dynamics

The context of therapeutic work in which therapists did not feel reciprocal sexual attraction towards their clients appears to be interesting on several accounts. First, it seems that it puts the therapist in a very powerful position which is not always easy to experience. Participant 2, Alex, spoke about this most directly by highlighting how unnerving it would have been to have contemplated that she had so much of an impact on the client. Further, subsumed within it, lack of sexual responsiveness seems to have activated an aspect of therapists' experience best described as the conflict between how they felt and what they thought they should feel in their role as therapists.

Most directly, participants talked about it as being 'rejecting', struggling to find a way of reconciling feeling personally disgusted with the client with her role as the therapist. As Pippa put it, the struggle involved a question of how to find an authentic and empathetic way of responding to the client when you do not feel the same way.

How do you say to somebody you disgust me...

or

... sense of "Yes, I have sex but not with you", ... [a sense of] rejecting.

And finally, a theme which I have come to see as a response to this power imbalance, in situations when participants did not feel sexually responsive towards their clients sexual attraction, they reported being preoccupied with their incompetency, fears of being at fault, or making a mistake. I found this one of the most striking findings, possibly because it didn't feel 'rationally' explicable.

Pippa talked about this dynamic in a most direct way by recalling a time when she was a relatively inexperienced therapist when, without quite knowing what she might have done, she had a generalised fear that her client's sexual attraction towards her was somehow her fault.

Most surprisingly, perhaps, even participant 4, Sarah, who came across as the most confident in her ability to work with sexual dynamics, described a moment when she doubted herself and wondered whether she had made a mistake by not anticipating a client's desire for a hug and then not being able to prevent it.

I have also noticed that this worry over making a mistake was accompanied by participants' anxiety about exposing or naming the dynamic of male client's attraction towards themselves, fearing that it could potentially be experienced as shaming for the client. Although, at the time of the interviews I simply accepted this explanation, therefore revealing something that is unconsciously understood between us, in retrospect, I started to wonder why the exposition of male sexual desire would necessarily be experienced as shaming.

The fact that the participants feared being put down by the clients in some way suggests that power plays a significant part in this dynamic. For example, participants feared either being made to feel 'silly' by the client who would deny his sexual attraction, or presumptuous by being made to feel that they gave themselves more credit than they deserved.

Linking these findings with the literature which talks about the capacity to provide or withhold sexual availability as being very powerful, and thus very dangerous (Mitchell, 1988), I have come to see this sense of responsibility, fear of being made to feel at fault or being put down as well as denying or turning a blind eye to the sexual dynamic as therapists' reactions towards being a more powerful positions over their client and as attempts to redress, rather than work through the conflict.

Interestingly, inequality in power between my participants and me within the research process was also something I found difficult to address and openly discuss. For example, at times, during the interviews I felt very insignificant and somewhat powerless whilst on other occasions, such as in the process of analysis, I experienced quite a significant discomfort in having power, making me fear the possibility of being ridiculed for being either incompetent or presumptuous. My own discomfort with power inequality meant that I found it difficult to bring it up for discussion, resulting in prolonged periods of 'paralysis through over-analysis' and delays in the research process.

Using the notions of 'mirroring' and 'enactment' in research (Chamberlayne, 2005; Halling, 2005) I used this experience to help me think through the potential parallel processes between the content and the process of interviews and the potential impact of interpersonal dynamics on the co-construction of narratives (Bager-Charleson, 2014; Etherington, 2011; Murray, 2015). The parallels between participants' sense of caution and discomfort in being in a power position *vis-à-vis* their clients and my experience in the role of the researcher *vis-à-vis* my participants were remarkable.

The main implication of this finding for me includes the need to consider the possibility that therapists discomfort might be a reflection of the wider tension existing in the society in which the power held within the personal, professional, and societal roles occupied by professional women may not necessarily be aligned and congruent with each other. I believe this to be particularly true for the psychotherapy profession in which a female therapist and male client reverse societal norms of power relating.

Power dynamics: society, psychotherapy, and gender configurations

Most fundamentally, the psychotherapeutic relationship is inherently unequal (Pilgrim, 1997) because of the different roles the therapist and the client occupy within it. It is the psychotherapist who sets the frame for the work and any negotiation of it is undertaken from a position of power. When clients enter therapy, they place themselves in a position of vulnerability relative to the therapists which in addition to therapists' relative anonymity further contributes to the power of the therapist's role. In addition to role differences, there might be other structural differences between the therapist and the client (e.g., of class, ethnicity, and age) each exerting pressure in terms of the power relations between them (Totton, 2000). My study has suggested that gender configuration might also be one of those relevant differences.

The way in which the power is experienced is found to be a product of a complex interplay of factors residing in the structural context of the therapeutic role and the intersubjective encounter of the therapist and the client (Day, 2010). Furthermore, given the complexity of the phenomenon, in any one situation there is potential for the experience of it to be conflicting and confusing (Day, 2010). I see my study as providing one of the therapeutic examples in which the intersection of the role power, dynamics of the work, and structural relations combine to make the experience of power particularly complex and potentially conflicting for female therapists.

Furthermore, as mentioned above, in addition to holding the ordinary power of the role, female therapists working with male clients' sexual desire find themselves in a position to provide or withhold sexual availability which is in itself very powerful. However, given the deeply rooted meaning of sexuality in our culture as an expression of male dominance, the aforementioned power of the female therapist may be experienced as being in conflict with the male client's power, when viewed through the structural lenses of our society. As suggested by Russ (1993), our social convention says that for women, sexuality is often equated with being the object of desire, whilst to be powerful means rejecting the receptive position and refusing to be regarded as a sexual object. Going further, Russ (1993) and Gornick (1986) suggest that male patient's shame might be associated with being in a passive position *vis-à-vis* a woman and that the erotic transference of the male patient towards their female therapists can serve to 'turn the tables', functioning as a defence against feelings of humiliation evoked by the therapeutic situation, or against threats to masculinity spurred by the regressive pull of the pre-Oedipal transference (Gornick, 1986).

Seen in this light, the examples provided by my study (namely participants' preoccupations with potential shaming of the client, their tendency to blame themselves or experience themselves as incompetent, as well as denying or turning a blind eye to the sexual dynamic) could potentially be seen as manifestations of this underlying conflict about their own sense of role and power and as attempts to redress, rather than work through, the sense of this conflict. For example, Participant 1 – Pippa's difficulty in 'taking charge' in the context of feeling sexually attracted towards her male client, could be seen as a manifestation of her conformity towards the societally prescribed female way of being, as opposed to her taking up a professional role which would have necessitated a more authoritative stance.

Similarly, her suggestion that societal messages play a part in her feeling of 'being at fault' is in line with Guttman (1984) and Schaverien's (1997) suggestion that therapists' difficulties of admitting their arousal are linked with some sort of unspecified guilt, perhaps to do with fear of being blamed for causing arousal in men or being seen as needy and seductive like the female patients in early analysis.

A more recent research study by Penny and Cross (2014) reported fascinating results relating to this finding in my study. They explored the influence of the hegemonic societal norms of masculinity on male therapists working with female clients. Male therapists who were interviewed in this study talked about their female clients' sexual attraction as something which is pre-existing, something that they bring with themselves into the room and assault the men/therapists with. Whilst the female client is seen as an agent of the attraction, the man is a passive recipient of it. Furthermore, the hegemonic masculine norms require men to take back the agency and engage with this attraction. This means either acting on the sexual attraction or, as is the case with male psychotherapists who are ethically obliged not to act, reframing it. One of the ways in which this reframing can be done, as shown by Penny and Cross (2014) is to find a flaw in the female object or reframe her into a figure of ridicule. I found this finding fascinating because of its potential to explain my participants' sense of 'being at fault'. Looking through the lenses of this research, the societal norms could be seen as not only playing a part in accounting for my participants' sense that they were to blame for having done something wrong to cause the men's arousal, but perhaps also for the less concrete sense of their incompetency and inadequacy, which in my study was particularly pronounced in the situations when they did not feel reciprocal sexual attraction towards the clients. According to Penny and Cross (2014) this would be the exact situation which would require the man to reframe the situation and denigrate the woman in some way, thus potentially explaining my participants' sense of inadequacy.

Furthermore, my study supports Kolarik et al.'s (2016) findings which suggest that especially in their early careers, female supervisors and therapists, in response to finding their clients attractive, experience a sense of failure or not knowing how to handle it, suggesting that women carry a sense of self-blame related to their sexuality. They refer to Lester (1985) who proposes that female therapists do not explore sexual issues with male clients due to fear of appearing seductive or vulnerable to seduction, finding emerging from my study as well as a wider body of literature (Luca and Boyden, 2014).

Interestingly, above cited research by Penny and Cross (2014) can also potentially shed some light on this fear of being seen or found to be seductive, because as they suggest, if found to be sexually unavailable, a woman will be 'reframed' in a denigrating way. Consequently, it would be of no surprise that women would not wish to be in position of receiving sexual attention which they cannot reciprocate.

Finally, that this feeling of being at fault for attracting male sexual desire is deeply ingrained in our culture can be seen though a number of myths which depict its female characters as abusers of their power over men. For example, the myth of Medusa, a beautiful woman raped and consequently punished for her beauty by Poseidon, illustrates how the dominance of the male is violently reasserted against the illegitimate power of women (Beard, 2017). Similarly, Simkin (2014) in his book on cultural constructions of the Femme Fatale, compares Pandora, the first woman created by Zeus to punish Prometheus and bestow torment on humankind, with 'Femme Fatale', a more contemporary role for women in films, in which a beautiful woman lures a male hero into a dangerous situation by overpowering his will with her irresistible sexuality. In doing so, Simkin (2014) is illustrating how an ideological construction of women, such as the femme fatale, the Medea-like murderous mother or the Medusa-like monster, are very often and swiftly mobilised against women who are seen to transgress cultural norms.

These myths illustrate the weight of the cultural sanction for women who transgress the cultural norms relating to male and female sexual relatedness and the norms by which female therapists working with male clients who are sexually attracted to them may be influenced. Or as Penny and Cross (2014) state, these are the discourses (in this instance, cultural) which cause the conflict in individuals' identities and which need to be challenged. Rather than falling into the trap of resolving them along the lines of individual deficit (which could be seen as contained in participants' sense of being in wrong), the attention and challenge need to be directed towards the discourses that form the conflict in the first instance.

Links between the therapeutic context, culture as a whole and female ambivalence to own her power is also discussed by Benjamin (1998) and Flax and White (1998). Flax and White (1998) showed that female therapists have ambivalent feelings towards power by expressing the phantasy of a 'Wish to Be Powerful and Autonomous' at the same time as an unwillingness to be seen as a powerful, phallic mother. Benjamin (1998) linked this dynamic with the culture as a whole, in which male children may defend against the power of the pre-Oedipal mother by devaluing the qualities that evoke her power. She further suggests that the same dynamic may play a part in male clients' wish to 'turn the tables' with their female therapists. Because of the woman analyst's emphasis on the connection, in an attempt to maintain the connection to the male, she may actually disown her own power and sacrifice her own needs for autonomy which in turn may preclude the male patient's ability to integrate a view of her as an autonomous, powerful being.

Dhillon-Stevens's (2005) multi-dimensional, dynamic model of power provides one way of capturing the complexity of power relations. It highlights our multiplicity and simultaneous membership of a number of different 'majority' and 'minority' groups and sub-groups. It draws our attention to the potential to be simultaneously oppressed and oppressing and argues that an understanding and negotiation of power in the therapeutic relationship requires commitment to the continuous intra and interpersonal work to understand the complex interplay of any potential differences which at any one point in time may be activated in, and in interaction, with others.

My study therefore suggests that working with sexual dynamics is one of the therapeutic contexts in which female therapists need to be aware of their and their client's multiple roles, and have commitment to the complex work required for understanding and negotiation of their resultant roles and power relations. The role of training and clinical support for therapists in applying the learning from this finding cannot be underestimated. Therapists require institutional support, training, and clinical support to enable them to see, question, and act against the prevalent norms which might be contradictory or confusing and therefore interfere with their ability to work within their professional, therapeutic roles.

Reciprocal sexual attraction

The context of therapists feeling reciprocal sexual attraction towards their clients seems to create a potential for two different ways of relating to the client. On the one hand, participants reported sense of mutuality and love with the client enabling the experience to be used for the therapeutic benefit of the client. Equally though within this context, participants also reported a sense of conflict, this time, revolving around themselves as sexual women and as therapists.

Splitting as a way of terminating the conflict of roles

One way in which participants dealt with the conflict between their roles of being a (sexual) woman and a therapist was to terminate one of them. For example, Alex described the experience of their roles as women and therapists as 'clashing' to which she responded by either trying to completely remove the sexual desire from her considerations of herself or feeling the need to terminate the therapeutic relationship.

Therefore, it seems that experiencing sexual attraction towards the client can feel very dangerous. The mistrust in one's abilities to resist an impulse which might lead to sexual acting out can result in denying the dynamic or in terminating the relationship, neither of which are therapeutically sound outcomes. As discussed with Pippa, this can lead to a feeling of a 'no-win situation', affecting one's sense of confidence and competence as a therapist. In her example, she explained how she felt bad about herself because of feeling that it was her fault that she had caused the clients to feel sexually attracted towards her and afterwards, after terminating the relationship on the advice of her supervisor, she ended up feeling bad because she felt that she had made a therapeutic mistake in terminating the therapy prematurely.

Maternal transference – another way of resolving the conflict?

In the context of the above mentioned 'need to split the roles', I have further wondered whether exclusive focus on 'transference' and in particular 'the maternal transference' in the context of early infantile sexuality, might be a form of splitting of the therapeutic experience in the service of managing the therapist's personal feelings towards the clients. I wondered whether by focussing on the transference, the therapist is minimising the impact she might be having on a dynamic, and by focussing on the maternal transference she is focussing on aspects of the relationship which are clearly aligned with her role of being a therapist.

Interestingly, Sarah and Pippa provided counterexamples in which their reactions towards the clients did not take away from their sense of identity, either as a woman or a therapist, enabling those reactions to become a part of the work, available for examination and sense making. Sarah talked about her attraction towards the client without experiencing this as conflicting with her therapeutic role, whilst Pippa talked about feeling disgust towards the client but withstanding the tendency to feel rejecting or cruel as a result of it. It would seem that the fact that they did not need to defend against their reactions towards the clients enabled the clients' expression of their feelings and made the related therapeutic work possible.

Mutuality and love

Not all examples discussed by participants were characterised by difficult or defensive behaviour. As mentioned above, Sarah and Pippa described work with clients with whom sexual attraction was mutual and the work was felt to be successful.

Reflecting back on what might have enabled this, Pippa highlighted her sense of shared responsibility for the maintenance of the therapeutic relationship. She recalled the client being the first one to name the sexual attraction between them, which created a sense of mutuality in which they could enjoy the relationship, knowing the boundaries and being able to work at a deep and intimate level. What ensued was a 'relationship of equals which was very affectionate, enjoyable and productive'.

Both participants described these clients with reference to the strength of their adult 'self'. Pippa recalled her client as an 'adult who was bright, smart, had a lot of resources and was able to hold his own', whilst Sarah described her client as somebody with the capacity to be a man in the world and whom she could respect as a potential adult male lover. Sarah went as far as to conclude that it was this ability not only to love but to see her client as a potential lover which was the reason for the success of his therapy.

From these examples above, it appears as if the loving context enabled integration of therapists' maternal and sexual feelings. It seems that in their relationships with clients there existed a mutual appreciation of multiple roles and states that they both occupied. Whilst clients seemed to be able to see and respect my participants/their therapists as sexual beings as well as therapists without needing to take away their professional role from them, the participants/therapists were able to see and work with their client's child-like vulnerabilities as well as recognising and admiring their adult strengths, including that of being a potential lover.

This finding is very much in line with the most recent writing in the psychanalytic tradition as exemplified by Gerrard (2010), as well as with the existentialist writing of Smith-Pickard (2014a,b) mentioned above, all of whom in their own ways call for consideration of clients' post-Oedipal/adult sexuality and consider the role of the therapist in its exploration.

Gerrard (2010) argues for the importance of the analyst participating symbolically in patients' seduction, thus allowing the patient the moments of Oedipal victory. In addition to her original writing about the need for the patient to arouse our deepest loving feelings (Gerrard, 1996), she thus adds the need for clients to find that their therapist found him/her desirable.

Despite using very different language, I find Smith-Pickard's (2014a,b) notion of 'existential sexuality' similar in encapsulating the notion that sexuality is an embodied interpersonal phenomenon through which we seek existential validation by claiming some significance in the lives of others. Part of the role of the therapist is to open him/herself up to receive this unique otherness, somewhat like lovers would.

Finally, these findings have reminded me of the literature which stressed the importance of sexual feelings as an accomplishment, not as a defence – sexuality as an accomplishment in the effort to sustain somatic and erotic liveliness (Cornell, 2001), so very rarely talked about in those terms.

Integration of our sense of personal and professional selves – a way forward?

Overall, in considering how to think about the above-mentioned conflict between feeling rejecting or sexually attracted and a therapist, made me wonder whether in addition to the need to direct our attention and challenge socio-cultural discourses constructing the nature of sexual relating (Penny and Cross, 2014) discussed above, there is also a need to question the norms associated with psychotherapy practice. What is it exactly that is appropriate to feel as therapists?

There is a variety of literature which questions the normative notions of what it means to be a therapist and shows the need for therapists to be able to feel and process a wider range of positive and negative emotions. For example, drawing on Foucault (1988; in Hedges, 2010) who warned against acceptance of 'grand narratives' about ourselves or our professional and cultural pre-suppositions, highlighting the narrowing effect they have on our thinking and interacting with ourselves and others, Hedges (2010) warned that particular conceptions of what it means to be a therapist inadvertently narrow rather than expand available roles for clients. For example, he suggested that 'Wounded Therapist' produces a child-like client whilst 'Missionary Therapist' creates an incompetent client (Hedges, 2010).

The research on the importance of the therapist's therapy (Adams, 2014; McWilliams, 2013) further highlights the need for therapists to integrate negative feeling and withstand being made to feel 'distorted' in the service of the client's need to process intense negative feelings.

Finally, neuro-psychological research which stresses the importance of implicit right-hand brain communication in affect regulation, highlights the therapist's role in amplifying and resonating the client's affect (Schore, 2012) and in taking risks to respond authentically when our affective worlds collide

(Lichtenberg et al., 1996; Stern, 1985; in Schore, 2012). These examples show the need for therapists not only to enter the client's affective world, but also to be prepared to be shaped by it in ways for which professionally therapists may not be prepared, but for which they will have a way of responding on a human level, thus suggesting the need for greater integration of the notions of the person and the profession of the therapist.

Notwithstanding this literature, my research has made me wonder whether the qualities of a therapist's warmth, empathy, and love have become therapeutic imperatives – the therapist's straight jacket which prevents us from allowing ourselves to be human. Equally, it strikes me that these are the very qualities we associate with being a mother, making me wonder whether the current dominance of the relational school in psychotherapy with its focus on early mother-child relatedness, might have defined the qualities we currently value in therapists.

In this context, it is interesting to reflect on the research showing that sexuality within the mothering context is taboo in most cultures (Kulish, 1986; in Schaverien, 1996) and also, to question whether female therapists' focus on 'transference' and 'maternal transference' could be seen as a form of splitting of their therapeutic experience in the service of achieving this therapeutic ideal.

The de-sexualisation and feminisation of psychotherapy and the emphasis on the mother-baby relations as a proto-type for the therapist-client relatedness has been commented upon and criticised by a number of authors (Budd, 2001; Lemma and Lynch, 2015; Renn, 2013. Whilst some of the authors call for greater reintegration of Freudian and Lacanian ideas and an acceptance of desire and genital sexuality (Budd, 2001), others are extending it through different theoretical concepts.

For example, Target (2015) using the notions of 'mirroring' and 'mentalisation', explains that sexual feelings do not become mentalised to the same extent as other affects in childhood, because of the maternal failure to mirror them adequately. As a result, she proposes a way for therapy in integrating aspects of the parental and aspects of sexual relationships. By being similar to a sexual relationship, she sees therapy as providing recognition of sexual feelings without rejection whilst by being like a parental relationship, therapy helps clients develop and represent feelings without satisfying the desire for action.

Contemporary existential writing provides us with a different metaphor to symbolise the therapeutic relationship and as such helps us create different levels of openness towards the sexuality of our clients. For example, Smith-Pickard (2014a,b) uses the metaphor of 'lovers' and 'lover's gaze' to depict relatedness through psychological proximity and sexual feelings in the consulting room. As he highlights, this relatedness involves whole body responsiveness in an attempt to reach into a non-verbal realm and embodied inter-experience and construction of meaning. Not so much to bring sex into therapy but to acknowledge the ever-present background of existential sexuality which allows us to become metaphorically naked and vulnerable, like lovers do (Smith-Pickard, 2014a).

I am aware that these are complex clinical issues (e.g., see Schore (2012) for discussion on therapeutic enactments) and that thinking about them will depend on one's conception of therapy and the role of the therapist. I do not wish to argue against any one modality or research which highlights the importance of the therapist's personal qualities on the therapeutic outcomes but instead wish to raise the possibility that our conception of what we 'should be like' might prevent us from considering what 'we are like' which consequently takes away our and the client's individual as well as joint interpersonal understanding and development.

Ultimately, if we accept that the development of the capacity for communication of emotions is at the core of the therapeutic process, the development of the therapist's own ability to do that, regardless of what the emotion is, must be the first step. In line with already cited research as well as Henderson's (2003) thinking on the importance of integration of difficult feelings in developing a secure psychological identity, it would seem that one's capacity to incorporate different aspects of one's sense of self together with the conception of the therapeutic role is crucial in the ability to work with the sexual dynamic.

The question of prostitution

Finally, as a personal reflection related to the starting point of this project and my overall conclusion outlined above, I found it interesting to note that none of my participants mentioned any association with prostitution.

Experientially and explicitly in the conversations, they communicated the sense of shame and embarrassment associated with the topic but did not elaborate much on the nature of it. When discussed directly, it was considered in relation to the client's sensitivity when sexual attraction was not worked with requisite therapeutic mastery. The therapists' sense of shame was therefore linked with their sense of incompetency or fear of making a mistake, discussed above. Although very interesting in itself, this sense of shame is qualitatively different to that which I experienced when I found myself feeling like a prostitute.

For me, feeling like a prostitute was connected with being an object of sexual desire in the context of my job. One way of understanding the lack of similar reports in my participants' accounts is to wonder whether they shared the same 'job description' as me. Perhaps their focus on their *clients'* shame and their own fear of making a mistake could be seen as a way of reframing their role, of communicating that the *'competent'* therapist's job description is not to accept being an object of sexual desire but to sensitively and skilfully, without hurting the clients' pride, find a way of letting them know that the therapist is 'out of bounds'.

Although I believe that this is an important practical step (i.e., therapists creating and maintaining clear boundaries of their behaviour) in retrospect

I wonder whether there is more to this situation. Is it possible to conceive that a therapist's role might also include being a sexual object?

In retrospect, I realise that in my study, my thinking about the need to challenge the professional and societal norms was limited to what felt safe and comfortable to consider, residing within the frame of reference acceptable to an emancipated, educated, middle aged, middle class, 'strong woman' which I consider myself to be.

I did not conceive the possibility that there might exist the role of being a sexual object for a client and of it being therapeutic. I know that the idea of being a sexual object does not sit very well with me and equally, that I have not had many professional conversations or read much about it in the academic field to know with absolutely certainty that being a sexual object could not be therapeutically beneficial to the client. Lemma (2015) considers clients' use of prostitutes as a developmental step which helped them integrate their sexual selves into attachment relationships. However, whilst she discussed the role of prostitutes in mirroring client's sexual desire and desirability, she does not implicate herself in this dynamic. She mentions the lack of any erotic feelings in the transference and discusses her role in term of helping client mentalise their experiences.

Consequently, conducting this study has been very interesting and informative but the question with which I started, of whether other therapists sometimes feel like prostitutes and if that has its therapeutic value, has not been satisfactorily explored or answered. It somehow got lost.

Given the cultural context in which I was brought up in which being seen to resemble, let alone 'be' a 'slut', was the biggest insult imaginable to a decent, self-respecting woman, I could not conceive myself in that role. Consequently, I wonder whether as a result of it, I did not think to probe or enquire about it in participants' accounts or whether in these participants' account the experience simply did not feature. I believe this to be an interesting topic for future investigation.

What does this mean for the new and wider population of women?

Upon the completion of my study, reflecting on its relevance, I am caught up in a mixture of feelings. On the one hand, I believe it to be of great relevance to all working women who find themselves in positions of being seen as sexual objects, something which has been greatly exposed and discussed in the recent years in relation to a string of sexual scandals and the subsequent #MeToo movement.

If, as my study suggests, therapists, who are highly skilled and professionally supported women, find the experience as destabilising and de-authorising, disposing them to potential professional misjudgement, what hope is there for women who are not in positions of authority and who might feel at a mercy of men who are employing them? What kind of support needs to be given to help and encourage discussion when even the therapists who are operating within the profession which not only supports but stipulates personal supervision and therapy find it difficult to make use of that support?

Societal messages about female sexuality are mixed and therefore unable to offer proper orientation. Whilst on the one hand, the sexualisation of our daily lives is leading us to believe that to be sexual is a good thing, on the other hand, as uttered by one of my clients, the threat of becoming a 'Jezebel' is still so alive in our psyche, that even the thought of it disables us and disarms us from defending ourselves.

Many women talk about the shame and embarrassment associated with the misplaced sexual experiences which then prevents them from speaking about it. We need to overcome that shame, in order to have more conversations and appropriately place or replace that sense of shame. In this context, I find my study of great importance, as a reminder of the need to do more to encourage openness and discussion within and beyond the psychotherapeutic profession.

On the other hand, the current debate about the proliferation of gender identities makes me think about the narrowness and potential futility of my study. Of what use is a study about the interaction of binary, male and female gender roles in the world which potentially counts as many as a hundred different and new gender identities (e.g., The Sunday Times, 8th September 2019)? As a child born in 1970s, raised in a relatively traditional family, I grew up with the need to find ways of integrating my sense of self as an educated, professional, maternal, and sexual woman, something which manifestly got entangled when I found myself working therapeutically with a male client who was sexually attracted to me.

I am curious what might this identity challenge look like for younger generations, who define themselves as gender non-binary, trans or gender fluid? Does the challenge cease to exist or does it become even more complicated?

In the context of my study which showed that age plays a part in our readiness to talk about our sexuality, the challenge to explore these questions might be to include younger generations in the conversation.

Conclusion

The reflections around my own experience of feeling like a prostitute and the lack of proper investigation of it in my study has confirmed my conclusion that to work with sexual dynamics in therapy is a task requiring a great deal of willingness to question one's one conception of the self. The reason why erotic experience and sexual attraction might be a difficult and sensitive area of work might be to do with our own (rather than our client's) reluctance to put our sense of self to the test, to challenge or change it.

As Flax and White (1998) state in relation to gender identity, the way in which we are constructed as gendered subjects in our society limits our sensitivity to the various identifications in the therapeutic room, which by extension would mean that our ability to be sensitive and tolerant of various identifications in the therapeutic room must depend on our willingness and ability to challenge our primary gender role identity.

The personal implication of this finding was beautifully captured by Alex. She reflected on the impact of her own therapy, supervision, and process of aging in diminishing the impact of her sexual attractiveness on her sense of self, enabling her to work with male sexual attraction in a freer way:

> ... Maybe also knowing, in a strange way, losing my looks is giving me a bit more freedom... you know... that sense of getting older and seeing myself get older, although there is loss involved in that, I am also more free as a woman.

One of the clinical implications of this finding is the need for the willingness and commitment of therapists towards personal therapy or other ways in which they would continue to grow and challenge their own sense of identity in order to be open to ways of working with it with clients.

Overall therefore, I conclude that to work with sexual dynamics in the therapeutic relationship is a complex task requiring willingness and openness to consider a multitude of intra and interpersonal processes within and between ourselves and our clients, something which cannot be done without commitment to the ongoing learning that personal therapy and supervision provide.

References

Adams, M. (2014) *The Myth of the Untroubled Therapist*. East Sussex: Routledge.
Bager-Charleson, S. (2014) *Doing Practice based Research in Therapy*. London: Sage Publications Ltd.
Beard, M. (2017) *Women & Power, A Manifesto*. London: Profile Books Ltd.
Benjamin, J. (1998) *The Shadow of the Other: Intersubjectivity and Gender in Psychoanalysis*. New York: Routledge.
Berry, M. D. (2014) Existential psychotherapy and sexual attraction: meaning and authenticity in the therapeutic encounter. In: Luca, M. (ed.) *Sexual Attraction in Therapy, Clinical Perspectives on Moving Beyond the Taboo, A Guide for Training and Practice*. West Sussex: John Wiley & Sons Ltd, pp. 38–53.
Bodenheimer, D. (2010) An examination of the historical and current perceptions of love in the psychotherapeutic dyad. *Clinical Social Work Journal*, Published online: 10 September 2010, Springer Science + Business Media LLC 2010. https://philadelphiatherapy.net/wp-content/uploads/2015/03/examination-of-love.pdf
Budd, S. (2001) 'No sex please – we're British': sexuality in English and French psychoanalysis. In: Harding, C. (ed.) *Sexuality, Psychoanalytic Perspectives*. East Sussex: Brunner-Routledge, pp. 52–69.
Chamberlayne, P. (2005) Inter-subjectivity in biographical methods: mirroring and enactment in an organisational study. Paper at the conference on *'Biographieforschung im sozialwissenschaftlichen Diskurs'*, Georg-August Universitaet Goettingen, 1–3 July, 2005.

Cornell, W. F. (2001) There ain't no cure without sex: the provision of a "vital" base. *Transactional Analysis Journal.* 31(4), 233–239.
Day, A. (2010) *Psychotherapists' experience of power in the psychotherapy relationship.* Doctorate theses available from Middlesex University's Research Repository: http://eprints.mdx.ac.uk/13049/1/ADay_thesis.pdf.
Dhillon-Stevens, H. (2005) Personal and professional integration of anti-oppressive practice and the multiple oppression model in psychotherapeutic education. *The British Journal of Psychotherapy Integration.* 1(2), 47–62.
Etherington, K. and Bridges, N. (2011) Narrative case study research: on endings and six session reviews. *Counselling and Psychotherapy Research.* 11(1), 11–22.
Flax, M. and White, J. (1998) The erotic spell: women analysts working with male patients. *Gender and Psychoanalysis.* 3, 5–31.
Freud, S. (1915) Observations on transference-love, *Standard Edition of Complete Psychological Works of Sigmund Freud,* Volume XII (1911–1913): The Case of Schreber, Papers on Technique and Other Works, 157–171, London: The Hogarth Press and the Institute of Psycho-Analysis
Gabbard, G. (2001) A contemporary psychoanalytic model of countertransference. *Psychotherapy in Practice.* 57(8), 983–991.
Gerrard, J. (1996) Love in the time of psychotherapy. *British Journal of Psychotherapy.* 13(2), 163–173.
Gerrard, J. (2010) Seduction and betrayal. *British Journal of Psychotherapy.* 26(1), 64–79.
Gornick, L. (1986) Developing a new narrative: the woman therapist and the male patient. *Psychoanalytic Psychology.* 3(4), 299–325.
Guttman, H. (1984) Sexual issues in the transference and countertransference between female therapist and male patient. *Journal of American Academy of Psychoanalysis.* 12, 187–197.
Halling, S. (2005, April) When intimacy and companionship are at the core of the phenomenological research process. *The Indo-Pacific Journal of Phenomenology.* 5(1), 1–11.
Hedges, F. (2010) *Reflexivity in Therapeutic Practice.* Basingstoke: Palgrave Macmillan.
Henderson, D. (2003) *Shame as an achievement in analytic training,* Talk given to the Psychoanalytic Consortium on Psychotherapy Education, London, 8th March 2003.
Hollway, W. and Jefferson, T. (2008) The free association narrative interview method. In: Given, L. M. (ed.) *The SAGE Encyclopaedia of Qualitative Research Methods.* Sevenoaks, CA: Sage Publications Ltd, pp. 296–315.
Kolarik, M., Lecbych, M., Luca, M., Markovic, D. and Fulepova, M. (2016) How Czech supervisors engage in the supervisory process on sexual attraction and strategies used to supervise sexual attraction in the work of supervisees. *Polish Journal of Applied Psychology.* 14(3), 27–42.
Lemma, A. (2015) The prostitute as mirror: distinguishing perverse and non-perverse use of prostitutes. In: Lemma, A. and Lynch, P. E. (eds.) *Sexualities, Contemporary Psychoanalytic Perspectives.* East Sussex: Routledge, pp. 189–205.
Lemma, A. and Lynch, P. E. (eds.) (2015) *Sexualities, Contemporary Psychoanalytic Perspectives.* East Sussex: Routledge.
Lester, E. P. (1985) The female analyst and the eroticised transference. *International Journal of Psycho-Analysis.* 66, 283.

Luca, M. and Boyden, M. (2014) An elephant in the room: a grounded theory of experienced psychotherapists' reactions and attitudes to sexual attraction. In: Luca, M. (ed.) *Sexual Attraction in Therapy, Clinical Perspectives on Moving Beyond the Taboo, A Guide for Training and Practice.* West Sussex: John Wiley & Sons Ltd, pp. 193–209.

Maroda, K. J. (2010) *Psychodynamic Techniques, Working with Emotion in the Therapeutic Relationship.* London: Guilford Press.

Marshall, A. and Milton, M. (2014) Therapists' disclosures and their sexual feelings to their clients: the importance of honesty – an interpretative phenomenological approach. In: Luca, M. (ed.) *Sexual Attraction in Therapy, Clinical Perspectives on Moving Beyond the Taboo, A Guide for Training and Practice.* West Sussex: John Wiley & Sons Ltd, pp. 209–226.

McWilliams, N. (2013) The impact of my own psychotherapy on my work as a therapist. *Psychoanalytic Psychology.* 30(4), 621–626.

Mitchell, S. A. (1988) *Relational Concepts in Psychoanalysis, An Integration.* Cambridge, MA: Harvard University Press.

Murray, M. (2015) Narrative psychology. In: Smith, J. (ed.) *Qualitative Psychology, a Practical Guide to Research Methods* (3rd Edition). London: Sage Publications Ltd, pp. 85–108.

Penny, J. and Cross, M. (2014) The self-preservation society: a discourse analysis of male heterosexual therapists and discourses of sexual attraction. In: Luca, M. (ed.) *Sexual Attraction in Therapy, Clinical Perspectives on Moving Beyond the Taboo, A Guide for Training and Practice.* West Sussex: John Wiley & Sons Ltd, pp. 173–193.

Pilgrim, D. (1997) *Psychotherapy and Society.* London: Sage Publications Ltd.

Renn, P. (2013) Moments of meeting: The relational challenges of sexuality in the consulting room. *British Journal of Psychotherapy.* 29(2), 135–153.

Rodgers, N. (2011) Intimate boundaries: therapists' perception and experience of erotic transference within therapeutic relationship. *Counselling and Psychotherapy Research: Linking Research with Practice.* 11(4), 266–274.

Russ, H. (1993) Erotic transference through countertransference: the female therapist and the male patient. *Psychoanalytic Psychology.* 10(3), 393–406.

Schaverien, J. (1996) Desire and the female analysts. *Journal of Analytical Psychology.* 41, 261–287.

Schaverien, J. (1997) Men who leave too soon: reflections on the erotic transference ad countertransference. *British Journal of Psychotherapy.* 14(1), 3–16.

Schore, A. (2012) *The Science of The Art of Psychotherapy.* New York: W.W. Norton & Company.

Simkin, S. (2014) *Cultural Constructions of the Femme Fatale, From Pandora's Box to Amanda Know.*Palgrave Mcmillan.

Smith-Pickard, P. (2014a) The role of psychological proximity and sexual feelings in negotiating relatedness in the consulting room: a phenomenological perspective. In: Luca, M. (ed.) *Sexual Attraction in Therapy, Clinical Perspectives on Moving Beyond the Taboo, A Guide for Training and Practice.* West Sussex: John Wiley & Sons Ltd, pp. 67–80.

Smith-Pickard, P. (2014b) Individual therapy and Foucault's dark shimmer of sex. In: Milton, M. (ed.) *Sexuality, Existential Perspectives.* Monmouth: PCCS Books Ltd, pp. 251–262.

Stern, D. (1985) Affect attunement. In: Call, J. D., Galenson, E. and Tyson, R. L. (eds.) *Frontiers of Infant Psychiatry* (Vol. 2). New York: Basic Books.

Stolorow, R. D., Atwood, G. E. and Orange, D. M. (2002) *Worlds of Experience*. New York: Basic Books.
Target, M. (2015) A developmental model of sexual excitement, desire and alienation. In: Lemma, A. and Lynch, P. E. (eds.) *Sexualities, Contemporary Psychoanalytic Perspectives*. East Sussex: Routledge, pp. 43–63.
The Sunday Times, 9th Sep 2019 'BBC films teach children of 100 gender, or more'.
Totton, N. (2000) *Psychotherapy and Politics*. Sage Publications Ltd.
Worrell, M. (2014) 'Hot cognition in sexual attraction': clarifying, using and defusing the dionysian in cognitive behavioural psychotherapies. In: Luca, M. (ed.) *Sexual Attraction in Therapy, Clinical Perspectives on Moving Beyond the Taboo, A Guide for Training and Practice*. West Sussex: John Wiley & Sons Ltd., pp. 3–22.

1.2 Mapping the 'erotic' in the therapeutic relationship

Paul Hitchings

Introduction

Two intertwined concepts form the premise of this chapter; a broad conceptualisation of the 'erotic' and that of 'embodiment' as necessary for empathic engagement. These concepts are briefly discussed before presentation of a mapping of the erotic in the therapeutic relationship.

Conceptualisation of the erotic in therapeutic relationships

The influence of the Cartesian duality paradigm, separating mind and body, continues to permeate our professional culture. The effect of overly emphasising the cognitive/rational, can induce anxiety in the face of the 'erotic'. The resulting lack of inclusion of the 'embodied' into the therapeutic space is further confounded with the confusion of the broader 'general erotic' with the narrower 'genital erotic', the latter being associated with anxieties concerning boundary transgressions. I believe we are in the midst of a paradigm shift where the 'embodied' and the associated presence of the 'erotic', instead of being peripheral but rather becomes essential to our full relating.

The term 'erotic' in this chapter is as suggested by Mann (1997), where he argues for it as a positive and transformational influence, primarily a psychological more than just a physical process and relates to engagement with all our senses including sexual feelings. Thus, being fully present to the other means a fully sensual connection requiring more than that of our 'mind'. Psychotherapeutic engagement is not one of only managing the erotic, but rather directly aims to be an erotic encounter.

An erotic engagement is our 'embodied' presence to one another, which provides the necessary foundations for the processes that describe good psychological contact between individuals: for example, attunement, empathy, inclusion, presence, and relational depth.

There is of course a continuum, as proposed by Blum (1973), with the erotic taking a range of forms in relation to the 'other'; partially disengaged, engaged, curious, confused, being emotionally moved, loosely attracted to, admiring, being sexually curious to being strongly sexually attracted. Such experiences will exist in a changing dynamic in both parties at any one time.

Embodied relationship and empathic engagement

Many concepts in the psychotherapy literature are often difficult to precisely define with different authors, for different purposes, from different traditions, having their own variations. The term 'embodiment' has become increasingly commonly used over the last decade; whilst acknowledging differences in definition, Hauke and Kritikos (2018: 1), in a major work on the topic, offer the following generic definition:

> .....embodiment really refers to a process that produces a network, woven through the fabric of our body functions and cognitions and our behaviour, connecting us to the physical environment and synchronising us with the cognitions and behaviours of other people.

Aligned with this definition, embodied communication is occurring at many levels, in mutual influence, between two people in engagement. The Rogerian concept of 'psychological contact' (Rogers, 1957) (with parallel concepts in other approaches) demands attention with all of our senses and internal sensations, the felt sense of those occurring in the other, as well as our given and received verbal utterances.

Discussing the hallmark of Gestalt as an 'embodied' therapy, and the concept of 'inclusion' (being open to the 'felt sense' of the other), Joyce and Sills (2014) state:

> Inclusion is a cognitive emotional and implicit somatic resonance, that allows the counsellor to fully experience the intersubjective field in the here and now moment.
>
> (p. 47)

> This rich vein of communication can be lost or overlooked unless the therapist is actively sensitive to her own body process and keeps alert to the unspoken messages from the body of the client.
>
> (p. 147)

Dekeyser et al. (2009: 113) state,

> Empathy in the psychotherapy session is essentially a cooperative, dialogical process that is at the same time vividly grounded in the body.

Bohart et al. (2002: 102) state,

> Embodiment is the cornerstone of empathic engagement in the psychotherapy session, it allows for the practitioner 'to understand experiences rather than words'.

Mapping the 'erotic' 41

An embodied and erotic engagement will be different with each client; we have a unique relationship with each and every 'other'. We might be less or more engaged with one person than another and the erotic takes a different dimension. We might be working with a child, an older person, someone attractive to us, someone we are moved by, or someone we struggle to connect with. What impact do the 'real' and 'co-transferential' relationships hold? How might we conceptualise this? To reflect on this a mapping of different states is offered.

The map

A map, it is hoped, will be particularly useful to guide and ground clinical thinking, which is especially important as the erotic so easily triggers shame and fear for supervisors, therapists, and clients. A map, however, can never be the territory as it offers a simplification of a more complex reality, so this is offered as an imperfect and incomplete but hopefully useful tool. This map is formed across two dimensions to yield a four-cell matrix. Whilst this is presented as four discrete boxes, reality is not as neat as there is a graded continuum along each dimension. Despite these important caveats, it is presented in this way for the purpose of clarity.

The two axes of the quadrant are that of the non-transferential versus transferential relationship and the non-genital versus genital erotic. One or both members of the dyad may occupy the same quadrant, or an invitation by one member into another quadrant may describe the current dynamic of the two person relationship. A discussion with illustrative examples in relation to each quadrant follows the diagrammatic map (Figure 1.2.1) below.

Quadrant 1 –non-transferential and non-genital erotic relationship

This is the quadrant of relationship within which most therapy is conducted and although complex in its layers is largely free from the overlay of the 'genital erotic'. It is characterised by an emphasis on the working alliance and the real relationship, and the attempt towards full psychological contact within the dyad.

Full psychological contact, incorporates the mutual, mostly unconscious reciprocal impact on one another. Drawing on neuropsychology and the concept of mirror neurons, The Boston Change Process Study Group (2018: 301) state:

> the mirror systems in our brains are constantly, though non-consciously, registering micro-versions of the movements and affects of those around us. .... we live in the bodily experiences of others as we interact with them or even merely observe them.

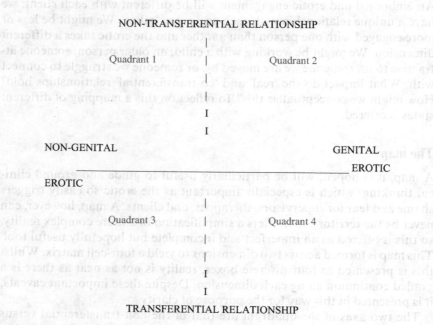

Figure 1.2.1 Four quadrants of 'erotic' relating.

How do we work with full psychological contact involving the full 'mind-body' dimension? Joyce and Sills (2014: 148–149) outline a four step process condensed here as: our own body awareness, our body awareness of the other, our bodily responses, and making tentative sense of the process which might inform our therapeutic responses. We are then in an explicit and implicit manner working in an embodied relationship that by definition incorporates the erotic. The presence of this ongoing engaged relationship is sometimes most obvious when we depart from and then return to such a connection. Such events can be considered as attunements and misattunements. Erskine (1998: 238) defines attunement as:

> a kinesthetic and emotional sensing of others .... to create a two-person experience of unbroken feeling connectedness by providing a reciprocal affect and/or resonating response.

Increased frequency of lapses in attunement coupled with changes in bodily experiences, are likely indicators of a 'push and pull' dynamic into and out of this quadrant into the transferentially flavoured Quadrants (3 and 4) with then an attempted return into Quadrant 1 (or 2). These mis-attunement shifts can be thought of as 'enactments' (Chused, 2003), or 'ruptures' (Safran et al., 2001) and potentially constitute part of the healing therapeutic process.

The dynamic described and the two example vignettes below will relate to much of the therapeutic process that we are all most familiar with.

Quadrant 1 Vignette 1

(taken from my own experience)

Beginning in an engaged way in the third session with a client, in the late afternoon, I began feeling unbelievably tired. My eyes wanted so much to close and my attention felt very foggy. Making every effort to waken myself; opening the window, tensing my muscles, moving and shifting in my chair, I managed to hold off my exhaustion to a degree.

Reflecting after the session I considered that possibly late afternoon was not the optimum time to see clients, that it might not be best ethical practice and resolved to monitor my energy levels and consider changing my working timetable.

The subsequent session was scheduled for early morning the following week, a time when my energy level was always high. Again a few minutes into the session the same sleepy state seemed to descend upon me. I began to notice the client's monotone manner and a repetitive hand movement that seemed almost hypnotic. Reflecting on the robustness of the client and our brief but broadly good working alliance, I decided with some trepidation to disclose my experience to my client. Prepared for a potential rupture, my client simply responded, 'Oh Yes, I think that I don't want people to really notice and see me'. The 'spell' was broken and we re-engaged with good contact and with alertness. We had travelled from the non-transferential to a transferential engagement and then back again.

Quadrant 1 Vignette 2

(taken from a supervisee's experience)

Towards the middle of a client session the therapist began to notice a set of tensions within her body. These same set of tensions had been familiar to this clinician, on certain rare occasions, both in her professional life and personal life. She felt thrown off balance and then momentarily reflected that such sensations usually signalled something of an urgent nature in the relational matrix. On both noticing the client's physiology (hyperaroused) and then confirmed with phenomenological enquiry, the client was indeed in a hyperaroused state. The therapist then suggested with some urgency that a GP visit might be wise. The outcome was dramatic; leading to an early discovery of a cancer, detected at an optimally treatable level of development.

Whilst this second example is somewhat dramatic, most practitioners will have common practice examples of moving in and out of full psychological contact involving the full 'mind-body' dimension. Of note is how the steps align with the four step process outlined above by Joyce and Sills (2014: 148–149):

1. Own body awareness: the therapist paid attention to a set of bodily tensions.
2. Our body awareness of the other: the therapist noticed the client's bodily state.
3. Our bodily responses: the therapist noticed their own bodily responses and that these had persisted and had amplified.
4. Making tentative sense of the process which might inform our therapeutic responses: the therapist choses an intervention.

Quadrant 2 – non-transferential genital erotic relationship

When the regularities, privacy, and intimacy of the therapeutic relationship are considered, it is normal and almost inevitable that some element of the 'genital erotic' will emerge for one or both parties. The 'genital erotic' needs to be thought of as on a continuum; from the quiet bodily admiration of the other to passing sexual thoughts and all the way along to considerable sexual desire.

The 'erotic' is always present in some form, sexual attraction contains within it the human desire for connectedness. We cannot easily pretend it away and if it is overly minimised this will be to the detriment of the therapeutic work. Premature closing down of the experiences of either therapist or client due to therapist anxiety can be counterproductive to the therapeutic process in exactly the same manner as closing down of any other experience.

Smith Pickard (2014: 67) notes,

> Sexual feelings within therapy are not only unavoidable, but attempting to deny them can be more problematic than accepting them.

If we can avoid panic and shame based responses then we are freed to consider what such sexual experiences within the therapeutic relationship might mean for us, the client or indeed both. Such material may well need time to emerge in the relationship so that such meanings might be seen and discerned.

A question in a particular therapeutic situation will usually be 'From which person does the 'genital erotic' emanate?' Whilst we may hold a philosophy that it belongs in some way to both parties; the question of from whom does this primarily originate is one that remains useful to consider. For clarity of discussion, the subsections below consider 'Cupid's arrows' flying from one or the other participants even though we know that it may well be not that simple, indeed the arrows can be flying in both directions!

The 'genital erotic' energy from the client towards the therapist

The reader may at this point struggle with this category being placed into the 'non-transferential' rather than the 'transferential' category. This is a difficult question to resolve, as the erotic is completely understandable given the 'here and now' conditions of the therapeutic relationship and will also likely have some transferential elements embedded in it. Mann (1997: 30) in considering this knotty issue notes,

> '……these problems are solved by a change of perspective. I propose that there is no difference between transference love and normal love, …' and later notes, 'Transference love is still a muddle for psychoanalysis.'
>
> (p. 52)

Perhaps, as may be expected, this is far from uncommon, with 73% of therapists reporting having had the experience of clients showing sexual attraction towards them (Pope and Tabachnick, 1993).

The therapist needs to be alert to what usually is the slow unfolding of the more 'genital erotic' in verbal and non-verbal communication.

Therapists need to have the sensitivity and courage to allow the erotic to emerge more clearly, and then it is essential not to close up the 'talking about', whilst also holding that the boundaries will not be blurred or transgressed. As there is likely to be significant meaning for the client in terms of their psychological histories and/or current life circumstances, the therapist must bear being the object of desire (for further discussion the reader is referred to McIlwain (2014)). Therapists need to hold themselves in the place of the 'disappointing lover' (Messler Davies, 2003), whilst simultaneously inviting discussion, making connections and encouraging meaning making. A particular concern here is to make efforts to avoid shaming the client.

The literature is sparse on the management of a client's attraction. There appears to be a gulf between knowledge, intent, and actual practice.

Kirby (2019), in her summary of research interviewing therapists on this topic, noted that therapists were aware of the erotic communications from clients:

> … clients as embodying unspoken erotic feelings through their eye contact and body language. …clients showering them with compliments, dropping hints about meeting outside sessions, trying to glean personal information about them…. All were described as having a strong attachment to their therapist: all hinted at rather than declared their erotic feelings directly, and all tried to push the boundaries…

In contrast, to whilst knowing theoretically the importance of working with the erotic, they seemingly attempted to ignore it:

> the therapists and their clients were both disempowered: the therapists felt awkward and frustrated, and the clients were left with deep feelings of longing than were not acknowledged and that they felt confident only to hint at and fantasise about.

We can safely assume that this negatively impacted the therapeutic outcome. The management of the 'genital erotic' is challenging. Ignoring the erotic and hoping it will go away to allow the 'work' to proceed should not be an option.

The following vignette, taken from my supervisory practice and a reference to an example from the literature evidence what good practice can achieve.

Vignette

The female attractive therapist began to notice that her male client almost always used the bathroom at the start of the therapy session. He would emerge into the therapy room and whilst standing close to her, before settling into the client chair, would be completing the buttoning of his trouser fly. The level of her mouth and his trouser fly for these moments would be in a horizontal plane within reasonably close proximity. Initially, she considered this as not meaningful, but this gave way after a number of sessions to some unease. After supervisory consultation, whilst internally acknowledging her own anxiety, she gently began to enquire of the client about his relations with women. It quickly emerged that they were almost always over-sexualised and used as his only means of making contact. The eroticised dynamic between them, could then be surfaced and talked about which led to a safe non-shaming discussion concerning the ways in which this pattern negatively impacted his romantic life.

In similar vein to this clinical vignette, Lotterman (2014) gives an excellent, engaging, and detailed account of her work using a relational perspective, with a male client who had strong sexual feelings towards her, that resulted with a healing outcome. She notes the almost inevitability of ruptures in the work and their healing potential,

> ...using a relational model was especially helpful when we experienced ruptures in our treatment – both because he was uncomfortable with his

sexual feelings toward me and because I was somewhat uncomfortable with them as well.

Both of these examples illustrate openness to the client, the therapist's acceptance of their own unease, sensitivity of timing, and management of the complexity of encouraging open discussion whilst holding the therapeutic boundary to maintain safety for both. This is a complex dance for which there maybe broad guidelines but no perfect formulae.

The 'genital erotic' energy from the therapist towards the client

Our sexuality is a core part of our humanity manifest across the continuum from deeply felt warmth all along to full genital erotic desire. Given a sufficient number of clients seen in our practices across months and years in the profession, how could we not find some of them genitally erotically desirable? We might pose to ourselves the question, why would we not have such feelings?

This whole area remains pervaded with guilt and shame, despite the ordinariness and this being what should be expected. Such experiences do not necessarily mean that we wish, or indeed will, follow through with physical intimacy.

Worrell (2014: 7) drawing upon the concept of 'thought-action fusion' from Cognitive Behavioural Therapy notes an example of the manifestation of this erroneous thinking process:

> if I experience a thought, image or feeling, this must mean something about me, it means that I must want to do this thing and am in danger of doing so.

He further notes that avoidance or suppression of thoughts leads to an increase in their potency. Consequently, in contrast to holding the stance of being the 'disappointing lover', we now need to hold the metaphorical stance of being the 'disappointed lover' (Messler Davies, 2003), holding our reflexive stance and not being pulled into the whirlpool of shame, guilt, and secrecy.

Linked to our reflexive stance, freed from the oppression of shame, we can engage with some useful self-supervision questions: What might this mean about me? About them? About us? How might this experience positively and/or detrimentally impact our process? What if anything needs to be done?

Smith Pickard (2014: 78) gives his useful internal guideline:

> ...own internal compass for working safely in what can feel like a relational free fall is asking myself how easy it is to bring this to supervision. If it is difficult, I am either outside the boundary of therapy or too close to the edge.

A final question here is whether we communicate our feelings to the client. The literature is almost univocal that we almost certainly should not, Mann (1997: 60) states,

> The main task of the therapist in these circumstances is to be able to have erotic desires objectively. That is to say, the therapist should feel but contain them.
> ... Erotic fantasies should not be shared with the patient.
>
> (p. 66)

Vignettes

There are two vignettes given below, one poorly managed with a damaging outcome (related by a colleague) and another from my personal experience as a therapist, where I believe good management facilitated the therapeutic work.

1. A Colleague, when in his twenties, was an extremely handsome gay man who partly due to estrangement from his family, financed himself through his education by having an older wealthy 'patron' to whom he twice weekly gave sexual favours. In his personal therapy, with therapist who was a gay man of similar age to his 'patron', he often discussed his unease and the wish to make a decision to bring this sexual/financial arrangement to a close. He was consistently persuaded by his therapist otherwise. In retrospect he considers that his therapist never fully recognised their own desire for him and instead casually elicited details of his sexual practices with his 'mentor'. The client now considers that his therapist at the time whilst never overtly violating a sexual boundary nevertheless did so at a psychological level by proxy.

2. When Richard entered my consulting room I was immediately taken by his handsome looks, attractive demeanour, and charming manner. I felt almost spellbound, self-conscious, simultaneously wanted to look at elements of his body and to avoid looking at those aspects. With both of us self-identified as gay men, my client will probably have known the likely effect that he would have had on me. Psychologically thrown well off balance I used my supervision to talk of my desires, hesitation, guilt at being 'caught', and desire to refer him on quickly. What emerged in supervision was that this was my opportunity to paradoxically accept my private genital erotic desire whilst learning not to 'sexualise'. This was initially challenging but the tension subsided which led to energy being freed to do the therapeutic work. Some months later into our work together, a moving therapeutic gain was evidenced when my client said, 'I don't easily get seen in the world, noticed yes...noticed very very much... but seen, really seen ... you have (with both of us in tears)'.

The reader may well consider that the first vignette with the seeming vicarious gratification indulged in by the therapist, might equally well have been placed into the fourth category below; that of the 'Transferential and Genital erotic'. This is certainly the case as these categories are not 'watertight' there is a continuum and there are no 'discrete' categories, the latter are maintained only for purposes of simplification and clarity.

Quadrant 3 – transferential and non-genital erotic

This quadrant of the erotic is often characterised by 'boundary crossings' which can be considered as situated on a continuum moving towards 'boundary violations'. 'Boundary crossings' can be 'harmful, helpful or benign to the therapeutic process' (Fasasi and Olowu, 2013) whilst boundary violations almost always have a damaging outcome.

Before discussing harmful boundary crossings and more blatant 'boundary violations' some discussion of benign and helpful 'boundary crossings' will provide some clarification. Examples of helpful or benign 'boundary crossings' include: the waiving of the notice period when the client is in critical medical treatment with unknown hospital appointment requirements, acceptance of a token gift, making extra time in a situation of urgency, and self-disclosure appropriate to the situation. On this issue, Cooper (2008: 109) gives a range of research and clinical argument that supports the concept of 'going the extra mile' as a helpful factor identified by clients.

Generally we are likely to be able to differentiate between helpful and harmful 'boundary crossings'. In 'erotic transferential' infused relationships, we are susceptible to unowned or unaware elements that are likely to propel us into the type of 'boundary crossings' which may be harmful to the overall therapeutic process. These might consist of those at the 'softer' edge of boundary blurring (e.g., regularly going a few minutes over time) to potentially unhelpful or harmful (e.g., not challenging, keeping client in therapy beyond an appropriate point, enjoying the client as storyteller, being overly curious about the next 'episode' in the client's story, significantly stretching the session time boundary).

Vignette

Some six sessions into work with a female, attractive, engaging, very likeable, and confused client in her mid-30s who was in a life career transition and a relationship bereavement situation, I experienced a strong protective parental countertransferential fantasy. I wanted to give her a home – my home! I wanted to mentor her, generally protect her, parentally love her, and give her what she had lacked in life. Discussing my powerful countertransferential responses in supervision in order to make some sense of them, it became evident that what the client needed was the encouragement and opportunity to experience her own agency and begin to develop 'her own mind'. Whilst the client was chronologically in her late 30s there seemed a developmentally young adult need for parental support to trust that she would find her own way. The supervisory engagement allowed for discussing these embodied erotic responses in a non-shaming atmosphere. Without such a discussion, whilst my countertransference responses would not have resulted in such a full 'acting out', nevertheless the therapeutic work would have likely been infused with an over-caring atmosphere, to the detriment of the therapeutic process.

Quadrant 4 – transferential and genital erotic

Clearly there is gradation between the 'non-transferential genital erotic' (Quadrant 2) and the more obviously 'transferential genital erotic' (Quadrant 4). Perhaps each are differentially characterised by being associated with the ability to hold a greater or lesser reflective stance. Much of the material written concerning Quadrant 2 will have some relevance in this section.

Vicarious boundary violations

The literature in this area (Black, 2017; Celenza, 2010; Sarkar, 2004) mostly refers to overt 'boundary violations'; however it is my belief that it is also worthwhile to consider (as in the first vignette in Quadrant 2) the vicarious forms of 'boundary violations'. Based on both clinical and supervisory experience and from discussion with colleagues some examples include; eliciting an overdetailed account of the client's sexual life, encouragement or failure to challenge risky romantic/sexual engagements, challenging a client to widen their sexual repertoire in directions not wanted by the client.

Vignette (presented in a supervision session)

A young client in a weekly gay men's therapy group complained that they had considerable anxieties in regard to their ability to maintain an erection, especially in the area of casual sex. The therapist offered a solution: that of learning to enjoy 'passive' anal sex, where the erectile concern would be considerably lessened. Despite the client explaining that this was not an activity that they wished for or fantasised about, the therapist held to a highly directive stance and invited other group members to endorse the suggestion.

In the supervisory engagement on this issue, it became clear that the therapist in question found this client highly desirable and had the passing fantasy of engaging in such activity with this client. Whilst they would not transgress the sexual boundary, it emerged that this was likely a vicarious form of boundary violation.

In the above clinical and supervisory management this seems an example of what Celenza (2010: 62), refers to as 'finding some aspect of yourself in the patient, driven by your need .... a self-other confusion'. This is similar to what Clarkson (1992: 157) refers to as a 'destructive pro-active countertransference', where the client acts out the therapist's predominantly unconscious desires. This could be expressed more graphically as a metaphorical rape of the client!

Overt boundary violations

Over the last couple of decades, there has been a considerable increase in awareness and prohibition of these events, across many helping professions, these are far from a recent phenomenon. Blechner (2014) lists numerous famous analysts across many decades, who either had sexual relations with or married their patients. Such behaviour is now seen as exploitative and a flagrant abuse of trust. It seems that it is always damaging to the patient (Seto, 1995) to the clinician themselves and to the reputation of the profession.

Attempts at an estimate of the incidence of events of sexual involvement with clients is very difficult to ascertain as surveys relying on self-reporting are likely to be an underestimate, and ethics board hearings will reflect only those brought to their attention. However based on what literature is available it would appear to reflect a figure of approximately 5–10% of practitioners with female patients constituting 80% of victims, (see Alpert and Steinberg, 2017; Pope et al., 1986; Sarkar, 2004). These figures are obviously significant.

Celenza (2010: 68) reminds us that 'No one is immune from these basic needs, temptations, and experience within the analytic setting'.

However, an important question concerns what factors might help practitioners manage good boundary maintenance? Conversely, what factors might we be alert to that might precipitate practitioners becoming vulnerable to such transgressions? There seem to be a cluster of factors under each category that we can attend to discussed under headings below.

Supervisory engagement

Despite knowing the importance of skilful management of the 'genital erotic', McIlwain (2014: 58) reports one participant in a study stating that that material concerning a client's attraction towards them is one where they would consult 'immediately with a supervisor' whereas if it were their attraction to a client, stating 'I don't think that I would speak with my supervisor'. This latter response reflects the shame inherent in the profession in regard to sexual attraction towards clients which in turn becomes a risk factor.

As supervisors then we need to reflect on any noticeable lack of presentation over time of the 'genital erotic' and avoid shaming responses. Similarly as supervisees to reflect on the presence or lack of presentation of erotic material over time and monitor our self for relationally based shaming experiences.

Maintaining self-reflective practice

Note taking as an aid to self-reflective practice and clarity concerning boundary choice and maintenance will support the practitioner. Also, essential is attention to maintaining our own emotional well-being and reflection on our bodily experiences and view of our own sexuality. Further monitoring through self-assessment instruments can yield material for reflection and supervision: for example, Boundary Violations Index (Swiggart et al., 2008).

Boundaries and the 'slippery slope' concept

Boundaries serve to protect the therapeutic space. The 'slippery slope' concept was a term coined by Gutheil and Gabbard (1993) which suggested that small boundary incursions led to increasingly larger events which paved the way towards significant boundary violations. However, withholding any boundary changes, in the belief that this protected from potential violations comes at a cost to potential therapeutic benefits (see 'Going the extra mile' earlier). Whilst, this concept is now considered as too rigid to apply as an absolute and the correlation is not supported (Gottlieb and Younggren, 2009) it may still be used for our reflective awareness as a question; might I be allowing the boundaries to slowly drift? The answer might well alert to a potential counter-therapeutic occurrence.

Stress and depletion

Being stressed, being overworked, managing significant personal crises, and lacking support and intimacy over significant periods of time seem, not unsurprisingly, to make us much more vulnerable to falling into 'genital erotic' boundary violations.

Once on the edge of such happenings it is increasingly difficult to retract. This is in part based in our physiology, as described by Fisher, H. (2008) in her TED talk 'The Brain in Love', where she points out that once this particular reptilian core of the brain is activated, 'you're willing to take enormous risk for huge gains and huge losses...', there is a 'willingness to risk it all', and 'you distort reality'. This is dramatically enacted in the HBO series *In Treatment*, (2010) in which Dr Paul Weston, a deeply personally deprived practitioner, describes to his supervisor his love for his client Laura, and he states, 'I love her. I want to be with her and I don't care what it means and I don't care what it costs...'

Especially for our clients, the lesson for us all is to ensure that we take sufficient self-care of ourselves and of those in our professional community that this point of almost 'no return' is not reached.

Summary

Whilst this chapter focusses on therapist-client relationships, much here is relevant to supervisory and training relationships as well. The structure offered can lend itself to training, supervisory, and reflective purposes for practitioners. Hopefully this map will challenge the shame that dominates this area and instead encourage a brave and open recognition of the erotic and our embodied engagement in the work that we do.

References

Alpert, J. L. and Steinberg, A. (2017) Sexual boundary violations: A century of violations and a time to analyze. *Psychoanalytic Psychology*, 34(2), 144–150.

Black, S. C. (2017) To cross or not to cross: Ethical boundaries in psychological practice. *Journal of the Australian and New Zealand Student Services Association*, 25(1), 62–71.

Blechner, M. (2014) Dissociation among psychoanalysts about sexual boundary violations. *Contemporary Psychoanalysis*, 50, 23–33.

Blum, H. B. (1973) The concept of erotized transference. *Journal of the American Psychoanalytic Association*, 21, 61–76.

Bohart, A. C., Elliott, R., Greenberg, L. S., and Watson, J. C. (2002) Empathy. In J. C. Norcross (ed.) *Psychotherapy Relationships That Work: Therapist Contributions and Responsiveness to Patients*. New York: Oxford University Press, pp. 89–108.

Boston Change Process Study Group (2018) Moving Through and Being Moved By: Embodiment in Development and in the Therapeutic Relationship. *Contemporary Psychoanalysis*, 54(2), 299–321.

Celenza, A. (2010) The analyst's needs and desires. *Psychoanalytic Dialogues*, 20, 60–69.

Chused, J. F. (2003) The role of enactments. *Psychoanalytic Dialogues*, 13(5), 677–687.

Clarkson, P. (1992) *Transactional Analysis Psychotherapy an Integrated Approach*. London: Routledge.

Cooper, M. (2008) *Essential Research Findings in Counselling and Psychotherapy – The Facts are Friendly*. London: Sage.

Dekeyser, M., Elliott, R., and Leijssen, M. (2009) Empathy in Psychotherapy: Dialogue and Embodied Understanding. In Decety, J. and Ickes, W. (eds) *The Social Neuroscience of Empathy*. London: MIT Press, pp. 113–124.

Erskine, R. G. (1998) The therapeutic relationship: Integrating motivation and personality theories. *Transactional Analysis Journal*, 28(2), 132–141.

Fasasi, M. I. and Olowu, A. A. (2013) Boundary transgressions: An issue in psychotherapeutic encounter. *IFE Psychologia: An International Journal*, 21(3), 204–224.

Fisher, H. (2008, July) *The Brain in Love* [Video] TED Conferences. https://www.ted.com/talks/helen_fisher_the_brain_in_love

Gottlieb, M. C. and Younggren, J. N. (2009) Is there a slippery slope? Considerations regarding multiple relationships and risk management. *Professional Psychology: Research and Practice*, 40(6), 564.

Gutheil, T. and Gabbard, G. (1993) The concept of boundary violations in psychiatry. *American Journal of Psychiatry*, 150, 188–196.

Hauke, G. and Kritikos, A. (2018) Building a body of evidence: From sensation to emotion and psychotherapy. In Hauke, G. and Kritikos, A. (eds) *Embodiment in Psychotherapy – A Practitioner's Guide*. Switzerland: Springer, p. 1.

HBO series 'In Treatment' Season 1 Episode 20, (2010) Dr Paul Weston declares his love for Laura. www.youtu.be/qop5YMwnmi4

Joyce, P. and Sills, C. (2014) *Skills in Gestalt Counselling and Psychotherapy* (3rd edn.). London: Sage.

Kirby, V. (2019) Seduction in the counselling room. *Therapy Today*, 30, 5.

Lotterman, J. H. (2014) Erotic feelings toward the therapist: A relational perspective. *Journal of Clinical Psychology*, 70, 2.

Mann, D. (1997) *Psychotherapy, An Erotic Relationship*. London: Routledge.

McIlwain, D. (2014) Knowing but not showing achieving reflective encounter with desire – A relational psychoanalytic perspective. In Luca, M. (ed.) *Sexual Attraction in Therapy* (pp. 53–66). Chichester: John Wiley.

Messler Davies, J. (2003) Falling in love with love. *Psychoanalytic Dialogues*, 13(1), 1–27.

Pope, K. S., Tabachnick, B. G., and Keith-Spiege, P. (1986) Sexual attraction to clients: The human therapist and the (sometimes) inhuman training system. *American Psychologist*, 41(2), 147–158.

Pope, K. S. and Tabachnick, B. G. (1993) Therapists' anger, hate, fear, and sexual feelings: National survey of therapists' responses, client, characteristics, critical events, formal complaints, and training. *Professional Psychology, Research and Practice*, 24(2), 142–152.

Rogers, C. (1957) The necessary and sufficient conditions of therapeutic personality change. *Journal of Consulting Psychology*, 21, 95–103.

Safran, J. D., Muran, J. C., Wallner Samstag, L., and Stevens, C. (2001) Repairing therapeutic alliance ruptures. *Psychotherapy*, 38, 406–412.

Sarkar, S. P. (2004) Boundary violation and sexual exploitation in psychiatry and psychotherapy: A review. *Advances in Psychiatric Treatment*, 10, 312–321.

Seto, M. C. (1995) Sex with therapy clients: Its prevalence, potential consequences, and implications for psychology training. *Canadian Psychology/Psychologie Canadienne*, 36(1), 70.

Smith Pickard, P. (2014) Role of psychological proximity and sexual feelings in negotiating relatedness in the consulting room – A phenomenological perspective. In Luca, M. (ed.) *Sexual Attraction in Therapy* (pp. 67–79). Chichester: John Wiley.

Swiggart, W., Feurer, I. D., Samenow, C., Delmonico D. L., and Spickard, W. A. Jr. (2008) Sexual boundary violation index: A validation study. *The Journal of Treatment & Prevention*, 15(2), 176–190.

Worrell, M. (2014) 'Hot cognition in sexual attraction' clarifying, using and defusing the dionysian in cognitive behavioural psychotherapies. In Luca, M. (ed.) *Sexual Attraction in Therapy* (pp. 3–21). Chichester: John Wiley.

1.3 The meaning of the asking
James Agar and Brian Fenton

Introduction

The two of us have gotten to know each other in a monthly clinical supervision group over a ten-year period. Our original interest in writing this chapter came from noticing how we as male psychotherapists manage erotic edges and sexual attraction in our clinical practices. More recently we have seen our work through the lens of intersubjectivity within a 'two-person psychology' (Stark, 1999). Intersubjectivity (Stolorow et al., 1987) addresses both client and therapist's unique subjectivity and the flow of energy and information between the two people. As a participant within the therapeutic dyad, we believe that the therapist is always subtly disclosing aspects of self either implicitly or explicitly.

This perspective directly implicates the subjectivity of the practitioner in what emerges in the room, including experiences of attraction. It also seems clear to us that attraction is an area of experience where there are dimensions of relatedness, and one where both client and practitioner are potentially at risk/vulnerable. A meaningful, ongoing supervisory relationship is therefore essential to the practitioner for the client's well-being.

We hold a wider consideration in our chapter about whether the formal years of psychotherapy training can in fact prepare practitioners to access and harness these powerful forces, or whether this capacity is mainly acquired through supervised practice.

In preparation for writing this chapter we found that we enjoyed the process of discussing the ideas so much that we would write the chapter in a discussant style. Whilst the chapter is not verbatim, the content in part emerged from our relatedness, which mirrors our clinical practice styles.

We describe our learning from our clients in the context of our own personal and professional development over the years through training, therapy, and ongoing supervised practice. Clinical examples are composite profiles which have been anonymised to preserve client confidentiality.

Setting the scene: the erotic as sensual experience

We believe that healthy adolescent and adult sexual desire arises from the embodied sensuality of childhood play, from the inside out. In this way we resonate with Celenza's (2019) 'approach to everything in the world as erotic'. She defines the erotic as sensuality and invites us to think about the way in which we 'gaze into the world, receive it and let it penetrate us'.

The erotic as sensual experience then links with Physis, 'the force of nature, which eternally strives to make things grow' (Berne, 1968, p. 89). In adolescence sexual awareness and desire grow out from the sensuality of pre-adolescence. Freud (1912) ascribed to "sexual life *all manifestations of tender feelings* which originated from the source of primitive sexual emotions" (italics added).

We think, however, that what gets constellated under patriarchy as adult sexual desires are in fact culturally sanctioned expressions of the erotic that are almost exclusively genitally oriented, hetero-normative and one-dimensional. Think: Naked Attraction (2019). By contrast, Holly McNish takes us beyond these binary restrictions to a rich and nuanced experience of the erotic with her reading of her poem, "Bricks" on YouTube (2014).

Additionally, Mann (1997) reminds us that everyone is born from a mother and that the mother-infant relationship is an embodied, sensual, and erotic one. In this way we can think that everyone's first relationship with their mother is their first love affair, whatever the circumstances. Whatever we get the first time round is what we get.

Writing this chapter heightens the authors' awareness of our intensely hetero-normative scripting and assumptions as middle-aged men about sexuality and desire, which are based on what Hedges (2011, pp. xiii–xiv) calls 'the many myths and just-so stories' where '…boys and girls, men and women are *naturally attracted to one another* so that they can be married and have babies to perpetuate the species. The end'. Hedges advises psychotherapists to identify and question every aspect of sexuality and gender to help our clients 'get beyond their just-so stories'.

Brian: Sexuality is a broad subject and quite daunting. It's always there in some form, whether we notice it or not. As practitioners, sexuality calls out to us in many ways, including when we are excited or even turned on by a client who is our 'type'; when sexualised behaviour is the client's (or therapist's) primary way of making contact; or, at times, when it emerges unexpectedly over time through growing affection within the nature of the engagement itself.

Thankfully being powerfully attracted to clients isn't an everyday occurrence. That said, Rogers (2011) found that 90% of therapists reported having been sexually attracted to at least one patient, and Martin et al. (2011) found sexuality to be a common aspect of the therapeutic relationship.

While we don't have space in this chapter to comment on all aspects of love and desire, and their interrelatedness, we will reflect on how we, as psychotherapists, take responsibility for our own sexual desires, attitudes, and prejudices in the consulting room so as to provide a climate which encourages fluidity of self. A climate where the risks sexuality brings to the dyad can be mindfully considered in supervision.

Jamie: We've come to understand sexual desire holistically and systemically, as involving both psychological and biological processes. We hold aspects of desire and biology as figure and ground, bringing one desire into awareness while others reside in the background.

And like Little (2018), we see no distinction between normal love and transference love. All love is hormonally driven and illusory and brings the hope and possibility of transformation.

In our research for this chapter we've tried to understand the theory of relativity in relation to a two-person psychology (Stark, 1999) and in particular the challenges of direction of effect or influence. Below I recall a scene from my past which evokes this strange kind of experience. Like when I'm on a train and another faster train comes alongside, there are a few intensely disorienting moments when I don't know which train is moving which way; when it seems even like my train is stationary, or a moment when it seems like my train is suddenly going backwards!

Power dynamics and the direction of effect: who is hitting on whom?

1986. This is a scene from the pre-digital world of my youth, before the advent of smart phones and generating our fantasies of others through a screen.

It's midnight and I'm heading home from a late shift in a residential project. I am sitting on a night bus parked in Trafalgar Square. Up top in the double-decker next to me is a very enticing, attractive young woman dressed in stylish Goth gear and makeup. I can see her face in profile and she is facing the other direction. I imagine myself to be stealing glances at her and looking away again, although I'm sure my gaze is much more obvious than that. I'm entertaining a vague erotic fantasy of something happening, I'm not sure what but I find her very attractive in her black gear and eyeliner and feel excited.

Suddenly she turns her head and looks directly at me. She then crooks her finger in my direction and beckons me towards her.

I gasp with embarrassment and look away. I look anywhere but in her direction!

This vignette reminds me that another person's subjectivity can actually be destabilising and even frightening because it refers to their intentionality: What does she intend with me?

When I think of how this occurs clinically I'm reminded that psychotherapy can be something dangerous you do without leaving your office (Bromberg, 2011)!

Brian: In your example I can see discord in the supposed power dynamics between the sexes. In this scene you, the male, appear to be following heterosexual norms as the seeking or penetrating one. But suddenly she calls you out, and you are exposed as the inexperienced one. What you imagine suddenly becomes real; you are overwhelmed, frightened, and even ashamed.

With regard to direction of effect, I find the metaphors from relativity and quantum theories fascinating, unshackling, and enlivening in their non-linear framings (Marks-Tarlow, 2008). Your disorienting experience on a train links nicely to one of Einstein's thought experiments (Khutoryansky, 2011). He described a situation where if we place two objects in a vacuum they each have no way of knowing which is moving and which is still, until some other force is present. For me this highlights the need for a 'third' as a form of friction to disrupt the vacuum of the therapeutic dyad. This third supports us in figuring out who is moving which way and who is influencing whom. This reference point for therapists is clinical supervision. In terms of the attraction a question might be, 'Who is hitting on whom?'

Wondering together about where our minds wander in the therapy hour led us to the title of this chapter: 'The Meaning of the Asking'.

Jamie: Wallin (2014) coins a self-reflective acronym that he calls WAIT: 'Why am I talking?' This acronym alerts him to listen and reflect in the midst of the action of the session.

Brian: How wise. As intersubjectivity situates the subjectivities of both the therapist and the client as being relevant to what emerges, I'm wondering if Wallin is searching within himself in the waiting?

Jamie: Yes, exactly. His acronym reminds me that I have to shut up first so that I can do that searching inside! Wallin (p. 233) goes on to pose a further overarching question: 'What am I actually doing with this patient?' followed by two others aimed at deepening our understanding: 'What are the implicit relational meanings of what I'm doing?' and 'What might be my motivations for doing what I'm doing?'

Brian: Those questions remind us that we can have motivations which are hidden from ourselves.

Jamie: I'm interested in what is in the field between the client and myself that is being conducted outside of our conscious awareness. Especially that which carries an erotic charge. For me this is where good supervision is essential.

The supervisory space is where I lean into my uncensored fantasies. I am vulnerable when I trust my supervisor and ask for help. I can then scroll into my process and begin to know better what the client brings me to learn.

This is especially poignant with long-term clients, who often in my experience symbiotically mirror back to me some aspects of my core issues, like shame and unresolved grief. If I can know what the client stirs in me then I will know better how to help the client. But for a long time we stay in the soup resonating back and forth with each other.

I observe the adage that the clients who stay with me have something to teach me and if I learn it then I will be able to help them. Then they might or might not be resolved enough to leave therapy. By this I mean that my responses to my clients are *mine*, *my* feelings, *my* trouble. When I describe myself as feeling stuck with my client, I recognise that that is *my* stuck-ness to know. When I am with my clients I roam the terrain of my own preoccupied and unresolved shame-based attachment styles and strategies. The client and I resonate with each other's longing for goodness and disgust with badness. If I can lean into what I find difficult to know in myself then I am better available to the client. That is my third-ness.

Who we are matters: the personal in the professional

Jamie: Now in my 60s, I feel released from testosterone and historical longing, which have been driving forces throughout my early and middle adulthood. I now feel able to begin to know the benefits of earned and learned secure attachment and a greater capacity to learn from the experiences I find most difficult.

Looking back, I can identify with the belated and notorious jazz trumpeter George Melly's (1989) comment on turning 70 and finding himself impotent. He said he felt like he was 'unchained from a lunatic'.

In a recent discussion I was interested that a post-menopausal female colleague could identify with Melly's sentiment.

Brian: You remind me, Jamie, of a gay feminist commentator who, after having hormone treatment of testosterone, left hospital and immediately noticed being markedly sexually aroused by the women walking by. She laughingly identified what she imagined it was like to be a man, and points us perhaps to differences between male and female lust systems. Hormones though, are only one influence on sexuality, and while we do tend to simmer down with age, the power dynamics and attitudes forged in our developmental attachments remain enduring parts of who we are as people.

Jamie: I'm interested in human sexual development in the late teens and early to mid-20s. This transition period from late adolescence into what I call full adulthood involves struggles with sexuality, aggression, and loneliness. I regard these as critical individuation tasks for early adulthood, and work with many middle-aged clients who come for therapy realising that they have somewhat 'unformed' adult selves which date back to this earlier time. I am always interested in reflecting with them on where they got to in their struggles with love, work, and being alone.

Brian: Sexuality and aggression are critical in forging identity during adolescence, and with it the destabilising impact of these parts of the self when they aren't met well.

Jamie: In writing this chapter I've become aware of how loneliness in my childhood influenced my sexual development so that in my reading of source material, I am drawn to authors who describe this experience, like

Atlas (2016, p. 16) when she writes that 'Sexual longing presupposes a sense of loss and the hope of refinding'.

This quotation speaks of my youth and a passive longing to be received and loved. I was an intensely lonely teenager growing up as the son of an autistic and very unhappily married Presbyterian minister.

Masturbation equated loneliness and unrequited longing in my world. In a pre-internet age I had to tolerate the lurking shame when buying 'top-shelf' soft porn at the newsagent. I had several homosexual encounters in my teens which both excited and scared the hell out of me. I was raging inside and terrified of my own destructiveness.

Using a developmental model of sexuality like Hedges (2011), I can resonate back to an early symbiotic rupture when my mother entered full-time work and left me in the care of my autistic father. During my early adolescence my elder siblings left home and I experienced more profoundly the Oedipal cost of my parents' violent and hostile-dependent marriage. I sometimes joke that the only thing my parents could agree on was that they both hated Catholics.

I was stuck in the middle, immobilised and frozen like a bug in amber. I felt constantly pulled to collude with my mother righteous rage while receiving my father's modelling of passive retaliation as 'top-dog' to her 'under-dog' (Clarkson, 1989, p. 92).

As an adolescent I believed that because my parents hated each other, that I was born from that hate and therefore I was hateful.

In adolescence I reinvented myself with drugs, independent travel, and jazz and blues music. I listened to bluesmen hollering the poetry of shame, pain, and loss through call-and-response lyrics like those of Elmore James's 'Done Somebody Wrong' (1960). In James's lyrics, he sings that something is wrong with him, and he hopes his luck will change.

My luck did change, eventually. In my family of origin I had my three much older siblings to remind me that my parents were the crazy ones and help me to leave home by providing alternative parental support and containment that kept me from going completely off the rails. Their influence and my foreign travel eventually helped me to reinvent myself and relocate to another continent.

Brian: Sounds like a challenging beginning, Jamie. How refreshing to see the word luck in there. And yes, we cannot discuss sexual attraction without considering our pasts, as we remain vulnerable to our developmental process pulling on us as we make meaning of anything. We see through our minds, as they say.

Jamie: After 30 years in private practice I begin to understand retrospectively how I was, and still am at times vulnerable to enactments (Bromberg, 2011) with couples and individuals as a consequence of those beginnings.

Brian: Yes, our parents' conscious and unconscious relationship patterns shape our Oedipal decisions. I'm the youngest of four children raised in a Catholic-of-sorts family. I was fortunate enough though to have a mother who was originally Protestant allowing me a reflective angle on difference from the very beginning. Our family resided in a working-class area of Glasgow, where at that time sexual identities were defined within stark binaries. For example, there were no openly gay children at my schools, which I realised in later life meant that those children who were gay were then forced to live fearful existences like fugitives or double agents. Whilst sexuality was seen as personal and private, this was done in a backdrop of hostility towards difference (disguised within humour).

So sexuality was private and my own but it needed to be within the parameters of hetero-normative sameness. Expressions of love and affection within the family were encoded and left plenty of room for misunderstanding. This was problematic when we consider that sexuality is a self-defining feature of our lives, and one we need support to manage. Sexuality is also an early signal of separateness through, for example, differences in preference, and with difference comes the risk of disapproval and oppression (Hart, 2019). Talking of which I recall the excitement of discovering porn magazines too, which in its way was liberating (as is often the case, liberation for one can be oppression for another).

Oedipal anxieties being a two way street meant that my parents' own anxieties manifested in mindless prohibition, and set the scene for me to make my own meanings. My siblings were all a good bit older than me and my parents' marriage was emotionally distant, so that I felt I had no competition for my mother's affection, up until around aged 7. It was then I think it fair to say that I did a psychological and emotional runner (I think that you and I Jamie share an experience of too much mother and not enough supportive father). Being left to one's own developing sexuality is not ideal in relation to managing primitive anxieties, which in my case resulted in a tendency to project out what makes me anxious. 'It's not me it's you!' Whilst having lots of friends, in relation to my Oedipal experiences and sexuality, I became an inwardly lonely, inept young man with little sense of impacting others, most likely due to my identifying with my distant father. This was complicated by my maintaining a grandiose sense of expectancy regarding being desired, followed by much disappointment in that it took time (a long time!) to realise other women weren't my mother, and that the breast was not coming to me! (Both these processes impact my clinical work, and these understandings have transformed my couples and group work.)

Like most of us though I managed to fumble my way into lust and sex, but remained devoid of narrative or outward expression of love. This awkwardness, combined with a lifelong distrust of authority, is the Brian I arrived in psychotherapy training with.

Learning from clients Michelle, Ma Belle

Jamie: I remember a client whom I shall call Michelle. I saw her for counselling and group work in a residential rehab in the late 80s, so this is also a story from my early adult life. During this period in London I had qualified as a counsellor and was beginning my training as a psychotherapist. I was in my early 30s and worked in a long-stay, second stage residential rehab in Camden for recovering alcoholics.

Michelle was a middle-aged woman who arrived in the project from an intensive post-detox hospital programme. Soon after meeting me she announced that she had made a new boyfriend who lived locally, and, lo and behold, *his* name was Jamie too.

Each week's counselling session consisted of elaborate details about their relationship – their activities, conflicts, hopes and dreams for the future, meeting his family. Being newly qualified and inexperienced I was partly curious but mostly naive. I tended to believe what clients told me as both real and true, so I took her narrative at face value.

After about a year I moved positions within the same charity to another project. Near the end of our final counselling session Michelle informed me that there was no other Jamie and that she had made him up.

We had no time to talk about her disclosure in the session and I was finishing in the service in a few days' time. I had also finished with our external group supervisor the previous week.

When I think back to Michelle's relationship throughout her year with me I imagine her pleasure in giving shape to what would have been a fantasy at the outset. This was done through speaking it aloud to me and to her fellow residents.

While I felt thrown in the moments following her disclosure, I then felt righteously annoyed and ashamed. My manager was amused. I'm astonished in hindsight that no one else in the service, the manager, our psychoanalytic supervisor, or even the other clients voiced doubts or suspicions about the veracity of her story through the entire year. I now think that *we* believed it because *she* believed it. The story only stopped being real when I was leaving and it couldn't be fuelled and elaborated with my ongoing physical presence in her life.

I imagine her elaborating on the details as she sat facing me week after week in groups and individual sessions so that *this* Jamie (who had a professional role and a separate life outside the project) became *that* Jamie (in her mind) *out there* with whom she could construct a life together. I almost can imagine her actually travelling to Peckham and walking the streets with me in her mind, putting flesh on the bones of the story, having me secretly in this special way where *she* was in charge. *She* could co-create this life with her fantasy Jamie on those streets of her native London.

Brian: I'm wondering what Michelle represented for you regarding your Oedipal experiences?

Jamie: Immediately I begin to consider the fictitious name 'Michelle' that I have given this client for the purposes of this chapter. I initially thought of the Beatles' love song (1965) as an expression of the erotic in our relationship which could not be openly expressed by *her* to me. But of course in the actual song Lennon and McCartney are writing about *his* desire for her.

So I have to think that she *could not express to me that which I couldn't bear to know*. She was a woman almost twice my age, almost my mother's age in fact. I was beginning my counselling career and had not been given any training or clinical guidance in managing the erotic in a residential service where the client lived, ate, and slept?

At this age I was both a boy and a man who was inhibited from expressing love by profound shame about my erotic life. Personally and professionally I would have felt frightened to think about it in a transference/countertransference frame. Too hot to handle.

Brian: I'm struck by who you and Michelle became for each other. Only she knows what that was for her in the fuller sense. However, it seems to me that her fantasy had a function of maintaining her connection with you as someone she could hold onto and put her love into. I imagine this detracted from a hopeless emptiness which her addiction had previously filled.

Learning from clients Ben: your phone's off the hook (but you're not)

Jamie: This leads me to my recent work in private practice with an older male client I shall call Ben. This vignette is taken from a complex and involved long-term psychotherapy relationship. Ben came to therapy via his doctor because he experienced alternating periods of intense anxiety and depression. He had recently been forced to take medical retirement from his work.

He reported that he had recently diagnosed himself via social media as 'incel' (involuntary celibate). I was intrigued and began to research this phenomena: a person, especially a man, who identifies as being frustrated by a lack of opportunities to have sex (Collins, 2019).

After some months Ben also began to tell me about his compulsive masturbation and addiction to online pornography.

Following my summer holiday he disclosed that he regularly rang my answer phone during my break in order to hear my voice on the recording but hung up without leaving a message. We explored the meaning and purpose: after the initial excitement of making the phone call, he reported feeling relieved and contained that I was a professional and that he was in my care – the voice of my answering machine message reminded him of this.

I wondered aloud if there was more to it, whether the anticipation and execution of the call might have created an erotic or even sexual dopamine hit, like his use of porn. He was shocked and vehemently denied this. For him, these anticipatory feelings could only be construed as 'anxiety' or 'stress'. Hearing my voice calmed and reassured him, he insisted.

Ben returned the following session, angrily telling me that he had been looking on my professional registering body's website for their ethics policy and codes of practice. He wanted to complain: how *dare* I suggest that *his* behaviour was erotic! He came to see me *because* there would be no risk of this being a sexual relationship!

This rupture became quite a major impasse and took some time to contain, repair, and build upon. I sought help from my supervisor and my group over a period of months. I had to find and own my disavowed 'incel' in order to help Ben to find and reclaim his lonely sexual teenage self.

In the longer term this served to help the two of us to negotiate our relationship as boundaried adults – and even *sexual* beings – between which there would *never* be a concrete sexual relationship, however. In time this proved to be a developmental milestone for the client who had rigidly preserved a core identity in his fantasy life as that of a young adolescent to disavow and ward off terror and shame for his deeper unfulfilled and dangerous erotic desires.

Brian: I can see also how calling an answer phone is one-way traffic and a process Ben felt in control of, as his initial use of porn would have been. With porn addiction I've found that discussing the particular genre they are addicted to can at times yield meaningful relational dynamics.

You take us also into the worrying arena of complaints. Offering an empathic experience can generate longings and desire in clients (and therapists), particularly where their partners are neither sensitive nor emotionally available. The thought of a complaint threatening my reputation is bad enough, but the threat to my income also frightens me just as much. In the past this threat has impacted on my freedom to make challenging interventions, particularly where there were inter-agency funding concerns to remind me just where I stand.

The training years

Brian: I remember my initial psychotherapy training in the early 1990s teaching me about here-and-now relatedness as attachment-based love or agape. We did not learn much about sexuality, the erotic, and lust. As trainee transactional analysts in terms of developmental dynamics much emphasis was placed on the lack lustre Script Matrix (Steiner, 1974). This is a schematic model which describes various forms of relatedness between a child and their caregivers and influences the child's core beliefs about self, others, and the world. For me, the model lacked vitality and dynamism. We did have the Drama Triangle (Karpman, 1968) though, which is a model using the three positions of Persecutor, Rescuer, and Victim for analysing repetitive patterns of behaviour which we use to maintain life scripts. This is an excellent tool for reflecting on familiar relational binaries and our part in them. These binaries, perhaps deriving from Oedipal failures on themes such as separation anxiety, difference, oppression, and disempowerment, again though remained absent of framing desire and sexuality.

In those days there was much placed on physical holding and reparation through meeting need, as in a '1½ person psychology' (Stark, 1999), a mode of therapeutic action which emphasises the provision by the therapist of a corrective or developmentally needed relationship. Looking back, I feel that this emphasis swamped and sanitised the dyad, leaving little space for noticing the longings and desires you speak of, Jamie. We were not trained to think about the erotic as part of a developmental drive towards self-definition and differentiation (see Mann, 1997) in ways that you and I have tried to do here.

Jamie: I remember my training psychotherapist providing intense warmth, empathy, and challenge, and I learned a great deal from her, for which I feel gratitude and appreciation.

But now, almost 30 years on, I think that she responded almost exclusively to my presenting infantile hunger, rage, and confusion with nurturing, containment, and physical holding in group and individual sessions. Neither she nor I gave much consideration to my identity as an adult sexual man, especially in the here-and-now of my marriage.

In the ensuing years I have learned that as a male psychotherapist I can powerfully communicate empathy and containment to my clients without physical touch. This is of course after years of supervised practice and learning from mistakes.

Learning from clients Angela: an inoculation

Brian: Like you then, the combination of my developmental context, my initial training and my personal readiness didn't prepare me for the road ahead. In an immediate experiential sense though, maybe nothing can.

I think back with regret to my work with a client very early on in my career. At the time I felt shame that being sexually attracted to a client was wrong and did not have a coherent narrative to manage the situation effectively. I also felt and still feel shame that I added to the process instead of containing it (Atlas, 2016), as I will describe below.

I was a training therapist working as a counsellor in a public setting with an attractive female client, Angela.

Angela wondered if she had been sexually abused as a child. She had been informed by her mother that she herself had been sexually abused by her father, Angela's maternal grandfather. Her parents were separated, and her father was a distant figure in her life, so Angela was often read bedtime stories by this grandfather. She wondered about the nature of the physical closeness they shared. At the time I had little or no experience of the erotic being a normal part of relatedness or as a process activated as a defence against intimacy and related vulnerabilities.

As the work progressed, Angela spoke of emotional distance in her marriage, and I found myself imagining being her partner. With each session I became increasing attracted to her and looked forward to her sessions. In my mind the dilemma I faced in this work was to remain focussed on the process Angela was bringing and to try and ignore the palpably obvious but unspoken attraction I had for her.

At this point I didn't consider that my feelings were requited. I certainly had no idea that the process between us may be significant in relation to Angela's intrapsychic and interpersonal worlds: she was emotionally distant with her husband as she had been with her father. I did not understand that hiding my sexual feelings in this therapeutic relationship might indicate countertransference information related to Angela and her grandfather. In brief I had little sense of wondering about the meaning of the questions I was asking. In this way the attraction and arousal remained disorganised, and both consciously and unconsciously I was subtly fanning the erotic fire with her. With hindsight I realise that I enjoyed this attention and didn't want it to stop.

The situation became more problematic when the designated number of counselling sessions came to an end and I arranged to take Angela into my private practice. My agency supervisor agreed this arrangement was fine and I informed Angela.

However, my training supervisor thought this transition unwise.

My memory is impaired as to what occurred in this training supervision for this decision to be made, but I hope I had enough presence of mind to reveal some of my feelings towards Angela. My supervisor and I both decided that I was not psychologically equipped at that point in time to proceed, and that the therapy hadn't been going on for long enough to warrant pressing on. In particular we did not have a strong enough therapeutic alliance. Although this brought problems for Angela it still seems right. I will never forget how difficult it was to inform Angela that it would be best if she were to continue therapy with a more experienced therapist. We had one session after this to end our work together. In this session Angela asked to see me outside therapy. I viewed this as devastating for her treatment. There was now no space within which she could explore and deal with her feelings or her disillusionment with me. Leaving her I'm sure, feeling wrong, as I did myself.

Jamie: What would you say now to that younger self, the trainee psychotherapist?

Brian: I guess I would adopt an understanding attitude as my supervisor had done towards me. At the time I comforted myself with the fact that I had not transgressed physically by agreeing to see Angela outside the therapy room. In this way I believe that she had experienced a non-abusive experience within an asymmetrical relationship with a man she trusted.

I had no sense that the role of therapist itself would stimulate these types of feelings, or that at times these types of feelings needed to happen. Or that if I had been one step ahead we could have worked through the situation, or at least I could have held it differently. I realise now that my feelings may or may not have been relevant to Angela's story, and much may also have been about us.

In a way I consider this experience as an inoculation of sorts. Not an inoculation in terms of my thinking that this experience could prevent this type of entanglement from happening to me again. (The unconscious is always at work.) I think of it as an inoculation which alerts me to the need to take these fantasies and feelings of love to supervision as early as possible so as not to become isolated with them, and to prevent things taking hold. I think too that some clients need their own inoculation. They need an experience where erotic longings and attractions are recognised as normal and can become symbolic, not through gratification, but through talking about them. Whether this process means self-disclosure regarding the therapist's feelings of attraction I remain unsure.

From this situation as a trainee I began developing an experiential narrative on erotic process, and have come to notice that these Rescue fantasies can indicate that I am sexually attracted to a client but not registering it'. (Rescue fantasies being a role doled out to men within patriarchy.)

Jamie: I'm curious to know what the eroticised role of Rescuer (Karpman, 1968) means more personally for you, Brian.

Brian: For me the Rescuer role can be a diversion away from erotic feelings, or the opposite in Rescuer being a role within patriarchy where powerful me(n) will help vulnerable you down from that tower (and legitimately have sex with you at the bottom!). In my case both apply, and my vulnerability is personalised in that I felt that my role as son was to rescue my mother from her despair.

Jamie: As a supervisor I would rarely force an end to a trainee's clinical work due to the risk of harm being done to the client by this action. Trying to refer the client to an experienced therapist rarely works in the way it is theoretically intended, unless the agency actually had offered her an appointment with another experienced therapist within the same service so that she felt contained. But I can see that you and your supervisor agreed that you were not trained and experienced sufficiently for the potential transformation from what was an unwitting transgression.

Brian: I was disappointed in the therapy not being able to continue, and also relieved regarding my own anxiety. I cannot overstate how mindless I was in the area of sexuality at this point in time, and expect my training supervisor picked up on some therapy issue I wasn't aware of. Perhaps some hangover from my Oedipal situation such as a difficulty symbolising attraction, or a longing to embrace a scarce opportunity for love, or maybe just a part of myself I wasn't sufficiently engaged with. Frommer (2006) suggests that sexuality is a self-state which holds hidden parts of ourselves. In daily life this may be fine, but as therapists we are required to be self-aware beyond the norm.

I used this client's example deliberately as it seems to me that training and newly qualified therapists are most vulnerable to mindless transgression and to causing harm to their patients and to themselves.

Jamie: This supports our hypothesis that as psychotherapy trainees tend to be preoccupied with academic and psychological developmental tasks, learning to work with sexual attraction intersubjectively in the main occurs through the hard graft of supervised practice following accreditation.

Don't search for the answers... Live the questions now. (Rilke, 1929/2012)

Brian: 'Never be sexual with patients', bellows Yalom (2002, p. 194). I understand him to mean don't actually have sexual relations with patients. He does not mean that sexual feelings should be prohibited in a non-reflective manner. I, too, find adopting this clear boundary helpful in managing issues of attraction.

Without wishing to tidy up chaos or to kill off ambiguity, my current thinking in dealing with sexual attraction and the erotic is to make a commitment to myself to 'never' entering into a concrete sexual relationship with a client or supervisee. The absoluteness of the word keeps me within an ethical frame which supports non-maleficence and beneficence. It also has the theoretical benefit of providing a container where potentially anything can be talked about. Without this line I feel the anxiety would be too inhibiting and distracting for both parties in the dyad. One might counter this position by saying that this line is as unreal as the vacuum in the Einstein metaphor above, and that in life nothing is really still, or totally safe.

Jamie: My motto is 'Once a client, always a client'. I could never have a social relationship with a former client because the power differential does not change for me. Adopting this position is a way of creating certainty in a post-modern world, as paradoxical as this may sound.

Brian: And paradoxes are windows into the unknown, and reminders that theories are just that. Post-modernism is a theory; one which better suits the human condition, but a theory all the same. Applying some certainty to this area of relatedness to manage a boundary feels right for me. It also provides a container for dysregulated feelings.

Certainty seems especially important here as love is a situation where the mind gets taken over, and we cannot be expected to trust our own feelings or motivations. The closeness felt in therapy can lead to succumbing to attraction and love, and to us telling ourselves what we want to hear, and as with all authority we are vulnerable to suiting ourselves.

For me 'never' provides a protective atmosphere within which the project of developing self can be undertaken and where I can manage my end of the bargain.

Jamie: Helen Fisher's extensive research (2005) shows us that romantic love is a drive and highly addictive. She likens it to maternal preoccupation. When two people are in love they are biologically programmed to notice their similarities rather than their differences.

Brian: Yes, and an addiction we are all vulnerable to. I expect that a small minority of transgressors are manipulative abusers, with the majority being well-intentioned characters that fall into an existential trap set within power dynamics they have lost sight of. And as you point to above, countertransference can at times be indistinguishable from here-and-now feelings.

Jamie: 'Real' love and transference love are simultaneously an illusion and hormonally driven. 'What you feel is real, but it's not necessarily true', I tell clients.

Brian: Without this clear boundary there is then a loss of the capacity for protecting clients and ourselves from the conditions of relating in psychotherapy (i.e., the attractions stimulated by asymmetry, the harm done through getting the mother, father, teacher, and with it the loss of reflection on temptations and desires the boundary offers). 'Never' provides the freedom to consider in supervision our fuller human existence, including our exploitative elements where we consciously or unconsciously use and objectify others for our benefit.

I can't deny the word 'never' stimulates a grief in me. But there's loss in acquisition too as in loss of desire. Put simply in this scenario for me it's better to regret something I haven't done as opposed to regret something I have.

The asymmetrical nature of the therapeutic encounter and the exaggerated attention of one for the other provides a hyper-reality (Oakley, 2019). Therapy is not intended to be mutual in the sense of openness. The therapeutic relationship itself then is contrived to support development and lacks naturalism. In this space our very personal ways of managing sexual distance, which are woven into our everyday life are discouraged, and as such clients are invited to disarm (i.e., 'we can talk about anything here').

How could a client have confidence to speak their mind in the therapeutic process if there were the possibility that the therapist's desires were to be included in the mix in a concrete way?

Jamie: Change can be understood metaphorically as the 'analytic child' (Mann, 1997, p. 7). 'The analytic couple, therapist and patient, have an analytic baby, the psychological growth of the analysand (and often the therapist, too)'. Mann goes on to suggest that this metaphor has at its heart the 'prohibited erotic desire' of the Oedipal scene, with potential for both danger and creativity.

Brian: When managing attraction then, do we speak it within the frame of never making the attraction concrete? Do we contain it? Do we believe that disclosing these types of feelings is important?

Jamie: I would take that on a case-by-case basis. Why would I with this person, why wouldn't I with another?

And, saying that, I have had the experience of falling in love with a client who was in love with me. Things in both our lives got very confused and messy and ethically required me to speak openly and honestly and take responsibility for my transgression. I'm glad to say that we recalibrated our relationship successfully after a period of disillusionment, sadness, and anger on her part. We didn't have sex but we made a baby, to use Mann's metaphor.

This experience was in the years following the therapy undertaken during my training which I have described above. I think now that my erotic transgression with this client followed from my lingering naivety and confusion of my own therapy experience. Working out the misunderstanding and owning my part with this client was a defining experience for me.

Brian: Yes, our training and personal therapy will influence what we feel is our task as therapists, and shape our own version of how to conduct the work. We both felt that for us there was lack of emphasis on the sexual aspect of attachment. I think, though, with some theories, such as psychoanalysis, there had been an overemphasis on sexuality and perhaps a lack on attachment and love in a wider sense, and the curative aspects of here-and-now relating. This situation has been addressed in part by the move from classical psychoanalysis to object relations. It is currently being furthered by relational perspectives, which seem to me to be working on how to include the subjectivity of the therapist from a two-person perspective (see Cornell and Hargaden, 2005).

For me the task of therapy is to support expansion of mind. To become more able to live with the uncertainties of life, to be more emotionally and psychologically flexible, and to reclaim the capacity for intimacy (Berne, 1972), including sexuality. My function is to provide my mind and heart to reflect with, and not to be the provider of need be per se, and certainly not sexual need.

Again, more questions: what do 'need', 'provision', and 'being sexual' mean? Do we not at times contain projective identifications, which include erotic feelings for our clients? As with intersubjectivity, sexuality is existential and to use your term Jamie, we are awash with it. Whether we directly refer to it or not, sexuality is always in our minds if not always on them. Do we as therapists ever have to make our own feelings of attraction explicit? If so, why?

Ultimately, given that all meaning is personal and co-constructed, the answer rests on each individual presentation.

Jamie: I agree. Each individual client constellates a unique dyad with me. As a rule of thumb I would trust myself to supervision in these matters. To use Mann's metaphor of therapeutic sex, the baby is more likely to be born healthy with meaningful supervision. I assume that when I take something that bugs me to supervision then I make it coherent and it begins to be ready to be known and perhaps addressed explicitly with the client.

But I have been known to act first and then have to deal with my actions, as when I naively suggested many years ago with a client dealing with complex memories of childhood sexual abuse, that she ask her husband to join us for a one-off session to ask him to refrain from sex while she was doing the therapy. B-A-D intervention. Boy, did he get angry!

Supervision and the hive mind

Jamie: I call a highly functioning supervision group a hive mind, where many minds work together as one. Throughout my career groups have been my preferred predominant support structures – supervision, therapy, and professional development groups, although I have had extensive individual working relationships as well. My groups are longstanding affairs, lasting between 10 and 20 years. Some are ongoing. These have become my "reconstituted family" imago (Clarkson, 1993, personal communication), within which I have co-created profound sibling affiliations and deeply personal professional attachments. Rarely have I socialised with any of these colleagues and yet I feel their friendship as a constant support in my daily psychotherapy practice.

I feel this way with you, Brian. You're part of the internal supervisory group mind I carry with me from my network of my professional attachments. This has become a familial container body within which I can be uncensored and refer my most troubling and shameful lust and disgust. Our former group supervisor, Charlotte Sills (2008, personal communication), once said to me that she 'keeps me honest'.

In this way Charlotte speaks for and requires me to answer on behalf of our profession's registering bodies. This accountability calls on me to define my own ethical stance and mitigates against my consciously or unconsciously suiting myself and going rogue.

Brian: Renn (2012) talks of building a platform in supervision. I take this to mean engaging in a way which allows practice for dealing with challenging areas of relationship. I have been profoundly inspired by my colleagues' courage to speak their truth in supervision. Within ongoing supervised practice I've learned to tolerate better being caught off guard in enactments, and their potential for shame.

I felt a distinct vitality and edgy aliveness in my initial post-training relational supervision group (see Hargaden et al., 2009). We engaged in deep reflection on split-off parts of ourselves, including feeling repulsion, attraction, and exclusion, as well as seductive parts. While considering these elements as potential countertransference, we were encouraged to take ownership of such elements of being within ourselves, leading to reduction in othering. In a sense, managing our own anxieties is a powerful tool in managing risk itself. By this I mean talking about feelings in an uncensored manner as you describe Jamie, makes acting them out in concrete manner less likely.

From early in my training to the present, supervision groups have equipped me for understanding the need for others in managing our feelings, and also at times in working out who's mind is who's (see Maroda, 2004). Utilising this type of space requires a degree of trust in our colleagues, and a tolerance of differences in ourselves.

You pointed us above to relativity, post-modernism and intersubjectivity, Jamie. From this perspective, where all is situated and biased (including all of the literature on sexuality), we have come to understand that there is no normal sex, no good or bad, only that in which there is mutual consent, how it feels for you, and how you are able to tolerate the situated opinion of others. And as you cite above, Hedges proposes that one of our central tasks is the deconstruction of the 'many myths and just-so stories' of sexuality. Aside from the incest taboo, the erotic has to contend with familial scripts, cultural taboos, bonds of loyalty, and developmental power dynamics.

Our capacity to be therapeutically intersubjective and to manage anxiety in the consulting room is shaped by who we are as people. In considering my attitudes I have recently been referring to notions of group mind (i.e., the group has a different agenda from the individual); and how in part we prefer *our* group (Elliott, 2016).

The notion of cultural jouissance expands on this situation of group mind (Zizek, 2016). Jouissance means 'physical or intellectual pleasure, delight, or ecstasy' (Oxford Dictionary, 2015), with related activities differing across cultures.

Between groups there are incompatibilities regarding sexual practices based on cultural, religious, or gender differences, which potentially elicit disgust and fuel alienation and feelings of exclusion and retaliatory attack. Other groups are also a convenient target on which to project out our own personal envy and inadequacies. It is vital to keep waking up to these wider issues through for example, personal therapy *and* by creating opportunities for real relationships with people of difference, including political difference.

In your intro, Jamie, you described the erotic as 'culturally sanctioned'. Foucault, too, points to the societal influencing our attitudes and shows us that sexuality itself is political, and in this warns against therapists adopting the role of confessor or permission-giver.

Foucault (1978, p. 103) directly links sexuality with power in describing sexuality as a 'dense transition point' of power. I take this to mean that we are told what we are supposed to desire or not desire within the patriarchal landscape when defining what is proper for a man (assertive penetrator) or a woman (passive recipient). Patriarchy with its double standards makes hypocrites of us all though. Hence our need as therapists to continually search within ourselves to be aware of our situation, as the human desire to maintain power is a significant phenomenon. Foucault also points to words themselves as defining, confining, and reducing experience, which is pertinent to the indefinable erotic.

In our reasonable minds then, we may agree that we are all of equal value and be willing to share power. This mindset, however, may well be in tension with our unconscious processes, where jouissance and cultural norms supporting who has power, pull us to favour our grouping. This situation can lead to processes of oppression towards difference which are outside our conscious awareness. For me, concepts such as *jouissance* and *transition points of power*, open up avenues for reflection, and enhance my capacity to manage the challenges of my own prejudices.

We are all vulnerable to splitting and oppression, so developing a mindset where we are able to wonder about our own processes is important. We can then bridge distinctions within ourselves between what we say we are thinking and what we are really feeling. Offsetting these oppressive elements allows more fluid identifications with the other, freeing us from inhibition and allowing more empathic capacity and habitation of perspectives.

These ways of understanding also support a position where difference is accepted and valued. Without the existence of difference, development truly is defunct. In my mind it is important we know that power is always at work. This is particularly so in today's world where the battle of the sexes has expanded to include multiples of gender distinction, and where genitalia no longer define who we are sexually.

The world of sexuality and gender distinction, more than any other field I engage with, alerts me to many unhelpful presumptions, and highlights Mann's assertion that the erotic pulls us towards greater self-differentiation. The process of self-differentiation itself is to my mind a particular expression of the dialectics of relatedness (see Fenton, 2016), and the working *out and away* from what might be termed proto-binaries.

To conclude

We think it's fair to say any two middle-aged, white, heterosexual, male therapists writing on this subject would find quite a different focus when considering attraction in the consulting room. That said, we believe that the processes described here will be relevant to many practitioners because 'power dynamics' exist within all therapeutic encounters.

We have described some learning from our own clinical errors, and have shown that attraction is multi-dimensional and intersubjective. As such, the practitioner needs the minds of others in ongoing, structured settings (via clinical supervision, professional reading groups, personal psychotherapy, etc.) to manage these feelings.

While the meanings of attraction are wide and varied, more constant is that attraction itself is a rich source of data. Power dynamics between client and therapist are influenced by culturally sanctioned patriarchal rules, and stimulated by the asymmetry of each unique therapeutic relationship. Both parties are vulnerable to these processes.

We agree that our trainings would have benefited from more teaching on potential meanings of love and sexual attraction in the consulting room, although trainees' emotional availability to learn this material will vary. We also know that learning from clients is vital and that no one can be fully equipped to deal with the intimate and confidential arena of psychotherapy.

While accepting that all meaning is personal, we feel that clear external boundaries have a developmental function, and a function of providing safety within which the work can be conducted.

There are many questions remaining. In particular, we are left wondering: if, given the nature of asymmetry in psychotherapy and the likelihood of clients becoming attracted to therapists, can there be such a thing as 'here-and-now attraction' in the therapy room? And if attraction just cannot exist simply as a pleasurable part of therapeutic relatedness, then is it not always about something else?

References

Atlas, G. (2016). *The Enigma of Desire: Sex, Longing, and Belonging in Psychoanalysis*. London: Routledge.

Berne, E. (1972). *What Do You Say After You Say Hello: The Psychology of Human Destiny*. New York: Grove Press.

Berne, E. (1968). *A Layman's Guide to Psychiatry and Psychoanalysis*. New York: Simon & Shuster (Originally published in 1947 as *The Mind in Action*).

Bromberg, P. (2011). *The Shadow of the Tsunami and the Growth of the Relational Mind*. London: Routledge.

Celenza, A. (2019). Erotic transference and countertransference. Online module in webinar series: *Working with Sexuality: Bodies, Desires and Imagination*. www.confer.uk.com.

Clarkson, P. (1989). *Gestalt Counselling in Action*. London: Sage.

Clarkson, P. (1993). Personal communication.

Collins (2019). Online English Dictionary. www.collinsdictionary.com/dictionary/english/incel.

Cornell, W. & Hargaden, H. (2005). *From Transactions to Relations: The Emergence of a Relational Tradition in Transactional Analysis*. Chadlington: Haddon Press.

Elliott, J. (2016). *A Collar in My Pocket: Blue Eyes/Brown Eyes Exercise*. CreateSpace Independent Publishing Platform.

Fenton, B (2016). The dialectical interplay between modes of relatedness. In Hargaden H. (Ed.) *The Art of Relational Supervision* (pp. 26–44). Oxon: Routledge.

Fisher, H. (2005). *Why We Love: The Nature and Chemistry of Romantic Love*. New York: Henry Holt & Co.

Foucault, M. (1978). *The History of Sexuality, Volume 1: An Introduction* (Trans. Hurley, R.). New York: Random House.

Freud, S. (1912). Chapter XI: Concerning "Wild" Psycho-Analysis from *Selected Papers on Hysteria and Other Psycho-Neuroses* (Trans. Brill, A.A.). New York: The Journal of Nervous and Mental Disease Publishing Company. Online edition pub. 2010. www.bartleby.com/280.

Frommer, M.S. (2006). On the subjectivity of lustful states of mind. *Psychoanalytic Dialogues*, 16, 639–664. doi:10.1080/10481880701357289.

Hargaden, H. et al. (2009). *The Evolution of a Relational Supervision Group*. Relationalta.com.

Hart, A. (2019). Attending to sexuality in the psychoanalytic relationship. Online module in webinar series: *Working with Sexuality: Bodies, Desires and Imagination*. www.confer.uk.com.

Hedges, L. (2011). *Sex and Psychotherapy.* London: Routledge.
James, E. (1960). *Done Somebody Wrong.* A-side of 45 rpm single. Fire Music catalogue no. 1031, USA.
Karpman, S. (1968). Fairy tales and script drama analysis. *Transactional Analysis Journal,* 7(26), 39–43.
Khutoryansky, E. (2011). *Albert Einsteins Theory of Relativity.* YouTube – Physics Videos.
Lennon, J. & McCartney P. (1965). *Michelle.* Song from the album *Rubber Soul* (Parlophone Records). Northern Songs Pub, UK.
Little, R. (2018). The management of erotic/sexual countertransference reactions: An exploration of the difficulties and opportunities involved. *Transactional Analysis Journal,* 48(3), 224–241.
Mann, D. (1997). *Psychotherapy: An Erotic Relationship Transference and Countertransference Passions.* Sussex: Routledge.
Marks-Tarlow, T. (2008). *Psyche's Veil. Psychotherapy, Fractals and Complexity.* Sussex: Routledge.
Maroda, K.J. (2004). *The Power of Countertransference.* Hillsdale, NJ: Analytic Press.
Martin, C., Godfrey, M., Meekums, B. & Madill, A. (2011). Managing boundaries under pressure: A qualitative study of therapists' experience of sexual attraction in therapy. *Counselling and Psychotherapy Research,* 11(4), 248–256.
McNish, H. (2014). Bricks // Spoken Word by @holliepoetry. www.youtube.com/watch?v=NCyyYY_pDC8&t=4s.
Melly, G. (1989). Quoted in *The Male Libido is Like Being Chained to a Madman.* https://quoteinvestigator.com/2014/03/15/chained/.
Naked Attraction. (2019). British dating game show broadcast on Channel 4. 5th series. Produced by Studio Lambert.
Oakley, C. (2019). Sexual desire and analytic time. Online module in webinar series: *Working with Sexuality: Bodies, Desires and Imagination.* www.confer.uk.com.
Oxford Dictionary (2015). Oxford: Oxford University Press. eISBN 9780191727665.
Renn, P. (2012). Moments of meeting: The relational challenges of sexuality in the consulting room. *British journal of Psychotherapy,* 29(2), 135–153.
Rilke, R.M. (1929/2012). *Letters to a Young Poet.* London: Penguin Classics.
Rogers, N.M. (2011). Intimate boundaries: Therapists' perception and experience of erotic transference within the therapeutic relationship. *Counselling and Psychotherapy Research,* 11(4), 266–274.
Sills, C. (2008). Personal communication.
Stark, M. (1999). *Modes of Therapeutic Action: Enhancement of Knowledge, Provision of Experience, and Engagement in Relationship.* Northvale, NJ: Jason Aronson.
Steiner, C. (1974). *Scripts People Live.* New York: Grove Press.
Stolorow, R., Brandshaft, B.J. & Atwood, G. (1987). *Psychoanalytic Treatment: An Intersubjective Approach.* Hillsdale, NJ: Analytic Press.
Wallin, D. (2014). We are the tools of our trade: The therapist's attachment history as a source of impasse, inspiration and change. In Danquah, A. & Berry, K. (eds) *Attachment Theory in Mental Health: A Guide to Clinical Practice* (pp. 235–239). London: Routledge.
Yalom, I.D. (2002) *The Gift of Therapy.* London: Harper Collins Publishers.
Zizek, S. (2016) *Against the Double Blackmail.* London: Penguin, Random House.

1.4 Gender identity and sexual attraction in the therapeutic encounter

Michelle Bridgman

Introduction

Psychotherapy, in all its forms, shapes, and nuances, is built on the relationship between the therapist and the client. The basis of this, as in any relationship, is trust. Without trust there can be no progress, no journey, no breakthroughs – often no conversation. Despite clients seeking a supportive and trusting relationship, the therapist's couch is where clients can feel most vulnerable, afraid of reaction, judgement, or shame.

When trust is there, a relationship is created and can grow. The intimacy that this affords, however, is often an issue in itself. The relationship, already alight with understanding, closeness, familiarity, and vulnerability, can lead to the development of sexual attraction between therapist and client. What happens when sexual attraction becomes figural in the therapeutic relationship? And what happens when there is an added layer of complexity, created when those involved are trans?

This chapter explores examples of the challenges encountered by a trans therapist and trans client, when sexual attraction becomes figural in the therapeutic relationship. A key discussion will be the interplay between sexuality and gender, and how it impacts on both trans therapist and client. Of equal interest, however, to me is the relationship between cisgender therapist and trans client. How are these different? Should they be considered as different, or not? How important is it to those concerned, and ultimately to the relationship itself, that a flexible viewpoint is maintained in order to accommodate these different issues?

Two points inform this exploration. First, it is important to bear in mind the impact of male privilege from two different perspectives. Such privilege affects both trans men and trans women and impacts on how sexual attraction may be experienced. Such attraction can be confusing to either or both parties. Secondly, it is also important to consider the impact of shame, and how the trans therapist may themselves be using energy to remain in stealth.

This chapter is informed by personal experience and is therefore a very real consideration of what may or may not happen in such a therapeutic relationship. My personal story is that of a psychotherapist who is also a trans woman. I have experienced sexual attraction in the therapeutic relationship, and it is this that gives me confidence when exploring how transgender affects therapeutic encounters.

Background

Men have lived as women, and vice versa, for hundreds of years and for many different reasons and needs. Power, desire, sexual manipulation, and even pure survival are all reasons why the human condition feels a need to reassign their birth identity. Physical reassignment however, the transgender that we understand today, was not within medical grasp until fairly recently.

The earliest documented modern-day surgery to reassign no keep reassign someone's sex from male to female was in 1912. However, this rudimentary surgery was unsuccessful. It was not until 1930 that a Danish trans woman – Lillie Elbe – underwent five separate surgical procedures to reassign her sex. Born Einar Magnus Andreas Wegener, she was a successful artist (under her original name) and publicly accepted as Einar's 'cousin'.

These pioneering operations were performed over two years under the supervision of German sexologist Magnus Hirschfeld. They were experimental in the extreme, as dangerous as any surgery and with the added complication of inexperience. Elbe finally died from complications involving an attempted uterus transplant.

Hirschfield's surgical procedures are generally accepted as successful, in that functioning genitalia were created, albeit very basic. Over the years of course the surgical processes of sex reassignment have improved greatly, and it is interesting to chart the progress of acceptance over the years alongside this.

The clinical treatment of *gender identity disorder* (or Gender Dysphoria, as it is now classified in manuals such as DSM 5 (2013) and ICD 11 (n.d.)) is a relatively new phenomenon. Harry Benjamin, an American domiciled German psychologist, pioneered the modern clinical treatment. His seminal work on the subject is 'The Transsexual Phenomenon' (Benjamin, 1967). Benjamin drew on his work with clients whom he described as having a variety of "sexual disorders". The sixties was a decade of both freedom and great repression, morally and legally, when gender identity was either male or female and would be confused with sexuality. For this reason, Benjamin was one of the first to make a distinction within the non-heterosexual sector. He argued that transsexuals as people who had a cross gender identity were then called, were distinct from both transvestites (heterosexual men who dress as but who do not wish to become women), and homosexuals. His work influences current clinical treatment to this day, although as a field of medical science it is rapidly evolving.

Thirty years on, the 1990s saw the emergence of the transgender phenomenon. This was heralded and championed by those individuals who took up the non-binary baton in challenging the idea that there was only a binary gender model. They believed and promoted the belief that transsexuality was too narrow a definition for the range of different sexual identities that occurred in humanity. Other individuals, notably Kate Bornstein in 'Gender Outlaw: On Men, Women and the Rest of Us' (updated, 2016) also challenged the accepted belief that there was 'no in-between'. Her work explored the concept that it was possible to possess a birth identity that was neither rigidly male nor female.

The emergence of the Transgender Identity offers an alternative to the early binary model. It provides an opportunity to explore different elements of what Bornstein describes as the 'gender spectrum' (Bornstein, 2016). Commenting on a trans woman who had decided against surgery, Robert Hill states "The validity of her self-definition rested on a crucial distinction she made between anatomical sex and subjective gender identity" (Hill, 2013).

When clinicians formally recognised and accepted this development, in the 2000s, there was a paradigm shift in the thinking and diagnosis of people presenting with gender identity incongruence. This was clearly demonstrated when the label 'Gender Identity Disorder' was removed from DSM V and replaced with 'Gender Dysphoria'. This shift was intended to herald a shift from pathology to identity and signifies the most recent thinking and attitudes towards the transgender phenomenon.

In summary, attitudes have changed over the years to match the gender fluidity that is now accepted. Removing this barrier of non-acceptance and inhibition from the therapeutic relationship results in a greater freedom to explore and discuss gender identity and sexual issues.

Identity and sexual attraction

When considering the history of what is now accepted as gender dysphoria, it is clear that gender and gender identities are constantly redefined. It is also true that the distinction between gender and sexuality often becomes blurred.

Perhaps an easy definition is 'Sexuality determines who you go to bed *with* whereas gender determines who you go to bed as'. When I wrote these words in 2014, I felt it was a clear if slightly tongue in cheek, definition. However, five years on, I believe it is far too simplistic, and a rather trite way to explain the complexities of gender and sexual identification. To explore this further. A trans therapist or trans client may have experienced their sexuality as heterosexual when in the gender role assigned at birth, but as a consequence of changing gender they may find themselves with a sexual identity which is by definition lesbian, gay, bisexual, or other. Their *sexuality*, however, may have actually remain unchanged.

The reverse may also be true if a change of gender results in a hitherto gay, lesbian, or bisexual sexual identity becoming, by definition, heterosexual. One outcome of my recent research into this reality (Bridgman, 2019) was that many participants reported their sexuality altering, or becoming more fluid, after a period of sustained hormone therapy commonly experienced before surgery.

Hormone therapy usually begins shortly prior to (or during) the individual living in the acquired gender role. It is therefore not clear whether the hormones altered their sexual preference, or whether they had been suppressing a sexuality that was now been released as a result of their gender expression. However, it is true that whether this releasing of a sexual identity is as a result of suppression, hormones or any other factor is less important. What matters more is an appreciation of the emotional adjustments that a client (or therapist) needs to make. Any client (or therapist) who may be transitioning or has transitioned between different gender roles, including non-binary identities, will be affected by this as well as the more obvious adjustments to acquired gender roles.

Boundaries

We have looked at the history of transgender and its route to the more fluid gender identity that is accepted today and seen how the issue of identity is key to the therapist/client relationship. What, however, is the particular relevance for a trans therapist, particularly in the situation of a real sexual attraction in the therapeutic encounter?

Irrespective of gender identity, there needs to be clear boundaries in the relationship between psychotherapist and client. These boundaries naturally change over time, as trust is built and the client feels able to 'open up', giving more information about their emotional state. Governing bodies have varying guidelines, but all hold the view that a psychotherapist is in a unique position of power. All behavioural guidelines take this as a starting point and are designed to guard against the abuse of this power. It is vital that the psychotherapist does not exploit or abuse the relationship in any way, but particularly (as the UKCP guidelines put it) "for sexual, emotional or financial gain" (UKCP, 2017, p. 3).

The trans-identified psychotherapist is no different from a cisgender therapist. However, their experience is different, and this experience is of value when dealing with conflicted gender identity and the development of sexual attraction. Any accompanying activity immediately places them in a different category. In the same way that their client is on a journey of discovery, the trans therapist is also on a personal journey. They may, for example, still be adjusting to their gender role, to the change of physical gender. Perhaps most interestingly they may still be adjusting to their relationships with both men and women.

This will of course affect the ways that they build the counselling relationship with their client, whatever their gender. While counselling their trans client, the trans psychotherapist may themselves feel vulnerable particularly if they are (as they may be) living in stealth.

Shame

Trans clients may often experience and/or present with shame. One of the challenges for the psychotherapist is in establishing whether this shame is as a result of the *world's* attitude to the transgender experience; or whether shame is the root cause of the client's unhappiness.

Patricia DeYoung (2015) describes the challenge faced by the trans therapist as follows. She says, "Therapy becomes a risk but when the client experiences me as being accepting it has an even bigger impact than it would normally". This is an important theme that will be explored in more depth later, but it is obvious that the therapist, and/or any other clinician would be foolhardy not to address shame in a therapeutic relationship. It should be explored and given sufficient attention in any treatment program. Few experiences can be more shaming than an individual being taunted or ridiculed for looking or behaving differently, being at odds with the gender role expressed or feeling that they do not fit any gender stereotypes.

DeYoung goes on to quote Danielian & Gianotti:

> When a child's vulnerable self is not met with safe nurturance, support, and appreciation, the child must neutralise the shame of this absence. He or she must manufacture through fantasy and imagination and idealised version of self, one that is over determined, absolute in its standards, and compulsively driven.
>
> (Danielian & Gianotti, in DeYoung, 2015)

Nichols (1992) reminds us that shame can act as a protector from both physical attack and psychological intrusion. He also points out this is effectively a shield for our self. Bradshaw gives one of the most practical descriptions when he describes shame as "the feeling of being exposed and seen when one is not ready to be seen" (Bradshaw, 1988). This is of course relevant to trans people in transition, but at a deeper level Bradshaw makes a significant and poignant point when he says, "perhaps the deepest and most devastating aspect of neurotic shame is the rejection of self by the self". This is when there is the potential for a transgender individual to feel shame over their transgender identity.

When shame becomes this shield, it becomes an identity in its own right. DeYoung perhaps expresses this concept best when she points out shame is "I am" whereas guilt is "I did" (DeYoung, 2015).

Vulnerability

The experience of transitioning in an unaccepting world has always carried risk. Historically this is marked by a higher than average incidence of suicide in the transgender population. Over the years, groups have worked hard to change the opinions of a society held fast in traditional mores, with some success. The result is greater acceptance of diverse sexuality, transgender, non-binary, and gender fluidity. Suicide rates and suicide attempts have (thankfully) declined over the years. However, this demographic still demonstrates the worst suicide statistics of almost any other group. Just twenty-five years ago, in the mid nineties, it would have almost been rare to speak with a trans person who had never felt suicidal.

A report by the Scottish Trans Alliance (2012) asked 311 transgender people whether they had thought about ending their lives at some point – 84% of participants replied that they had. Similarly, a US survey of Lesbian, Gay, Bisexual & Transgender (LGBT) youth (Mustanski and Liu, 2013) found not only that two out of three respondents had contemplated suicide in the past but that they were ten times more likely than other groupings to reattempt suicide within a year.

In a different survey in the same year, the authors reported "Psychological and physical gender abuse is endemic in this population and may result from occupational success and attempts to affirm gender identity. Both types of abuse have serious mental health consequences in the form of major depression" (Nuttbrock et al., 2014).

Shame, vulnerability, and a propensity for suicidal thoughts are all elements that can manifest in the therapeutic relationship. The psychotherapist working with a trans client, particularly one on a journey of exploration or transition, should be mindful of this fact. Extra vigilance may be required.

Trans clients

We have seen how this grouping is historically vulnerable, particularly susceptible to low self-esteem, shame and invulnerability. One issue in the transgender/psychotherapist relationship, constantly expressed by trans identified clients, is that therapists can fall into the trap of assuming that gender identity must be their problem to the exclusion of everything else.

One possibility that is hard to acknowledge is that they may feel uncertain, unsure around their sexuality. They may therefore look for affirmation from the therapist in the form of compliments. They may wish for reassurance that they are still sexually attractive to others. However, this rarely translates into overt flirting or inappropriate behaviour, in fact the reverse is true as clients are likely to be reticent, reluctant to talk, possibly ashamed, and certainly vulnerable.

As a therapist working with this client grouping, I believe that it is particularly important to allow a client, trans or otherwise, to find their own place. Phenomenology is of the utmost importance (perhaps dependent on the genre of therapy being applied) and so it is vital to allow for the client's phenomenological process in any therapeutic relationship.

Trans therapists

Trans therapists also develop at their own pace and are prey to doubts and vulnerability. When they meet a client and begin building the trust and knowledge needed to make the therapeutic experience a positive one, it is important to remember that they may themselves be dealing with issues. These issues may be similar to their client's, or as all trans experience their journey in different ways, in opposition to them.

Whatever the stage of their journey – mentally and/or physically – no therapist is immune to the dangers and pitfalls experienced by trans clients. This is however a challenging dichotomy. In order to gain trust from their client, a trans therapist must appear a 'safe' pair of hands. A client will assume that the therapist, the person with whom they are entrusting their thoughts and problems is completely grounded, knowledgeable, and extremely experienced both in their work and as a 'successful' trans person. There is little room for the feeling that their therapist is also vulnerable.

However, this is of course true in any therapeutic relationship. The transgender psychotherapist is equally as grounded and/or as vulnerable as any gender therapist. In other words, they are no more or less likely to face the same challenges that cisgender therapists face in the therapeutic encounter.

Power and male privilege

Male privilege

There are three perspectives to take into account when considering male privilege. First, that of the person brought up as a female, the trans man perspective. Second, the person brought up as a male, the trans woman. Thirdly, the person brought up as a male or female but who identifies as non-binary. The experiences and emotions of these groups are deeply felt, but often the experience becomes implicit in behaviour or attitude and is therefore difficult to convey with words. It is therefore challenging for these groups to communicate with those lacking this experience, or not sharing this perspective.

To demonstrate this, it is necessary to look at the experiences that shape the trans man's perspective of the world, and how it treats him. The trans man will not necessarily be fully aware of a lack of privilege prior to transition. If, however, they have been brought up in a patriarchal system, they will soon realise what they had been denied when they attain the privileges of being male after transition. These privileges range from the minor to the major. Experiences such as getting a table in a restaurant, or attracting a waiter's attention easily, may seem minor compared to getting better paid and empowered employment as a man. Each experience however underlines the differences society places on male and female. It is well documented that nowadays those living as women, still do not have the equal pay and job opportunities that are generally accepted to be the norm for men.

Turning this on its head, this may of course seem a good deal for those transitioning from female to male. However, the trans man does not have the benefits experienced by cisgender males (born male and identifying as a male), which has been gathered through a life experience of living as a male, an upbringing where society engenders and constantly reinforces the advantages that being physically male brings.

This contradiction in how the genders are perceived by society, in both the small subtle ways and the way in which lives may be changed through greater/fewer opportunities, is itself another adjustment for the trans person, mentally and emotionally. For example, a prominent activist, a trans man, reported that many trans men in his experience struggled with the levels of assertiveness expected from a man by others.

Conversely, a trans woman will have spent her life until transition experiencing society's forms of male privilege. Following transition however she finds that getting the waiter's attention is more challenging. She finds herself in an employment market that is unforgiving, with less opportunities to progress. She finds herself passed over in the workplace, expected to field menial tasks or considered not as mentally capable as her male colleagues. One client reported the experience of having men talk over them in business meetings, as if their opinions were not as valid as their male colleagues. She also found that she was treated with more aggression on the road, by both male and female drivers. These changes in society's perceptions and treatment can be a new and daunting challenge for the trans person, exacerbating an already difficult situation of adjusting to a different body and way of living.

These experiences of course underpin the feminine gender construct argument, which argues that the societal perception of gender keeps women in a subservient role. It supports and encourages the questioning of the right of trans women to call themselves 'real women'. How can they be so when they have not experienced a patriarchal system in childhood? Or found, growing up, that their choices were more limited? How can they be 'real' women without having to fight to be noticed or appreciated in business? If they have lived as a man, how can they understand how the world works when you are female?

Trans clients

One of the biggest bugbears expressed by trans identified clients is that therapists will often assume that gender identity alone is their problem. It is as if this is a given, an inevitable problem that needs to be addressed before any other issues – emotional, empathic – can be considered. As we have seen however, this grouping is historically vulnerable, particularly susceptible to low self-esteem, shame and vulnerability. It is particularly hard for them to acknowledge that, on top of everything else, they may feel uncertain or unsure around their sexuality.

This lack of confidence in turn may lead to a need for approval. They may therefore be looking for this affirmation from their therapist in the form of compliments, a more or less constant reassurance that they are still sexually attractive. The therapist is an intimate, someone to whom they have (or are prepared to) admit their doubts and talk about their innermost feelings. Proximity, need, and a sympathetic ear is often all that is required for an initial spark to become a flame, a desire for the other. This does not mean that a trans person is likely to flirt, or be sexually overt, expecting a reciprocal response by sharing their feelings. The reverse in fact is true. The client is more likely to be reticent, possibly ashamed, and certainly feeling vulnerable. Much of what has been said assumes the trans person is either in transition or recently transitioned from one gender to another. At this stage, sexual attraction is possibly going to be the last thing on the client's mind as their gender expression is likely to be paramount. A trans person who has completed their gender transition journey may well be confident and not seeking affirmation any more than the rest of the population.

In any therapy situation, I feel it is particularly important for the therapist to allow the client to find their own place. Even if phenomenology is high on the list, depending on the genre of therapy being applied, it is important to allow for the client's phenomenological process at their own pace.

Trans therapists

As we have discussed, the therapist may also be on the trans journey, and therefore at risk from the same feelings of vulnerability. Supervision will clearly be a necessary and valuable support. Depending in which stage of their lives they find themselves, the trans psychotherapist is not immune from any of the dangers and pitfalls experienced by trans clients. Indeed, there is an added challenge in that there is a need to be 'strong' for their client. The client's expectation of their therapist is that they are completely grounded, very knowledgeable, and extremely experienced in their work. There is therefore no room for the therapist to be anything but strong in their sessions with their clients. There is no opportunity for indulgence, or a self-seeking approach.

However, it may be argued that a transgender psychotherapist is as equally as grounded – and as vulnerable – as cisgender therapists are. In other words, they are no more likely to face the challenges that cisgender therapists face in the therapeutic encounter. Whilst this may be true, it is also worth recognising the trans Psychotherapist may have been on a journey that provides particular beneficial understanding and insights; they may also benefit from supportive supervision where they can explore transferential feelings and sometimes erotic attachments.

There follow two brief case studies which illustrate some challenges for the Psychotherapist.

Case studies

Graham is a trans man in his late thirties. He is highly qualified, having attended university and left with a degree in Psychology. He then worked

Gender identity and sexual attraction 85

as a social worker for several years. When he was 29, he completed a social transition, from female to male. He found he was sexually attracted to both men and women; however he had not yet pursued a sexual relationship with anyone. This was because he felt that he was still in the process of having medical treatment and did not feel ready to enter into a relationship until this work was completed.

It was during this time that he decided on a career change. He began studying psychotherapy again and, having completed Integrative Psychotherapy training, began to work in private practice when he was 33. It was approximately three years later when he took on a client named Sheila. Sheila was a 28-year-old cisgender female who had entered into therapy to deal with the loss of a five-year relationship, terminated by her cisgender male partner. The reasons were fairly clear cut – she wanted children, but he had resisted any discussion about starting a family and had eventually ended the relationship. Since the breakup Sheila had been in a series of relationships with men, who were all initially committed to a lasting partnership with her but who had all been ultimately unfaithful. Unable to cope with this she had terminated the relationships.

As her therapist, Graham reported that it was after the initial sessions that the issues of inappropriate behaviour started. Sheila began to make complimentary remarks about him, initially commending his skills as a therapist but, in later sessions, commenting on his appearance. Graham felt these comments were not overtly sexual, but they made him feel uncomfortable. However, not wanting to challenge his client he decided on a strategy of not acknowledging these compliments, to see if they subsided.

Graham felt that Sheila, as his client, was simply fishing for compliments and seeking confirmation that she was still attractive to the 'opposite' sex. He deliberately refused to enter into any discussion on the topic, moving the conversation on to other matters. After four months of weekly therapy sessions where the client worked on her loss, Sheila told him that she was ending the therapeutic relationship.

When questioned, Sheila said that she felt that Graham hadn't really 'heard' her. She said she experienced him as cold and aloof, and that he did not seem to 'notice' her. Graham apologised for any miscommunication but was in fact relieved as he had felt uncertain about the way he had been working in counselling Sheila.

It was only after the therapy sessions had ended that Graham took the case to Supervision. When questioned as to why he had waited, he admitted that he had felt embarrassed by an inability to discuss his feelings about the work. He felt that he should have been able to do better and that the sessions required basic therapy tools alone. On the surface he felt that he had failed the client and that his work had not been of the standard that he expected from himself.

On further discussion however, Graham owned that the reason he felt inadequate was that he felt that he did not have the experience to deal with a client who he realised found him attractive as a man. This inexperience in relationships, both in and out of the therapeutic relationship, was a matter of regret.

Within a supportive Supervision environment, Graham was able to admit his own vulnerability and shame. He was able to acknowledge both his inexperience in dealing with such a situation and his inability to admit to his own feelings in the matter. With sensitive affirming supervision, Graham was able to work through and benefit from what he later described as an important experience. Indeed, he entered into psychotherapy to work through his own feelings and his own relationship with his sexuality. Graham reflected that, in his determination not to encourage or acknowledge sexual attraction in the therapeutic encounter and in order to keep boundaries, he had missed an opportunity to help the client explore her fears of inadequacy and rejection. By not being fully present in the dialogue and exploring the client's experience he missed an opportunity for a fulfilling healing encounter. Indeed, in his determination to avoid erotic transference and to give any encouragement to his client he had avoided her altogether. On the plus side, he had grown as a therapist and learned from a valuable experience.

Angela

Angela is a 43-year-old trans woman. She is an experienced psychotherapist with almost 20 years' experience in both a clinical and, latterly, a private practice setting. Angela's change of gender was completed both socially and medically some 15 years ago. She describes herself as heterosexual as she reports only ever being attracted to men, however she is aware that her sexual feelings maybe more fluid since she has been in her acquired gender role.

Angela is in a happy successful relationship with her cisgender boyfriend Robert, although they don't live together. She had been seeing her client Denise, a 30-year-old cisgender woman, for about two months. Denise had issues of both depression and bereavement as her mother had died a year earlier. The therapy was proceeding well, but Angela was aware that she found Denise attractive and began to think about her more and more between sessions.

Angela was clear about boundaries between therapist and client, and never felt there was any danger of her crossing the line. She was clear to herself that she would keep her thoughts private and not give her client any idea of her true feelings. Angela took the case to Supervision and questioned whether she should keep working with the client or whether she should find a way to end the therapeutic relationship. When discussing why she felt a cessation to be preferable, she admitted that she was confused about her feelings and worried that her client would pick up on what Angela now described as an infatuation.

It was suggested that Angela might benefit from entering psychotherapy herself, with a view to exploring her feelings. In the meantime, it was agreed that she would continue to see her client but that she would continue to bring the case to Supervision. In exploring her situation, Angela became aware that she was suppressing feelings that had been simmering below the surface. In her quest to adopt a 'normal' relationship with her cisgender partner she was suppressing feelings that then "leaked out" (her words) via her relationship with the client. Angela's experience illustrates the value of supervision as an aid to acknowledging her personal feelings and her personal shifting sexuality at the same time aiding her therapeutic work by helping her be more present with her client.

Supervision

Supervision, of course, cannot be the only filter when working with boundaries, transference, and countertransference. It should, however, provide a safe place for owning feelings and impulses. The Supervisor therefore plays an important role in helping to manage any embarrassment or shame and the successful owning of erotic feelings towards clients, when therapists are dealing with a client who they feel is sexually attracted to them.

While the therapist should be prepared to take their feelings into their own therapy when necessary, Supervision provides an exploratory space. Therefore, an important question for supervisors and supervisees alike is 'Does this space provide a safe container for frank exchange?'

One of the issues particular to this demographic is that of power and privilege. I have already discussed some of the issues pertaining to trans men and trans women, but Supervision should also provide a safe place for the trans therapist to own and explore their own unique vulnerabilities. We would do well to remind ourselves of the particular power held by the therapist in the therapy room. This may benefit from further exploration, both for the trans therapist who may have recently transitioned; or for the cisgender therapist who is working with trans clients. A psychotherapist colleague shared with me that when working with a trans client he had wanted to compliment his client on her appearance but had held back for fear of seeming 'over familiar'. I respectfully pointed out that his client may in fact have been affirmed by the comment, provided it was delivered in the right spirit.

What these case studies illustrate is that trans therapists and clients are both prone to precisely the same challenges and transferential issues as their cisgender counterparts. However, there is an experience unique to the trans therapist or trans client. Depending on their age, when commencing hormone therapy and socially transitioning, they will have gone through a form of emotional puberty and growth at an older age than their cisgender counterparts. They will have missed the experience of sharing emotional journeys with their teenage counterparts which is all part of emotional development and growing up. The therapist would do well to recognise the need for sensitivity and the potential to shame the trans client. Likewise, the trans therapist will benefit from a supervision environment that permits vulnerability and provides a space for ambivalence and exploration.

References

American Psychiatric Association (Eds.), 2013. *Diagnostic and Statistical Manual of Mental Disorders: DSM-5*, 5th ed. American Psychiatric Association, Washington, D.C.

Benjamin, H., 1967. The transsexual phenomenon. *Trans. N. Y. Acad. Sci.*, 29, 428–430. doi:10.1111/j.2164-0947.1967.tb02273.x.

Bornstein, K., 2016. *Gender Outlaw: On Men, Women, and the Rest of Us.*

Bradshaw, J., 1933, 1988. *Healing the Shame That Binds You.*

DeYoung, P.A., 2015. *Understanding and Treating Chronic Shame: A Relational/Neurobiological Approach.* Routledge, Taylor & Francis Group, New York.

Hill, R., 2013. Before transgender: Transvestia's spectrum of gender variance. Transgender Stud. Read. 2.

Mustanski, B., Liu, R.T., 2013. A longitudinal study of predictors of suicide attempts among lesbian, gay, bisexual, and transgender youth. *Arch. Sex. Behav.*, 42(3), 437–448.

Nichols, M.P., 1992. *No place to hide: Facing shame so we can find self-respect.* Fireside.

Nuttbrock, L., Bockting, W., Rosenblum, A., Hwahng, S., Mason, M., Macri, M., Becker, J., 2014. Gender abuse and major depression among transgender women: A prospective study of vulnerability and resilience. *Am. J. Public Health*, 104, 2191–2198. doi:10.2105/AJPH.2013.301545.

WHO, 2018, ICD11.

1.5 Editor's summary and reflection of the themes related to practice issues

Jasenka Lukac-Greenwood

Variety of definitions

One of the initial striking aspects of this section of the book, as well as in relation to the wider literature to which it refers, is the variety of ways in which the phenomenon of sexual attraction is defined and labelled. Given the practical focus of this book, this is not particularly surprising. However, what I found very interesting is the sense that authors' writing is more 'physical' and more 'genital' than the introductory definitions they chose to frame it within.

It is as if the authors illustrated the split between their 'theoretical' and 'lived' view of the sexual phenomena. I find this fascinating as potentially pointing out the discrepancy between teaching and working with the subject as well as the possibility that these authors might be 'showing' the changing nature of our thinking about sexual matters in therapy.

As mentioned in the Introduction, from the theoretical point of view, in recent decades, British object relations theory has been the prevalent way of thinking about the 'erotic' and 'sexual' in psychotherapy. It emphasised early, mother-infant relatedness and the view of sexuality as a manifestation of other, earlier relational needs, at the expense of the bodily experiences of the erotic phenomena, for me best illustrated by Mann's (1997) description of the erotic as "psychological experience", the very definition used by other authors in this section of the book.

In addition to the consequent de-sexualisation of the therapeutic relationship (Target, 2007; Renn, 2013) and splitting between the meaning and the bodily experience of the erotic phenomenon, this view, to me, suggested that working with sexual aspects of the therapeutic relationship is no different to working with any other aspect of it. This notion was a driving factor for my research.

Implicitly, this did not feel right. For me, working with sexual aspects of the therapeutic relationship felt different. To put it simply, it felt stronger. My research participants added that to them it felt deeper because it touches the core of our identity (Lukac-Greenwood, 2019). As a result, I crave a way of defining it and distinguishing it from our other ways of being with our clients. And at the same time, I realise this is not easy. As Mollon (2008) puts it, there is something inherently mysterious about sexuality, perhaps related to child's incomprehension of it. He illustrates this by saying that the loss of the "gleam in the mother's eye" in response to the child's sexual explorations is a lesson that not all experiences are admissible. Similarly, Target (2015), using the notions of 'mirroring' and 'mentalisation', explains that sexual feelings do not become mentalised to the same extent as other affects in childhood, because of the maternal failure to mirror them adequately. Not only does this cause problems in our ability to comprehend them, but it also causes problems in admitting them to the social discourse (Mollon, 2008), which then creates a problem in having a common and well-defined language with which to speak about sexual feelings. Shame, about which I will say more below, is also a foundation of this difficulty.

Consequently, I wondered whether the variety and inconsistency in the way the phenomenon is defined betrays this difficulty of linking the lived experience of sexuality with all of its mystery, incomprehension, and potential shame, with the attempts to give it a form and to find a common language. Notwithstanding, I see the actual lived experience of the authors described in this section of the book as more aligned with the more contemporary thinking on the subject which calls for greater acknowledgement and integration of bodily responses to the understanding of the sexual aspects of the therapeutic relationship. I believe this trend needs to be followed up. We need to grapple with all-encompassing notions, such as 'erotic', in order to claim, define, and ultimately integrate the bodily aspects of the sexual attraction in therapy in all of its various manifestations.

Shame

As mentioned above, in addition to the mystery of it, one of the difficulties in grasping sexuality is related to the shame associated with it. In 'The inherent shame of sexuality', Mollon (2008) draws our attention to Freud (1905) who was preoccupied with the peculiarity of the relationship between sexuality and repression; the bodily, 'organic' repression of sexuality. Freud pointed out that direct sexual expression is antithetical to culture and that the breakdown of culture and society always leads to rape especially during periods of war. In torture, part of the humiliation is to strip the person of their clothes, their physical and linguistic covering, and their linguistic identity when the person is reduced to a biological process. Finally, he points out that to shame someone is to render them invalid, taking away their role in the group life and human discourse, associating shame with aspects of self that cannot be communicated. In this way, Mollon (2008) links aforementioned bodily experiences of infant sexuality which are not adequately responded to by the mother and by extension, not easily communicated in the social realm, with the inherent sense of shame and repression.

Summary and reflection on Part 1

The sensitivity, vulnerability, and shame associated with sexual ways of relating is mentioned by all of the authors in this section. As Hitchings (Chapter 1.2,) puts it, *"This whole area remains pervaded with guilt and shame, despite the ordinariness and this being what should be expected"*. Jamie Agar (Chapter 1.3), using vivid personal examples, provides us with the image of himself gasping with embarrassment at the moment in which his inner sexual desire is being seen by the girl on the bus. Bridgman (Chapter 1.4) goes even further to consider shame on a number of different levels. In addition to the shame and embarrassment that the subject evokes in all of us, she writes about a transgender client group who might be particularly prone to the feelings of shame. She points out that their experience of difference and society's relative lack of appreciation and understanding of that difference exposes them to the heightened levels of vulnerability, in their day to day living as well as within the therapeutic relationship. Furthermore, if, on top of it, they live in stealth, they become the embodiment of Mollon's (2008) point that shame is associated with those parts of the self that are not allowed access to the social realm of shared discourse. Although the challenge for all therapists is to be very sensitive to the potential for shame in the work with sexual matters, Bridgman (Chapter 1.4) wonders whether that challenge might be particularly difficult for therapists who are transgender themselves and who are going through their own personal journey in relation to it.

I think Bridgman is right to raise this question for all of us, whether transgender or not. When working with clients who we perceive as presenting with similar issues to our own, the potential for over-identification, over-compensation, or the need to act as a role-model of strength in the face of our clients' struggle is always present. This is something that we need to work with in our own therapy and supervision. However, what strikes me as particularly interesting is Bridgman's point that with transgender clients, therapists might fall into the trap of assuming that gender identity must be their problem to the exclusion of everything else. In this context I wondered whether being a transgender therapist might actually be very useful. Given their understanding, knowledge, and therefore freedom to question and challenge the issues related to gender identity, they might be less likely to fall into this trap.

Put in a broader context, Bridgman's question taps into an issue brought up by all of the authors, being that of the person of the therapist.

The personal and the professional

Agar and Fenton (Chapter 1.3) say, 'Who We Are Matters'. They provide us with beautiful examples in which their personal stories have shaped their relatedness with sexual matters and with which they sit in their therapy rooms. Similarly, when considering ways in which clients impact therapists, Hitchings (Chapter 1.2) includes personal detail which partially explains that impact on him. In the example of his work with the client named Richard, the probability is that the impact and the subsequent therapeutic work would not have been the same had the therapist not been a gay man.

Similarly, Bridgman (Chapter 1.4) writes about a recently transitioned trans male therapist Graham working with a cisgender female client Sheila who was sexually attracted to him. Very poignantly, she describes that the difficulty that Graham encountered in working with Sheila was his lack of experience of being in a position of being sexually related to as a man. Unable to bear this, he refused to enter into any discussion of the topic which ultimately led Sheila to end the therapeutic relationship.

The examples provided by the authors in the section are very similar to the findings of my study which also suggested that a possible difficulty in working with sexual matters in therapy resides in the therapist's discomfort with their own sexual identity, whatever shape it might take. When we feel at ease with ourselves, we are less likely to feel the need to defend ourselves from the client's projections and resultant associations and instead are more likely to engage with them with curiosity, searching for the meanings behind them. Problems occur when, as in my own personal example, the therapeutic situation activated an image of myself as a prostitute, an image I felt I needed to defend myself from, which in turn paralysed me from talking about it.

A further compounding point found in my study, not mentioned by Hitchings or Agar and Fenton but touched upon by Bridgman, is the potential conflict between our sense of who we are and who we believe we need to be as therapists. Bridgman mentions this in relation to the question of whether as a trans therapist, one is supposed to be 'strong' for their clients, given their expectation of their therapist being 'completely grounded, very knowledgeable, and extremely experienced in their work'. I further wondered whether professional norms and standards stipulating therapists' own therapy and supervision, may add to this pressure to feel that as therapists, we should be 'sorted', leaving us with the sense that our own doubts and dilemmas are not a terrain of the work with clients but something which needs to be dealt with in advance of it. Adams (2014) in her book 'The myth of the untroubled therapist' explores this very issue.

My study made me wonder whether this incongruency between the personal and professional selves is particularly likely to appear in the context of work with sexual matters.

Female therapists who faced difficulties in working with sexual attraction in my study, reported a sense of conflict between their sense of themselves as 'sexual women' and as 'therapists', believing that its resolution lay in the termination of one of those roles. For example, they either denied the sexual aspects of the therapeutic relationship and continued to work by making themselves 'asexual' or felt that the sexual aspects of the relationship were all-encompassing which would lead them to re-refer the client and terminate the therapeutic relationship. Furthermore, they also reported tendency to behave in a socially prescribed feminine way which conflicted with their therapeutic role. This included taking a more passive role and waiting for the male client to take the lead in talking about sexual matters.

Conversely, in situations where female therapists did not feel reciprocal sexual desire towards their male clients, the conflict revolved around the therapists' sense of being 'rejecting' and 'therapeutic'. They grappled with ways of reconciling their negative feelings of disgust with their role as a therapist.

This difference in the female therapists' experience of working with male clients' sexual desire which appears to be related to the reciprocity of therapist – client feelings (or its absence) is in line with two additional and related themes mentioned by the authors in this section of the book. First, the question of 'Who is Hitting on Whom' (Agar and Fenton, Chapter 1.3) or 'Where are Cupid's arrows flying from?' (Hitchings, Chapter 1.2). As Hitchings puts it, *'whilst we may hold a philosophy that genital erotic belongs in some way to both parties, the question of from whom does this primarily originate, is one that remains useful to consider'*. In the context of my study, the direction of Cupid's arrows suggested the second related theme, the direction of flow of power in the relationship, an additional dimension of the therapeutic relationship which requires careful attention.

Power

Bridgman (Chapter 1.4) writes about gender power most explicitly, in ways which can help us appreciate and understand the complexity of the change that a trans person might be undergoing. She draws our attention to the fact that in addition to needing to adjust to their new body and ways of living, a trans person will also be experiencing changes in society's perceptions and treatment of themselves in relation to their gender. For example, she points out that a trans man may become aware of the ways in which they were denied privileges as a ciswomen but at the same time may come to realise and struggle with the different expectations placed on the role of men in our society such as their required assertiveness. Similarly, for trans women, the challenge may be related to dealing with the ways in which they are treated within the employment market, finding themselves with fewer opportunities to progress and with lower earning capacity.

Agar and Fenton discuss power to capture the discomfort of the reversal of societal power dynamics at a moment when Jamie, the male, who is supposed to be the dominant one, is in fact exposed as sexually inexperienced in front of the more sexually powerful woman. This leaves him feeling overwhelmed, frightened, and ashamed.

In my study, related to the point I raised earlier, when I found that female therapists who were not feeling the reciprocal sexual attraction towards their male clients experienced a sense of conflict in their personal and professional roles, I explored the possibility that this conflict was partially related to their discomfort in being in a more powerful position *vis-à-vis* their male clients. This grew out of the observation that therapists in this position particularly feared shaming and exposing their male client's sexual desire (as was the situation in which Jamie found himself, described above), something which I simply accepted as a 'truth' during our interviews (thus perhaps revealing something which is unconsciously understood between us) but which in retrospect, I started to question. Why would the exposition of male sexual desire necessarily be experienced as shaming? The fact that my participants, female therapists, also feared being put down by the clients in some way (either by being made to feel 'silly' by the client denying his sexual attraction or by being made to feel their presumptions because they gave themselves more credit than they deserved) suggested that power was a part of this dynamic.

Furthermore, I was reflecting that in addition to holding the ordinary power of the role, female therapists working with male clients' sexual desire find themselves in a position to provide or withhold sexual availability which is in itself very powerful and therefore dangerous (Mitchell, 1988). However, given the deeply rooted meaning of sexuality in our culture as an expression of male dominance, the aforementioned power of the female therapist may be experienced as being in conflict with the male client's power, when viewed through the structural lenses of our society. Seen in this light, the examples provided by my study (namely, participants' preoccupations with potential shaming of the client, their tendency to blame themselves or experience themselves as incompetent, as well as denying or turning a blind eye to the sexual dynamic) could potentially be seen as manifestations of this underlying conflict about their own sense of power and as attempts to redress, rather than work through, the sense of this conflict.

These examples from my own study as well as the chapters of the authors in this section of the book made me think that working with sexual dynamics is one of the therapeutic contexts in which therapists need to be aware of their own and their client's multiple roles, and be committed to the complex work required for understanding and negotiating their resultant roles and power relations.

Although in relation to my study I was thinking about the particular complexity that female therapists might be exposed to in the negotiation of these different role and power positions, Bridgman's chapter has lifted that complexity to an altogether different level. Her descriptions of the interplay between gender and sexuality and the fluidity of sexuality in the face of changing gender is extraordinary in its intra- and inter-personal complexity, even without adding the societal dimension. I was left thinking that the work required to grapple with this level of complexity seems to be particularly demanding for our trans colleagues. Equally, I was left thinking that we can all learn something from their work.

In particular, I was reminded of one of my study findings which suggested that part of the difficulty in working with sexual matters in therapy is related to the fact that it is such sensitive area of our own identity. Whilst majority of my participants commented on it being a sensitive area of identity for their clients, I was struck by what was discussed less directly, namely that in being such a fundamental aspect of identity, sexual attraction might be a more difficult area of work because of our own (rather than our client's) reluctance to put it to the test, to challenge or change it.

Bridgman's chapter (Chapter 1.4) made me consider the potential level of challenge to the sense of sexual identity which trans clients might pose to cis gender therapists operating from within the heteronormative standards of our society. The work in grappling with the complexity of personal and societal identity required for trans therapists in negotiating the power is equally required for cis therapists when working with trans clients. Consequently, Bridgman provides a beautiful and very concrete example for my study's conclusion that in order to be open to ways of working with sexual matters with their clients, therapists need to be willing and committed towards personal therapy or other ways in which they would continue to grow and challenge their own sense of identity.

Boundary violations, supervision, and therapeutic work

Finally, although the issue will be discussed in more detail in Part 3 of this book, at this point I simply wish to highlight the need to broaden our notion of boundary violations, something mentioned by all authors in this section of the book. Instead of simply paying attention to the overt boundary transgressions, for example, engagement in sexual acts with clients, authors in this section warn us against vicarious boundary violations in which the client is led to act out the therapists' predominantly unconscious desires, which in Hitchings's language (Chapter 1.2) is expressed more graphically as a metaphorical "rape" of the client.

As all authors suggest, the role of training, institutional, and clinical support for therapists working with sexual issues cannot be underestimated. These are the areas covered in depth in the other two parts in this book.

References

Adams, M. (2014) *The Myth of the Untroubled Therapist*. East Sussex: Routledge.

Freud, S. (1905) *Three Essays on the Theory of Sexuality*, S.E. 7:125–243, London: The Hogarth Press and the Institute of Psycho-Analysis.

Lukac-Greenwood, J. (2019) *Let's talk about sex: Female therapists experience of working with male clients who are sexually attracted to them*. Doctorate theses available from Middlesex University's Research Repository: https://eprints.mdx.ac.uk/id/eprint/27296.

Mann, D. (1997) *Psychotherapy: An Erotic Relationship Transference and Countertransference Passions*. London: Routledge.

Mitchell, S. A. (1988) *Relational Concepts in Psychoanalysis, An Integration.* Cambridge, MA: Harvard University Press.

Mollon, P. (2008) 'The inherent shame of sexuality' in Pajaczkowska, C. and Ward, I. (eds) *Shame and Sexuality, Psychoanalysis and Visual Culture.* London: Routledge, 23–35.

Renn, P. (2013) Moments of meeting: The relational challenges of sexuality in the consulting room. *British Journal of Psychotherapy.* 29(2), 135–153.

Target, M. (2007) Is our sexuality our own? A developmental model of sexuality based on early affect mirroring. *British Journal of Psychotherapy.* 23, 517–530.

Target, M. (2015) A Developmental Model of sexual excitement, desire and alienation, In Lemma, A. and Lynch, P. E. (eds.) *Sexualities, Contemporary Psychoanalytic Perspectives.* East Sussex: Routhledge.

Part 2
Sexual attraction and sexual identity in supervision

Part 2

2.1 The supervisory dimension
Jill Hunt and Charlotte Sills

Introduction

There is much excellent literature on the nature of the erotic and sexual attraction in psychotherapy – both in this volume and elsewhere (see, e.g., the reference list at the end of this chapter). It is a topic, perhaps like few others, that bring with it many subtle nuances in understanding and meaning – from the simply exciting to the sensual, from the infantile transference to the power play – to genuine here and now attraction. Space precludes us from examining them all here, so we have decided to concentrate on those elements of sexual attraction in practice that might be particular to supervision and the supervisory relationship, trusting that the ways of thinking about the emergence of the erotic will have been well treated elsewhere.

This choice begs the question: what might those particular elements be? We attempt to unpack this question here, writing from the perspective of the supervisor – for other supervisors – inviting us to think together about how the supervisory relationship might assist the supervisee to become more confident in discussing and managing this intense and important element of therapeutic practice.

So what is particular to supervision with regard to the issue of sexual attraction?

In most ways, supervising issues of the erotic is no different from supervising any other issue. The aim of the supervisory relationship is to provide a supportive environment for reflective practice in which both supervisee and supervisor are mutually engaged and participating. The aim of that engagement is the development of the supervisee, be that in knowledge, skills, personal self-awareness, relational competence, or ethical thinking. The ultimate aim is the improvement of service to the client.

Proctor (1988) describes three tasks of supervision: *Normative*, *Formative*, and *Restorative*. We use them to think about the supervisory tasks regarding the issue of the erotic and sexuality.

Restorative points to the necessity of supervision being a safe and non-judgmental container where anything and everything can be discussed.

Encountering sexual attraction in therapeutic work, be it their own or the client's responses, is probably the issue that supervisees find most difficult to bring to supervision. Perhaps, as supervisors, a question we need continually to be asking ourselves is whether the relationship with our supervisee is of the quality that can withstand the honesty and openness that is required of all involved, including ourselves. Supervisors need to ensure that supervisees experience the supervisory relationship as mutually respectful, trusting, confidential, and appreciative.

Formative involves the supervisor's duty – without shaming – to address the learning needs of the supervisee, providing some opportunity to think theoretically and clinically about the various possible meanings of the emergence of sexual attraction. This is important because, even now, it is a topic that is often missing in training. We allude to some of the possibilities at the start of this chapter and point to the other chapters in the book. But there are some issues that might emerge in the context of a supervisory discussion that pertain particularly to the topic. For example, the therapist may not recognise that they may be seen as having the power in the relationship. As therapists we create what we see as 'boundaries' or 'the frame', but which our clients, perhaps new to this peculiar relationship, might see as rules – even cruel ones. What effect may that have on a client and their sexual feelings or their sense of their sexual-selves? Do the rules become something to fight against in an attempt to feel powerful or does the client feel powerless and helpless in the face of them? Where is the place for flexing the boundaries, something that Maquet (2012) asserts is sometimes essential in the process of honouring the client and the relationship? His article is entitled 'The Frame as an Elastic and Dynamic Structure' and suggests that 'A good analogy for this [process] is a balloon. It is able, within certain limits, to undergo variations of pressure without exploding'. He goes on to say that 'the dynamics of the frame for any particular patient are related to that person's idiosyncratic psychic economy' (Maquet, 2012, pp. 20–21). As supervisors our task is to facilitate our supervisees to be able to hold this idea.

A supervisee was very concerned when a single male client brought her a personal present from his three-week-long trip to Asia and clearly enjoyed giving it to her, with the expectation that she would be pleased. Her concern when she came to supervision was that she didn't want to take the present as this could be seen as unethical. She was angry with him, saying, "he knows I cannot accept presents".

The supervisor pointed out to her that there may be another way of understanding his gift. What might this mean in terms of his attachment and relationship with her that during his break he had decided to buy her a present? Reluctantly she admitted that she had felt there was something happening between them for a while. It seemed as if he was wanting to make an impact on what he considered "these stupid rules!" She was relieved to have spoken about it and they were able to think together how about she could speak with him of what was happening between them. She reported later that when they had talked he had said, "How do I know I am in relationship with you if I know nothing about you?" This gave her further pause for thought with regard to how she could hold boundaries that took account of the individual relational dynamics of her clients.

The *Normative* element of supervision means helping the therapist be clear about those boundaries and limits to what he or she says or does. The therapist can actually feel more confident and held when there are certain guides in place. Our 'general rules' include the practitioner never explicitly saying that they feel sexually attracted to the client even if asked directly. There are so many parts or selves of the client listening – not only the adult but perhaps the abused child, the exploring teenager, and so on.

The Normative also requires us to be alert to the vulnerability of the supervisee to stray over boundaries. Gabbard (1997) says 'The main point I want to stress here is that given certain life stressors such as divorce, loss and other personal misfortunes any of us may become vulnerable to using patients as objects to gratify our emotional needs'. He goes on, 'Virtually all sexual involvement between analyst and patient begins with subtle breaks in the frame that progressively lead to more egregious transgressions of analytic boundaries' Gabbard (1997, p. 2). This topic is covered in depth in Part 3 of this volume.

These transgressive feelings and impulses are mostly not acted out, but they can muddy the frame. I (Charlotte) was supervising a woman whose husband had left her for a work colleague. The therapist was going through a vulnerable time personally – feeling humiliated and hurt as well as lacking in confidence in her own attractiveness. She could not help being warmed by the appreciation she felt from a client who was clearly captivated by being listened to and cared for deeply, probably for the first time in his life. She was able to speak about this in supervision and we talked about the possibility of her representing for the client the mother who needed to be made happy when his father suddenly left when he was ten. We assessed that this was not a problem at the moment; however it gave the supervisee pause for thought. The challenge came for the supervisee when she found herself feeling more than a little ambivalent when her client, no doubt in great part because of their deeply awakening relationship, met a woman at a party and started dating. Again, the supervisee found it helpful to explore the idea that she might be representing the mother who was both proud and pleased at her son growing up and leaving the nest, and at the same time finding it hard to let him go.

Whilst discussing these tasks we decided to speak with a dear colleague and the author of the model, Brigid Proctor, with whom we had an immensely fruitful and enjoyable discussion. One of the aspects that became apparent as we talked about our stories is the interactive nature of the three tasks – how both the Normative and Formative are Restorative, in that they relieve a supervisee of a lonely responsibility, and how the Restorative can free a supervisee to be able to hear and learn about the Normative, which can itself become Formative. And again, we recognised how vital the supervisory relationship is in the process, so that the three tasks are interactive not only with each other but co-created between supervisor and supervisee(s).

We also began to account for the multiple areas of focus that the supervisor and supervisee are required to hold in supervision and how we can understand and reflect together on the many and varied expressions of sexual attraction by clients and the responses of our supervisees and ourselves. We considered these by using Hawkins and Shohet's (1989, 2012) model – the 'seven-eyed model' of supervision, in particular eyes 3 through to 7. This model articulates seven areas of focus of attention in supervision: (1) the client or client's issue; (2) actions or interventions; (3) relational dynamic between supervisee and the client; (4) the person of the supervisee, with their personal and professional biases and proclivities; (5) the relational dynamic between supervisee and supervisor – including potential parallel processes; (6) the countertransference and responses of the supervisor; and (7) the wider world context.

At the end of our meeting with Brigid, she asked us to sum up what we wanted people to take away from reading our chapter. We agreed that we had two paradoxical wishes: first, we wanted to convey how very subtle, complex, and complicated these issues of the erotic and sexuality could be and how vital it is that they not be ignored; simultaneously we wanted to leave the reader feeling free and relaxed – able to say, 'Oh that ... well, of course'. We think that the following case example illustrates both sides of the polarity for the supervisory relationship. The issue of sexuality could not be ignored in the therapy – indeed it was very much 'in the therapist's face'. However, the fact that it was so deeply explored in the supervision was key to the success of the work. We also hope that the vignette illustrates the interactive strands of Formative, Normative, and Restorative as they arose in supervision as well as the flow of focus in the seven-eyed model. It is a composite vignette so that anonymity is protected.

David's story

Alice saw David for therapy for over four years, mostly twice a week.

David was in his early 30s when he came to see her. He said that he felt he had missed out on experimenting with his sexuality, that he had had no sexual experience before meeting his wife at college. His problem was that he wanted to have an affair but was unable to do so. He had seen two previous therapists who, he reported, had told him to 'just do it'. He said, 'if I *could* just do it I would have done it by now'. David had been married for six years and constantly complained that his wife did not want sex. They had one child.

David had been born in the UK, and at age seven he had moved to Canada because his father had gotten a new job. This did not work out, and they moved to middle America, when he went to a Jesuit school where the attitude to sex and sexuality was very negative, and there was a strong belief that sex before marriage was a serious sin. The message he took from it was that men were at fault and should curb their disgusting desires.

As the story unfolded, it became very clear that David's shame about and rejection of his developing manhood long pre-dated the Jesuits. He related some of his experiences with his mother, who seemed to close down on his sexuality from the start. He remembered a time as a young child when he was in the bath, with his sister. He asked his mother why his penis became hard – her response was to tell him that "It didn't". His mother also voiced her dislike of men – his father in particular – and he remembers being aware that he did not want to be like his father, whom he described as 'pathetic'. He had a clear memory of trying to tell his father how unhappy he was at school when they moved to Canada, and his father broke down in tears.

There was no physical contact in his family, no hugs or cuddles. As a teenager he spent many, many hours alone in his room playing with a baseball and glove, attempting to sublimate his sexual desire.

In his adult life, he reported many stories about girls and women fancying him; they had made that obvious, but he had been too scared in the moment to respond fully. Alice sensed that he was scared of what might be expected of him, both sexually and relationally, and that he was also experiencing the painful dilemma of both rejecting and yearning for a sense of himself as a sexual man. As he told her about these incidents in detail, she was aware that he wanted her to confirm that indeed the behaviour of these women was an indication that they desired him sexually.

After about a year of therapy David announced that he wanted Alice to have sex with him. It was clear to him that this is what he needed: someone to respond to him with desire. When she demurred, he assured her that no one would know.

In supervision, Alice discussed the client in a somewhat formal manner. She struggled to understand why he would want sex with someone 20 years older than him, nearer in age to his mother. As she reflected on this more fully rather than being dismissive and defensive, she began to understand the connection with regard to his relationship with his mother.

As they reflected together, Elsa (the supervisor) began to be interested in her own countertransference, which was to feel some disgust and revulsion as Alice described David. She was reminded of Dimen's (2005) 'Eew factor'. 'That sexual moment when you go, 'Eew! That's disgusting!' (p. 1). She offered her experience to Alice, who, with relief, admitted that she also felt like that sometimes. She felt able to respond empathically to David's child longing to be seen and loved, and felt very warm towards him at times, but she struggled to find a way to respond to his adult desire. She was not attracted to him in any way and when she thought about it she would become cold and unmoved internally – at times even disgusted by him, especially when he cried and was damp and messy. They discussed the notion of perversion; David's sense of his own sexuality had been perverted, first by his mother and then by his experience with the Jesuits. Being able to put words to this gave an enormous sense of relief and release to Alice who felt able both to shake clear of her own revulsion and also find greater understanding for David's strange behaviour.

At times Alice experienced his desire for sex with her as an attack, both on her and on the therapy. She was his therapist and therefore had a code of ethics! For a while, she hid behind the code of ethics in her refusal to have sex. She knew this was not useful as it was avoiding the issue. Her conflict was that she wanted to affirm him as a man, and yet she could not say that he was attractive; she did not find him so. She tried many interventions that interpreted his desire for her. However he seemed unable to work with the symbolic. He wanted and longed for gratification.

He decided to take short trips away, missing therapy in the process. He was clear that his aim was to have a sexual encounter. He also disclosed that he was attracted to a gay male friend of his. Alice was unsure whether David was really attracted to this man or to his apparent sexual freedom and enjoyment of his sexual encounters, which he relayed to David in detail – who again repeated them in detail to Alice.

Alice felt mixed about him travelling expressly in order to have a sexual encounter. She was concerned about the risk he seemed to be taking with regard to the effect on his marriage; she felt in some way she was being asked to collude with something unethical. Again a discussion in supervision helped her to be more aware of her sense that was something he was working through, even though it was not clear what. He would come and regale her with the details of his experience, sometimes in a way that demonstrated how attractive he was and at other times how pathetic he was. He did not have sexual intercourse with another woman, neither did he fulfil his desire to have sex with a man. There was a flavour of him bringing her something – like a cat who brings its owners a dead or injured mouse or bird as a present. Mainly these trips reinforced a loneliness and despair for him, which resulted in more demands for her to have sex with him. It felt important not to reject his stories of sexuality and his desperate longing, but at the same time she felt largely untouched and frequently he berated her for not caring.

Another break-through in supervision came one day when Alice talked about her guilt at not being moved by David's plight. He spent a lot of time railing and shouting at her for being cold and unfeeling and not caring. Alice indeed did feel cold and unmoved. And she questioned how could she be so unaffected? Yet she also felt that it was unfair of him – she knew she was a truly caring person. His particular outrage was that Alice could send him away, out of the room at the end of sessions. She had tried many ways of saying "I care and yet I will not have sex with you or hold you; and I will continue to care however much you criticise me". Elsa asked "Who says you are supposed to care for your clients?" Alice looked surprised, and then light dawned. She had been trapped in trying to be the 'good therapist' – her countertransference responding to the unconscious transferential demand by David to match his mother's purity and therefore keep her intact in his mind. When she stopped feeling 'bad' about her unfeeling states she began to realise that she was experiencing his projection of a cold, unmoved, and at best uninterested mother.

During the supervision, Elsa commented that sexuality is a therapeutic issue that is both psychological/emotional and also physical and that it was important to allow the physical into the dynamic between them. She noticed how Alice seemed to be sitting in a rather rigid way, seeming to lean forwards and backwards at the same time. She invited her to experiment with sitting how she sat when she was with David and to notice her internal feelings, then to sit how she would want to sit. Alice immediately softened her shoulders and back. She relaxed into her chair, uncrossed her legs, and slightly opened her arms.

Freeing herself from the pressure to be a caring therapist allowed Alice to say to her client that she did not see 'caring' as part of a therapy contract, that in fact she did care about him but that the work here was to truly understand what had happened to him. He was taken aback. But here too something relaxed after that and they went on to explore the tragedy of his unmet longing for both his mother and father to have shown that they cared for him and as parents to have supported and enjoyed his sexual development. He began fully to acknowledge the impact of his mother's denial of his sexuality, his father's lack of 'being a man' in a traditional sense, the reinforcement he received at Jesuit school, and the lack of any previous help for him to resolve his internal confusion and dilemma.

Of course, it was not all plain sailing. At one point during the work, David formed an attachment to a woman at his place of work. He would regularly report how he was sure that, if he wanted to, she would sleep with him. One time when his wife was away he went to dinner with this woman and worked himself up into a pitch of anxiety from which he propositioned her very awkwardly. She refused, and he became enraged and tried to persuade her. He was both ashamed of his behaviour and denigrating of the woman, calling her a whore and saying that she'd slept with everyone else, why not him?

Sometimes David related something to Alice that he had heard or read, which occasionally she did find erotic and arousing. For example, he told a story of a man who had hired two women prostitutes. He seemed both aroused by this story and disgusted by his arousal. He could not believe that Alice was not disgusted in the same way and railed at her for it – what sort of a person was she? It was as if he was testing her – on one hand wanting her to be aroused by the story and to affirm his sexuality and on the other condemning her for it.

In another supervisory discussion, Elsa and Alice explored the meaning of this pattern. They hypothesised that the denial and dislike of David's maleness, his masculinity, by his mother meant that he looked for that recognition in every relationship with a woman. When a woman paid attention to him, he sexualised the attention and when he did begin to form attachments or friendships, his feelings became sexual and the strength of these sexual feelings became overwhelming. Alice realised that she needed not only to convey that she was not disgusted by his stories, but that in the symbolic arena she could find the images sexually arousing – thus being a 'mother' who was not horrified by sexuality – either his or hers.

David finally left therapy, having made sense of much of what was going on for him. He had also released himself from the terrible bind he had been in about his sexual needs and felt much more comfortable being himself. He had not had an affair. However, he reported that his relationship with his wife had improved considerably. She was being kind to him. They were laughing together – and their sex life had increased a lot. David had also started going to football matches with his young son.

He left his last session slightly early, saying, 'This is a demonstration that what I have had from therapy has been enough'.

Reflection

Alice was very clear that without supervision, she could not have managed. It was this space to reflect that allowed her to work through and hold many things. Those interacting tasks – Restorative, Normative, and Formative weaved in and out of every session. Perhaps most important was the Restorative element – it was a place where she could own and name her countertransference, in particular her guilt at feeling unmoved at best and disgusted at worst, in response to her client. She had been experiencing herself as another 'abuser' in David's life and was horrified. When she was able to identify the feelings as projective identification, she was hugely relieved. Further, fully allowing the occasional feelings of revulsion allowed her to 'wipe them off' and return to thoughtfulness.

The importance of putting words to feelings and experiences, to not avoiding the 'sticky' was underlined. As Davies (1994) says 'What masquerades as analytic neutrality may in many cases represent the re-enactment in the transference of a countertransferentially induced gratification of the patient's eroticised masochism, rather than an enhanced capacity for intimacy and erotic mutuality.' (p. 162). In this case giving voice to some of the countertransferential and relational phenomena was not simply a therapeutic choice but Normative.

In addition it was very helpful to be able to think theoretically – it was Formative – for example to understand how the repression of sexuality can lead to perversion and how powerful those patterns of enactment can be. The supervisory conversations ranged over the areas of focus of the seven-eyed supervisor model (Hawkins and Shohet, 2012), from client conceptualisation (Focus 1) through to understanding the therapist's vulnerabilities of countertransference (Focus 4) to the relational dynamic and parallel process (Foci 3 and 5), including the supervisor's openness about responses (Focus 6), and, of course, the essential element of the 'situation as a whole', Wollants (2007) – the nature of manliness, the unsayability of the erotic in Western society, the implications of monogamy, and so on (Focus 7). Wollants states, 'person and world are inseparable and interdependent parts of a dynamic whole' (p. 2).

As they reviewed the case, Elsa and Alice wondered about the significance of their gender. What difference would it have made if one of them had been a man – or both? On a couple of occasions Alice had discussed the case in her peer supervision group – with four male colleagues – and their robust and normalising feedback had been very useful as they challenged her both to accept David's feelings towards her but also to be straight-forward in her firm setting of boundaries.

Counter-transference

We have talked above about how and when something ordinarily erotic and sexual becomes perverted. Gardner (1999) writes of a difference in working with clients who have been sexually abused as children. She describes the erotic transference as always being present. However the abusive experience has led to a perverse and negative manner in which it is conveyed. The relationship between the adult and the child has been perverse as it has been based on the 'gratification of an adult's desire at the expense of the child's needs' (p. 142).

I (Jill) was supervising Alan – an experienced practitioner working at a young person's service. Alan was a heterosexual man in a long-term relationship, who had been working at the service for several years. One day he came to supervision, sat down heavily, and put his head in his hands. He looked close to tears. Eventually he said, "I don't know how much longer I can keep doing this, I just don't feel like myself in my work with Daisy". (Daisy was a young woman in her early 20s.) He felt shame and described feeling horror with regard to what had happened to her as well as arousal, which disgusted him. 'I feel scared that I am a risk to her'. She had been open from the beginning that her reason for coming to the service was that she had been sexually abused as a young child. I recalled reading Fiona Gardner's article, and I began to speak of her section on 'A sense of mind of the abuser,' in which she states, 'Each patient brings their experience of the mind of the abuser to the therapist either through conscious memory or unconscious communication and fantasy' (p. 147). Alan took his head out of his hands, touched his head, and began to make sense for himself of what had been happening. He began to think and was able to say clearly, I think more to himself than me, 'I am not a risk to her.' His relief was palpable.

Going first

We have encountered many and varied responses from supervisees with regard to the erotic and sexual dynamics in their therapeutic work. These have ranged from outrage: "How dare he? I am his therapist!" to fear and terror of being found to be unethical. Supervisees have spoken of shame with regard to being excited and aroused, and also anxiety about being found sexy by raising the topic and appearing to encourage sexual feelings. Some supervisees have expressed guilt at finding themselves flirting with clients; some feel disgust and revulsion at clients' expressions of their sexual desires or admissions of attraction to their therapist. Others worry about the voyeurism in wanting to know more about clients' sexual encounters – or the envy they might feel of a client who has described a happy and fulfilling sexual relationship.

Given the potentially disturbing nature of the erotic transference and countertransference we thought therefore that there are some important things for the supervisor to bear in mind. The first, and perhaps most obvious but easy to forget task of the supervisor is to be willing to raise the subject of the erotic. Normally one would allow the supervisee to choose the focus of the supervision – especially with more senior supervisees. Because this topic is so taboo, it may be one that the supervisor needs to put on the table, direct attention to and inquire about. We need to 'go first' as Benjamin (2004, p. 8) puts it.

A simple statement of 'Perhaps he/she fancies you?' or even 'Of course he is in love with you.' or 'Do you find her/him attractive?', may be enough to open a reflective discussion. Sometimes the therapist themselves is the last person to become aware of their client's feelings towards them. As Dimen says, 'spark discussion so that the unspeakable can enter public discourse' (2005, p. 2).

As therapists and supervisors we deliberately aim to create intimate relationships which are deeply personal so is it not to be expected that the erotic will emerge within them? Schaverien (1995), citing Samuels (1996), says, 'Contrary to avoiding the erotic nature of the therapeutic situation then, it might be important to address the question: "Why is this person not lovable? or Why am I not aroused by this person?"' (1995, p. 40). As supervisors therefore should we from the beginning of a supervisory relationship 'be alert to the presence or absence of loving or sexual feelings just as we are alert to anger, envy or aggression' Schaverien (2006, p. 69) encouraging this topic to be an ordinary part of the supervisory conversation rather than extraordinary?

In the early days of my training I (Jill) was working with a young man who had clearly, I now understand, formed an erotic attachment to me. At the time I did not comprehend the nature of erotic transference and countertransference. I was uncomfortable, and I was desperate to discuss this in my own supervision. My supervisor's response was to tell me I had to stop working with him immediately. I felt criticised, a deep sense of shame, and that I had done something wrong. I did what I was told and ended the relationship. Looking back on that now I feel deep regret about what that experience must have reinforced for him. This was a young man who had not experienced a loving home environment; his mother had been unavailable. He was just developing a sense of his sexuality. I fear that the abrupt termination may have confirmed his belief that he was not loveable and that there was something wrong with him?

I am also now aware of how a rich opportunity was lost. First an opportunity to analyse the transference drama in a supportive supervisory relationship, to process what was happening for me, and to make sense of the client's experiences and feelings – both physical and emotional. And then perhaps to explore my supervisor's reaction and see what understanding that might have brought.

We need to aim for a supervisory relationship where there is mutual respect and lack of judgment. Everything and anything is welcome. In the freedom of the supervisory relationship, neither supervisor nor supervisee needs to mind their words. We as supervisors (as do trainers) need to encourage people to talk about sex, to play with meanings, to enjoy the energy that talking about sex brings, encouraging jokes and puns, experiencing the relief of talking openly, so that the process of naming becomes normalised.

Supervisors need to be prepared for their own feelings to be evoked and to share their responses to the erotic content brought by their supervisees, whatever the nature of it. They need to let go of any discomfort they may experience or concern about how they may be viewed. This may potentially be personally exposing, yet it is important modelling.

We think it is primarily the responsibility of the supervisor to notice the relational dynamics in both the therapeutic relationship and the supervisory relationship, raising questions such as: how is the supervisee relating to me as supervisor? How am I feeling as a result? What is it like to be with this supervisee and the material they bring? This may well reveal processes within the therapeutic relationship. Schaverien (2006) states that 'a variety of emotional and intellectual responses are demanded of the supervisor as spectator and attention to these very often reveals the parallel process' (p. 66).

Another important element of supervision of the erotic and sexual attraction is the supervisor's opportunity to notice patterns in the way supervisees do and do not bring issues of the erotic to the supervision.

- They may subtlety ignore (deny) the possibility of feelings between themselves and their client, by for example talking about another issue.
- They may reveal much in their bodily responses as they speak or the imagery and language they use about particular clients.
- They may have a general tendency to bring the same sorts of issue over and over again: for example to avoid erotic feelings by focussing on the

maternal love of an abused child and ignoring that this abused child lives in an adult body (we think we notice this more in women than men).
- They may ignore the existence of the erotic and interpret fascination with a client as some other distraction.
- They may reflect a cultural or societal trend that emerges in many supervisees (and to which the supervisor may or may not be contributing)

I (Jill) had a supervisee who brought the same client to the supervision group time after time, often the same issue. Gradually her feelings began to emerge strongly: she seemed to be enchanted by him – the client was all good; she admired everything about him. Although apparently at ease immediately following the session of supervision, having used it to regain her analytic mind, she seemed incapable of sustaining it. One day in the supervision group as she again spoke about the client, eventually (and it was after some time!) as the supervisor I said very forcefully, "you will not have sex with this client". She was shocked and surprised, and although this apparently had not been in her consciousness it was enough to break the enchantment. She was also clearly deeply disappointed by the breaking of the fantasy. And I noticed that I felt a little cruel to have cut through something. We discussed the meaning of unconsummated love and cruelty in relation to her client. She was able to go on to do some really good therapeutic work with this man, who was driven to charm and then cruelly abandon women.

A strongly erotic dynamic is inevitably likely to re-evoke the earliest, most pre-cognitive self-object experiences. It can easily become the 'madness' of being in love (Tallis, 2018) as our attachment centres are triggered and our NTA (ventral tegmental area of the brain) propels us to preoccupation with and need for the object of desire (Fisher, 2013). By definition therefore, it is hard to think rationally about and make sense of our feelings on our own. Supervision offers a supervisee time and space to think with the supervisor standing beside them, as an observer as well as participant. Clinical discussion about meanings and theoretical explanations can help the supervisee 'engage brain' and differentiate the subtle levels and implications of the experience. Theory can be a great support!

The previous point leads on to its opposite. Mann (1997) says 'I consider that the erotic pervades most if not all psychoanalytic encounters and is largely a positive and transformational influence' (Mann, 1997, p. 1). Gerrard says:

> Until and unless there can be felt moments of love for the patient by the therapist, the patient is not able to develop fully. I think it is only when a patient can arouse our deepest loving feelings (not empathy) that we can really hope for a truly positive outcome from our work.
>
> (1999, pp. 29–41)

A therapist can be enormously competent, ethical, and clinically subtle, but without the erotic element of delighting engagement, the relationship will not have the 'vital base' that Cornell (2001) describes: 'I have come to believe strongly that when we engage in therapy that is too nurturing, too careful, too sanitized and de-eroticized, we do our clients a disservice'. (Cornell, 2001, pp. 213–224). Here there is an echo of the words by Davies (1994) quoted earlier, about the possible abuse in so-called therapeutic neutrality. It behoves the supervisor to be alert to whether, for whatever personal reason, the therapist is not offering the sort of zestful relationship in which growth flourishes.

The supervisory relationship itself

As we have stated, supervision is an intimate and deeply personal relationship, usually with affection and a developing familiarity. It is likely that transference and countertransference will develop here, including the possibility of the erotic. So how do we manage this in supervision? We think that the supervisory agreement has to include the willingness to openly discuss the relationship dynamics that are happening between supervisee and supervisor. Again this is probably a situation in which the supervisor has to take the initiative to go first. As supervisors we also have to remember we will be seen by our supervisees as having the power in the relationship.

Both of us have had the experience of a situation in which a supervisee, someone we thought was good practitioner who appeared to become so fearful and mistrustful in supervision that all they did was report on and describe their client work. We tried everything we could to discuss what was happening but to no avail. We encouraged our respective supervisees to talk in their own therapy; it didn't change what was between us. As we think about that now we wonder if that was an abandonment of something vital in our relationship? Although this may not have necessarily been to do with direct sexual attraction, there certainly was something to do with a relational dynamic that could not be spoken of.

Frawley-O'Dea and Sarnat (2001) describe a relational model of parallel process 'in which relational patterns from either dyad can influence the other' (p. 195). In other words, a parallel process can not only be carried into supervision from the therapeutic relationship; it can also be carried the other way, so that either the inhibitions or the freedoms contained in the supervisory dyad can facilitate either a bind or a release in the therapeutic dynamic. They suggest supervisor and supervisee discuss three questions: (1) What is the relational pattern currently in play in the supervisory relationship? (2) What does it tell us about the relationship between this supervisee and this supervisor and their work together? and (3) What, if anything, does it suggest to us about the transference and countertransference of the supervised treatment?

It is important for the supervisor to initiate a reflective process without shutting things down or trying to impose a meaning before it has emerged. We need to model allowing the parallel process to emerge, so that feelings and experiences that develop within us as supervisors are available to the conversation. If we are uncomfortable with discussing the erotic we risk shutting down on the reflective space and the possibility of meaning becoming known. This then may be replicated in the therapeutic relationship.

This brings us on to perhaps the most common worry we find expressed by supervisees. A supervisee may have settled to the idea that something must be named, but wonders how to do it appropriately as an opening up of a space to explore rather than something that might at the very least foreclose on the process of discovery and at worst disconcert or even terrify her or him.

Finding the words to say it

Sometimes it is easier to respond to a communication that is clearly about sexual activity and gratification than it is to address one where the erotic is more subtly conveyed. People get stuck and unable to think of a response. One of the constant questions from supervisees is "How do I talk about this with my client?" They fear being seen as making an advance and that if the feelings are not mutual or recognised by the client, they will end up feeling stupid and humiliated. Alternatively they worry that they will be unable to find the words in the heat of the moment without them sounding overly explicit.

We like to stress that the supervisee should find their own words – not stick to a formula. If the supervisor has a strong personal perspective they may become rigid and attempt to force this on the supervisee. This book is full of examples of how therapists have had the courage to 'go first' in putting words to what is difficult to express. We think the important thing is that the therapist is willing to *say something*. The exact words don't matter – simply that a process is started whereby the possibility of talking about the erotic is brought into the room. We find it can help enormously if the container or boundary is set. When the boundaries are in place – boundaries of what the therapist will say and do – a container is created in which the therapist can feel freer.

We encourage supervisees (and here is where a supervision group can be hugely useful) to try out different phrases or offerings in response to client's comments, such as:

There's something charged between us
We enjoy each other
There is an exciting energy between us

Particularly challenging can be a direct question about the therapist's feelings of attraction to a client. As we have said above, we believe it is important not to be too personal in a response. For example a therapist might say:

You are a lovely woman (rather than I find you attractive)
I really enjoy working with you – I think you do too

In response to expressions of love or desire, we think it is appropriate to value the gift of the disclosure as well as clarify the boundary if necessary. So a response might be

'I feel deeply moved by you expressing your feelings – and nothing will happen between us'.

We can feel confident that creating a relationship of boundaried freedom when the clients themselves share the task of naming, such as when a male client said "My wife said it was alright for me to fall in love with my therapist".

Another said "In other circumstances I would have asked you out". The therapist answered "In other circumstances I may well have said yes".

In both cases there was a clear understanding that nothing would 'happen'. What the declaration achieved was a clearing of the air which made room for the enjoyment of a very productive therapeutic relationship.

We are aware that differences in gender and age might make a difference in what and how the therapist speaks. Sometimes race and ethnicity will also change the context. This also introduces the question of how much the gender, race, and sexuality of all parties involved have an impact on the efficacy of the supervision. In the example above where the therapist was told by her (female) supervisor to stop the work, would the outcome have been different if the supervisor had been a man? We wonder if a man may have understood this young man's developmental and early relational needs and facilitated the therapist to find words with which to talk with him. Or if supervision had taken place in a group with a mixture of genders and sexualities?

All this points to the need to be alert to the possibility of collusion as supervisors. As women would we be more likely to concur with a female supervisee's view of a male client's perhaps gendered behaviour or attitude? Or might we miss a possible powerplay in a male client's flirtatious humour. Would a (cis) male supervisor perhaps overlook the seductive element of a female client's fragility? And so on. What difference does the race, gender, and sexuality of supervisor/supervisee relationships make in their capacity to identify and find meaning in the erotic? Here is yet another argument for group supervision as a rich source of differing opinions, ideas, and responses. In Chapter 2.3 of this volume Di Hodgson explores this topic of diversity in depth.

In conclusion

We imagine it is clear to the reader that for us, the most important role of supervision in relation to sexual attraction is the provision of the supervisory relationship itself. If a space can be created where anything and everything can be felt, reflected on, experimented with, and verbalised, this will be not only interesting and enjoyable but enormously liberating for the supervisee and supervisor alike.

References

Benjamin, J. (2004). Beyond doer and done to: An intersubjective view of thirdness. *Pscho-Analytic Quarterly*, 73, 5–46.

Cornell, W. F. (2001). There ain't no cure without sex: The provision of a "vital" base. In: Cornell, W. F. & Hargaden, H. (Eds.) *From Transactions to Relations: The Emergence of a Relational Tradition in Transactional Analysis* (pp. 213–224). Chadlington: Haddon Press.

Davies, J. M. (1994). Love in the afternoon: A relational reconsideration of desire and dread in the countertransference. *Psychoanalytic Dialogues*, 4(2), 153–170.

Dimen, M. (2005). Sexuality and suffering, or the eew! factor. *Studies in Gender and Sexuality*, 6(1), 1–18.

Fisher, H. (2013). The anatomy of love. www.youtube.com/watch?v=Wthc5hdzUIs. Accessed 17th August 2019.

Frawley-O'Dea, M.G. & Sarnat, J. E. (2001). *The Supervisory Relationship: A Contemporary Psychodynamic Approach*. New York: Guildford Press.

Gabbard, G. O. (1997). Nonsexual and sexual boundary violations between analyst and patient: A clinical perspective. Paper presented at Scientific Meeting of the British Psycho-Analytic Society, November 5 (pp. 1–8).

Gardner, F. (1999). A sense of all conditions. In: Mann, D. (Ed.) *Erotic Transference and Countertransference: Clinical Practice in Psychotherapy*. London: Routledge. 139–149.

Gerrard, J. (1999). Love in the time of psychotherapy. In: Mann, D. (Ed.) *Erotic Transference and Countertransference: Clinical Practice in Psychotherapy*. London: Routledge. 29–41

Hawkins, P. & Shohet, R. (2012). *Supervision in the Helping Professions*. Maidenhead: OUP, 4th Edition (first published 1989).

Mann, D. (1997). *Psychotherapy. An Erotic Relationship. Transference and Countertransference Passions*. London: Routledge.

Maquet, J. (2012). From psychological contract to frame dynamics: Between light and shadow. *Transactional Analysis Journal*, 42, 17–27.

Proctor, B. (1988). Supervision: a co-operative exercise in accountability. In: Marken, M. and Payne, M. (Eds.) *Enabling and Ensuring Supervision in Practice*. Leicester: National Youth Bureau. 21–34.

Samuels, A. (1996). From sexual misconduct to social justice. Psychological dialogues. *The International Journal of Relational Perspectives*, 6(2), 295–321.

Schaverien, J. (1995). *Desire and the Female Therapist: Engendered Gazes in Psychotherapy and Art Therapy*. London and New York: Routledge.

Schaverien, J. (2006). Supervising the erotic transference and countertransference. In: Schaverien, J. (Ed.) *Gender, Countertransference and the Erotic Transference*. London: Routledge. 56–70.

Tallis, F. (2018). *The Incurable Romantic – And Other Tales of Madness and Desire*. New York: Hachette.

Wollants, G. (2007). Therapy of the situation. *British Gestalt Journal*, 14(2), 91–102.

2.2 The disturbance and comfort of forbidden conversations (sexuality and erotic forces in relational psychotherapy supervision)

Carole Shadbolt

Introduction

In this chapter I reflect upon some issues which arise in psychotherapy supervision concerning sexuality and erotic forces.

In his book *Awakenings*, Oliver Sacks comments that

> there were always *two* books, potentially, demanded by every clinical experience: one more purely 'medical' or 'classical' - an objective description of disorders, mechanisms, syndromes; the other more existential and personal – an empathic entering into the patients' experiences and worlds.
>
> (Sacks, 2012, pp. xxxvi)

My aim is to try for the spirit of the latter in this chapter which is about sexuality and the erotic as I have found them to be or not be in my work. There is, as we are becoming increasingly aware, no single way of expressing our sexualities and our erotic selves, so in that respect each supervisory encounter is likely to parallel this and be unique and individual, and unfold in its own way. Similarly, theories about how and why our sexualities and erotic desires and loves take the form they do differ widely, as do ideas about therapeutic direction. Here I speak and reflect on what made best sense to me as I worked both as a clinician and as a supervisor.

I take you through a supervisory relationship in which emerged a potential transgression. I reflect on that journey with my supervisee, naming some theories and processes concerning sexuality and the erotic which arose and sat alongside the unfolding drama. I will use other examples and vignettes as part of my reflections. I view all my examples and ideas as journeys in self-and-other discovery and self-with-other revelation.

Supervisory illustration

"The Hug"

I could immediately grasp the tension in my supervisee's demeanour as we started our time together.

That sense that something is in the air.

We had worked reasonably successfully together for a number of years, but in my own reflections I knew between us was a certain withholding. Not unusual.

I had known her since her training, years ago now and I respected her as a clinician and had no reservations about her integrity or commitment to her work and ethical and professional stance. She was a supervisor herself. Despite this, and although we had a good enough supervisory relationship, I would call our supervision functional, conventional, traditional, a duty I got the idea. She came regularly and kept herself firmly on the right side of ethical and professional requirements. In short she was a good, dependable, trustworthy psychotherapist who brought sometimes boring work to our sessions (like us all from time to time).

This all added up to nothing really amiss, nothing to bring up with her so I rarely addressed "us" with her, other than to enquire whether as far as she knew she was getting what she wanted from our supervision. She certainly did not bring up "us". When I did attempt to mildly wonder whether what was between us might be informative to the work she was bringing and therefore, quite possibly in parallel, or unconsciously countertransferential with her clients, inviting curiosity, my enquiry was batted back, politely but firmly. Dead.

She did not, would not, could not, allow that notion to take hold and to live in our explorations. We worked for some time like this, as she went from trainee to experienced clinician. She reported success and satisfaction in her clinical work, but nothing which came close to sexual aliveness or the presence of any erotic force in her work. In any case, the erotic or sexuality may not always be present a priori in clinical work as referred to by Susie Orbach's work on gender differences when working with female to female expressions and experiences of sexuality and the erotic (Orbach, 2000, p. 231).

We did speak about her clients' sexuality often, but it was usually a descriptive categorising reporting, that is, straight or LGBTQI, married or single, divorced, superficial assumptions made. As might be put on a 'front sheet' when presenting a case to a group or something of the like.

I am familiar with this process in both clinical as well as supervisory work, it's how it goes, eventually in my experience something will happen. I strive to be a patient clinician and supervisor and wait for my clients and supervisees, as my mentors have taught and waited for me. A respected voice from the past internally supervises me to be nevertheless attentive, "Carole, there is never nothing going on". And so it was in this case. I had naturally taken my own reflections about the deadness of our supervision to my own consultant. It was difficult, not straightforward because of my bothering about boundaries and differences between supervision and therapy, and as a result I had uncomfortable fears and was reluctant to continue to confront or wonder about the deadness between us. But I had begun to feel a note of dissatisfaction creeping into me at her carefully correct lacklustre style, which I had come to regard as withholding, and her slight agitation. At some point about this time, I was startled to realise that I was wondering about her hair, what shampoo she might use, and absentmindedly my hand went to my own hair and stroked it. As if I could be seen by her, I quickly withdrew it and shoved those terribly shaming thoughts away. But I caught the erotic communication or embodied countertransference, alive and present in our supervision session, who wouldn't, and though I didn't verbalise this, I immediately used my own therapy and consultation to address its meaning for the work. Something was coming to life.

This time there was no withholding, no deadness, though dealing with the issue was less straightforward. It painfully drew upon our supervisory relationship.

In summary, she had spontaneously hugged a client at the end of a session. The Hug turned into what she thought was an embrace redolent with sexuality and arousal apparently. The client returned the next session saying though they felt somewhat confused about "the fumbled hug" they were also thrilled and energised by its meaning. In their view, it signalled an exciting and more lively therapy which up until then, they were now aware, had been pedestrian.

She had immediately apologised and said as far as she was concerned that was the end of it she felt. "You hoped" I felt myself ruefully and wryly thinking, and sure enough, since the event she had dreaded the client arriving. She was 'on the back foot'; what was initially one uncomfortable session had become a therapy which was now intolerable for her. She felt ashamed and frightened, out of control with the client who, she told me she had come alive and was curious and pushing on boundaries. She felt inhibited and 'not herself'. The work had stalled as far as she was concerned and she didn't know how to proceed except in supervision she wanted to discuss how to end with the client as a way out of what she felt she could no longer manage. She was in uncharted waters, I saw it as my job, the supervisory task, to hold the frame whilst she thrashed about in them, confident that at last she was on course. Certainly not to end with her client at least not an ending driven by her fear of becoming ensnared in the very process she had, it was now clear, steered us and herself around so judiciously. All unconscious.

As I sat and listened my heart went out to her, I knew her to be a good therapist and woman, but I could tell that at this point she felt far from that herself. In the air now was 'smuttiness' and mistrust, and deeper still a precarious privacy which had been rudely exposed, an unfamiliar dreaded moment of emotional nudity, followed by withdrawal. Of having done something wrong, shamefully wrong at that. I knew too that engaging and attending to the meaning of this process, was where we needed to go to in the supervision, and no doubt she in her work with her client, reluctant as I felt then about doing so. To borrow the title from Cornell's relevant article *What am I getting myself into?* (Cornell, 2003) The aliveness, and its disturbing contents which I had explored in my own consultation, was now appearing between us. I remember thinking "at last, she and we have come alive, she and so we, are experiencing and bringing to life something which we cannot kill off".

Something of the forbidden, unbidden, the taboo, so present when working in the presence of sexuality and the erotic, had been carried into our supervision and had been up to that point unaddressed, unconscious, unknown, and uncertain to us.

It took the form then of me being not a little surprised at what she told me, I simply couldn't imagine her hugging or touching a client or anything remotely like it.

In answer to my enquiry when did this take place, I was taken aback to receive the answer… about a year ago. She had been suffering all this time without so much as a word to me, or me picking up any sense that in her work and life she was battling with this. Whilst I might not expect as with a client to know the details of her personal process I might have expected to know of her struggles which so affected her work well-being and self-image.

And there I would be wrong. I did know some of it very well in fact. It was there all the time, in the enacted deadness, the correctness and withdrawal, that I describe earlier. Whatever the nature of what had been powerfully dissociated from now emerging between her and her client was no doubt unconscious too shameful to even know until The Hug, it's parallels had found their way into our work and deadened it. It was working at its transgressive edge which transformed our supervisory relationship, which in turn addressed and fixed what was missing in the work between my supervisee and her client and had come alive and were pushing their way to the light in our supervisory relationship.

Approaching that 'transgressive edge', I respectfully enquired, got curious, invited her to reflect on what she had felt about The Hug. She couldn't say, other than that in her body she felt "pinned", could go neither forwards nor back, frozen. What's more she told me straight out she didn't want to. In a sense, though we both understood and respected the "not wanting to" we realised somewhere, somehow that this needed to be attended to. A genie was out of a bottle albeit a pinned and frozen genie.

As a way forward I got curious in my own mind and in my consultation about that polarity. That she felt "pinned" but also realised she needed to address The Hug and its meaning. I worked diligently. I imagined a sexual fumbling, an experimentation, the smuttiness, a certain unwelcome insistence as well as the familiar deadness. It also carried with it a feeling of distaste. As I reflected on that impasse, a deeper knowing about fragile privacy, exposure and, I imagined, deeper still of loss, painful perhaps, became clear to me. Alongside that the shame and fear that I would feel she wasn't a fit person to be seeing clients. That I would stop seeing her and stop her working.

Now of course the sexual metaphors, the power dynamic and the taboos and signifiers are all too obvious, but the forbidden and taboo are powerful diluters of desire and aliveness and when they enter the field they somehow make sexuality and aliveness invisible. Or at least shy. A through-a-glass-darkly atmosphere.

I spoke then to my thought of not being able to imagine her hugging anyone, which stood as a contradiction because of course she had done just that. I was curious about that contradiction in me I offered. I was interested to know her take on that. Somehow I don't now know how, she risked all by saying in fact she was excited by The Hug, she was sexually aroused, she knew the same was true for her client. Continuing, she spoke my imaginings and personal reflections back to me. There was more to this story than she had let herself be fully aware of.

Her own life, sexual or otherwise, was joyless, empty, and lonely in many respects – no partner or wish for one, no sexual expression; her work as a psychotherapist was everything to her, she told me. I "sort of" knew all that, it was just that I could not know nor say it in the fullness that now emerged. I was also mesmerised by the power of dissociated from forbidden connections. A curious clearing and focussing of my mind and between us was occurring as she finally made connections with The Hug, herself, her client's story, and their therapy time together.

At the time of The Hug, her client was going through a painful love-hate relationship and was by turns upset and jealous, confused or elated and joyous. One moment they felt unlovable and ugly and the next all was well. It happened that one day the client asked to show her a wedding photograph, evidence that her partner and she were happy and fine. She agreed and to her dismay she looked again on the face of a person she thought she had buried and banished from her heart long ago, there as a wedding guest. It brought "crashing back" love and loss, arousing emotions of that lost love and life in what felt, and was, a lifetime ago. She told me that she had been shamefully betrayed and deserted by that beloved treasured partner some years ago and for a while her life was extremely bleak and empty. She was unwanted and lost and in extreme psychic pain. Her trust had been broken as well as her heart and she vowed she would never again expose herself to such agony, and she never had. In my own feelings I was now sure that what had been reawakened was that unattended to loss that I had intuited, of relationship and love and had found a transferential expression as she, as it were, comforted herself and her client in their intersubjective pain and a locked away desire found its physical erotic expression between them.

Her blind spot, the dissociated from pain, was beginning to be addressed and given life by the awakening of her own sexuality and desires, as feminist psychotherapist Susie Orbach has intimated are often absent or deeply buried and dissociated from, in women (Orbach, 2000, pp. 230–232). My own blind spot as supervisor had been to not be able to imagine my supervisee having the desire to hug anyone, in other words, to have desires and be a sexual person, or the work to have anything other than a deadness to it. Or to be able to bring that to my supervisee, we had in fact co-created the very dead relationship which I describe earlier and caution against (though mercifully not completely) because of the powerful unconscious parallel process I now know.

I have written elsewhere about clients going only so far as their therapist has psychologically travelled "it is as if they know we couldn't take it if they did" (Shadbolt, 2018). Attending to her personal work as well as the inevitable teach/treat dimension between us was crucial. Exploring the intersubjective, that is, addressing the "what is happening between us?" question so long unaddressed, including the meaning of the deadness, brought our sessions full circle from that deadness to life. "The same applied to you", I said to myself from my internal supervisor as I accepted the parallel of my blind spot as I almost failed to imagine her other than she was. Although a necessary part of working through, I am always astonished by the power of that process, moving from unawareness of what is dissociated from material to them having, being given life. I always imagine I know what's going on only to find I never do! That delicious moment of clarity, of clouds clearing and meaning given, almost has an erotic quality of its own.

Sessions now included engaging with emotions and the erotic force in her work, she and I had dissociated from. From this she understood the root of the disavowal of sexual feelings and desire which had been enacted for so long and which had eventually erupted between her and her client, and had led her/them to almost transgress in the first place.

Expressions of hitherto forbidden and shameful sexual feelings emerged which she took to her own therapy and found their rightful place, seeing in turn how her clinical work was impacted transferentially. Connections made possible by our now alive relationship and supervisory space. Her clinical work, now in the realm of her clients emerging sexuality and desires, their own dreaded and repeated losses and longings for relationship were intermingled with her own and brought us to the 'transgressive edge'.

At one point she came to the horribly tumultuous idea that she had quite probably fallen in love with her client who frankly she had come to adore. It hit her like a thunderbolt. That thought and her words almost died on her lips as soon they were spoken. But they were out. In me I took her shameful horror and anguish seriously and cared for her in that place. In the way one might care for someone who is in the grip of an erotic obsession and 'in love'. Whether she was or not or should be was somewhat beside the point, that we now had a space, a relationship in which these tempestuous disturbances could be spoken of, honoured in some respects, examined as a legitimate, central part of her work with her client. We also knew its root, loss from which she had never recovered and its antecedents, and the root in her client: a dread that she was undesirable and would be and had been rejected.

In supervision sessions we navigated the inevitable teach treat boundary. Such clinical cold words to describe, and which somehow cannot impart the depth of human feeling, of how her own narrative played out, intersubjectively mirrored in her clients own losses and desires and how she contained them.

Supervision concerned approaching those multi-dimensional edges. Transgressive in part because of my parallel bothers about boundaries between supervision and therapy and in relational work their close often indistinguishable boundaries as well as attending to the very real pain her client wanted relief from brought us close to exploring those edges. The work was to find a way a space, between the binary of saying nothing and saying too much. To contain what sometimes felt uncontainable. In fact, over time as we unflinchingly (mostly) addressed those issues in our supervision, she found a new resilience and understanding of the co-transferences concerned with her client and the work became less fraught and difficult. Boundaries were respected – their edges not ignored nor shied away from.

In addressing the forbidden and becoming curious about those in herself she learned how holding its boundaries without denying them led to more understanding of what the feelings meant in her work and how to manage the roller coaster of ups and downs with her client which emerged from the intersubjectivity present between them. In at last feeling and taking ownership of her own dissociated-from sexuality and desire and her own losses, in her own therapy (and life!), her work with her client was transformed into a meaningful and real experience which, though useful, had also been lacklustre and superficial.

I came to have a deep respect for her and the journey. She had found courage, desire, and an absolute commitment to neither act out nor dissociate from the erotic intersubjectivity which had been revealed by the transgressive hug. Her work with me returned to her a sense of her integrity, goodness, and equilibrium, and a sense of inhabiting her own life. And comfort.

Reflections

Because sexuality and the erotic are as ubiquitous and changeable as the weather it should come as no surprise to psychotherapy supervisors that the topic should appear one way or another in their consulting rooms. Unlike the weather, at least in the UK, which is a topic of endless comment and preoccupation, sexuality and its impact on the practice of psychotherapy is less easily or freely commented upon or engaged with as I discovered. There are a number of understandable reasons for this: social, cultural, professional, and psychological. Matters of sexuality and the erotic carry elements of a forbidden territory, of taboos, and of the danger of transgression. The subject brings up disturbance and uncertainty.

So looking back it should also have been no surprise that when finding ourselves and our work in the domain of sexuality and erotic forces within

Psychotherapy and Psychotherapy supervision that there was indeed disturbance and uncertainty, whether it was in awareness or not. In this situation its presence out of full awareness took the form of silence, fear, and shame, which were themselves dissociated from and made dead.

What was also dissociated from, were the opposite forbidden erotic forces, that we can also be delighted charmed, excited, turned on, seduced, and reckless.

When sexuality and the erotic came to light in the manner it did my supervisee disconcertingly just did not know what to do or where to start, or whether she should be addressing these forces at all, either clinically or in our supervision, and so they remained unnamed and hidden from us both, 'out of harm's way'. As we learned, though, there was the potential for them to take root and remain unexamined. Until the rupture or emergence of unconscious material finds its way to the surface as in the case I describe and lived through in a sense with my supervisee.

This dynamic could have been seen as repeat of an original experience in the development of self-hood of her client's relationship with their sexuality and the presence of the erotic or absence of it and in which case regarded as an enactment in the present with the therapist and carried into the supervisory domain and relationship.

As I describe it was also an intersubjective dynamic, meaning that in this instance therapist and client were not separate from each other but mutually influenced each other and the work. In other words, what they made together was unique and in some respects a necessary part of a working through of them.

Although, or perhaps because, these disturbances may signify the importance of the presence and place of sexuality and the erotic in psychotherapy for the reasons I have highlighted above it can be a risky, potentially shaming business to accept these processes as existing in the first place in our consulting rooms. This applies to both being a supervisee and a supervisor. It can seem a rather large leap to accept them as legitimate or significant, let alone regarding them as healthy and an effective and perhaps inevitable part of the supervisory task and work when we become aware of them. As was the case with my supervisee.

Transactional analysis's creator Eric Berne speaks of the therapist's job and stance. He notes, and passes on, that as therapists our job does not necessarily include being made to feel, or make ourselves comfortable in that role or position. So true, and very applicable to the supervisory process as well. Engaging in a meaningful manner with the issues of sexuality and the erotic in supervision are a potential co-transferential minefield of unconscious process and probably means we are almost destined to be personally and professionally exposed to those less than palatable discomforts. My supervisee's shame and shock about The Hug and what it awakened in her and her wish to end the work because of that, her dread of sessions, her experience of the embodied frozenness were all examples of these discomforts and disturbances.

Coming to understanding that it is probably not always a comfortable experience but that it is always personal is probably a fundamental starting point for getting to grips with addressing the supervisory issues involved and until my supervisee came to know this and was able speak choice-fully to what might feel forbidden and seems transgressive but nevertheless *was*, our work was a rather sterile and perfunctory tick box affair, characterised by me, as a fragile unequal pseudo-power dynamic, conducted within an atmosphere of enmaddening, deafening, psychological relational silence. It is easy to see how this very likely repeats the therapist's clinical dilemma in the first place. It is also likely to be an intersubjective phenomenon. By which I mean mutually influential... and influencing.

The relational supervisory frame

"A place to say it"

As well as the above understandings also fundamental was building a supervisory frame and relationship in those issues can unfold and be addressed. Eventually my supervisee about whom I write and I formed a powerful meaningful supervisory working alliance so to speak which transformed the deadness which had prevented any genuine connection and understanding. As the supervisor I was also mesmerised by the dissociative presence of the forbidden, the taboo in the countertransference, the parallel process. So ubiquitous was it that it was almost hiding in plain sight. That process was worked through to reach the trusting supervisory relationship required to chase down the danger of any further uncontained enactment.

Ideally as a relational clinician, I draw and rely on the relationship between me and my client as a barometer to what might be present though as yet unnamed and sometimes is unknown. I see supervision in the same way. The constituents and principles of a relational supervisory relationship include uncertainty, trust, and mutuality.

They are fine liberating and aspirational ideals but they are also lived in experiences, subjective and relational rather than concrete objectivities and their presence is not always a forgone conclusion as my story of The Hug painfully reveals. Tim Bond captures their subjectivity when describing what he calls "the missing ethic of trust" observing that risk is an inevitable part of working as a psychotherapist but that it is sometimes overlooked or unacknowledged.

Indeed, sometimes it is actively undermined particularly when living and working with issues of sexuality and erotic, which are imbued with cultural prohibitions about violation of boundaries and fears of litigation and so on (Bond, 2006). The absence of trust, uncertainty, and mutuality, albeit unawarely, in my story was what challenged my supervisee who in the beginning trusted neither herself, nor our supervisory relationship nor probably her client. Ethically speaking she 'did no harm', which also meant in this situation 'take no risk', until that which had been unattended to burst upon her. The fact that she withheld her distress and held me at arms' length for some time through uncertainty about what to do is illustrative of that. Eventually we formed a strong relationship through the rupture and in her risk of revealing what had happened as uncertain as she was about its outcome. It also reveals her fear that I would stop her working also revealed her understanding and fear of the asymmetrical dynamic us, rather than understanding and trusting our mutual roles she believed that I would stop her working. There was a necessary working through, a living through that situation to get from mistrust to trust, from certainty to uncertainty, to get from detachment to mutuality as it were. A making of a unique to us supervisory space. Bond put it as follows: "one that supports the development of reciprocal relationship of sufficient strength to withstand the relational challenges of difference and inequality and the existential challenges of risk and uncertainty". His words fit so well with what a relational supervisory dynamic looks like.

A note about power

My supervisee's fear that I would stop her practising and that she had in some way committed a gross indiscretion and had been unethical but had been unable to bring it to either our supervision or to her own mind led me to think about power within the supervisory relationship. Power dynamics seem particularly relevant when sexuality and the erotic need in some way to be accounted for.

There are particular overlapping connections between sexuality, the erotic, and power, and they were evident in both the cases where I describe the supervision. These connections had psychosocial, cultural, and political dimensions, all of which were externally generated, 'carried in', implicit sometimes and explicit at others. Although our relationship was safe enough and good enough it sat within that 'outside' context which was influential and impacting. For example, my supervisee's own opinions and views about sexuality itself, her own desires, the client's desires as well as cultural aspects, both conscious and unconscious. Views about those matters, in wider society and within the psychotherapeutic community's approaches and values about how to work with sexuality and the erotic were influential both consciously and unconsciously understood.

There are wide and differing views about all those dimensions, but they illustrate that our supervisory relationship was not separate nor independent of those contexts, and bring with them power dynamics. Michel Foucault's work on power and sexuality is relevant and applicable. Elspeth Probyn's article speaks of Foucault's work which illustrates the psychosocial shaping and influences of our sexual and gendered selves (Probyn, 1997, pp. 133–145). Ideas of power concerning 'dominant discourses' meaning what is said to whom, who decides what action is required for example. These 'dominant discourses' map out reality that fix and name a 'normativity' that is a set of rules about what is allowable, what is normal. What is transgressive and what is not.

Thinking about that power and the dynamics between us, I returned to Orbach's ref questions concerning the absence of the erotic between women. I came across a quote by the late Audre Lorde in which she says,

> There are many kinds of power, used and unused, acknowledged or otherwise. The erotic is a resource within each of us that lies in a deeply female and spiritual plane, firmly rooted in the power of our unexpressed or unrecognized feeling. In order to perpetuate itself, every oppression must corrupt or distort those various sources of power within the culture of the oppressed that can provide energy for change. For women, this has meant a suppression of the erotic as a considered source of power and information within our lives.
>
> (Lorde, 1993, p. 339)

Lorde's powerful message seems to be entirely relevant to further understand the power dynamics of dissociation which featured so relevantly in our supervisory relationship. They were worked through mutually, albeit implicitly between us, supported by the ethical principles I have described above.

Embodied countertransference

The centrality of our bodies

When as supervisors we have a puzzling sometimes intense phenomenological physical reaction or arousal to what we are hearing and experiencing in the work, it is worth considering that they are most probably countertransferential and transferential process. The 'embodied', that is, that which is carried in and felt by the body, speaks of and communicates loudly and clearly but differently, and usually bypasses cognitive processes, most especially when matters of sexuality and the erotic enter the field. A different vignette illustrates this.

"How can speak to my client who has started to sit, legs wide open with her fanny showing?" said my supervisee. I was taken aback, mostly because of his out of character rather coarse turn of phrase which immediately put me on my supervisory guard. "Shall I just tell her to pull her skirt down, and cover up her bottom?" he went on. "Shall I say nothing?" "I am made to feel intrusive and she is being rude and flirtatious" "I'm just not at all sure what to do or what I feel about it, or what I'm being invited into" "She's leaving nothing to my imagination, and I'm afraid I will have a hard on soon and that will be her fault!" He had left nothing to my paralleling countertransferential imagination either. I didn't like his tone somehow, and I caught what I thought was a fleeting involuntarily snigger escape from him.

He sneered somewhat at his client's unawarely provocative exposure. Something repellent played across his slightly downturned mouth as he was telling me his experience. Of which he was just as unaware as his client was of her exposure. I was going to follow him closely I noticed I decided, and then put that aside to concentrate.

Working with uncertainty at what we were dealing with like this probably means not immediately answering such direct questions as a supervisor, but trusting that what was between me and my supervisee would stand us in good stead as we explored and opened up the space between us and made meaning of his probable embodied countertransference and my own parallels. I trusted that attending to his reactions and awarenesses would migrate into his work with his client. As they had already been doing no doubt. I asked for his associations, in my mind putting the client as I normally do in an imaginary empty chair in our work I waited, as it were with them, and watched, as might be said as a witness. Something in the realm of sexuality and erotic force hovered between us, something viscerally unsettling brought to life by this communication rather than its premature interpretation to provide a tidy certainty. As supervisor I carefully spoke to my own transferential parallels by asking what his embodied experience was without explicitly naming his involuntary snigger, his sneering coarseness, the curl of his lip, or my distaste and watchful wariness. He used our supervisory space to explore, be curious about, and name a potentially shaming roughness in him, an on the edge of abusive fascination came to his mind. He was also disgusted by the thought of his client's unaware exposure of her privacy, my own transferential response to his countertransferential experience had mirrored this unerringly. We came also to understanding that beneath this communication there was also the presence of innocence and trust, and his disgust gave way to a tender empathy. He explored things he would never say directly to his client but that he brought to life in supervision and which lived within him in his countertransferential embodied life with his client. All this needed to be said, experienced, and worked through within our good supervisory relationship which contained and heard what his vulnerable client probably could not name. Being away from his client in the safety and privacy of our supervisory relationship provided that place. The next session he returned, rather astonished. Though he had said nothing directly of his dilemma to his client, she told him she had been abused as a schoolgirl by a trusted older man, a friend of her family, where uninhibited play had led him to betray his place of trust and abused her. She had kept this entirely to herself all her life.

In asking and wondering how she had come to remember that now, she bravely said that something in his gaze had brought that time and somehow the abuser to her mind. Working at the transgressive edge, which is a respectful exploration, a coming close to the hurt place, rather than the original abuser's violation and abuse of her young spontaneity and no doubt sexual experimentation, he asked her whether it would be useful to talk of that between them? She told him that she dreaded that something she had done had led this older man on, was her fault, but she did not know what that could be; was she a bad girl without knowing it? She asked him directly whether she had ever done that to him? A crossroads presented itself, a moment of genuine relational challenge, and his client's self-esteem, well-being, and freedom rested upon his reply, and would be pivotal and important. None of this was lost on this good containing therapist, he understood the trust his client had in him and the risk she was taking and what was at stake. He was able, with truth and the tenderness he now genuinely felt, to tell her that even if she had enjoyed a physical freedom, a certain carefree experimental abandonment, with her abuser that was no invitation, excuse, nor permission for him to violate her young body. A moment of meeting between them. Fine work on his part. I could have cheered.

The co-transferential field

Understanding the co-transferential components and roots of sexuality and erotic played its part in deciding how to approach my supervisee's work here. These days there are wide ranging views which widen our and understanding of erotic transference and what to do about it therapeutically, rather than in traditional psychoanalysis where the erotic was and sometimes still is regarded as entirely the product of transference, an infantile love for the therapist by the client and not real as first described by Freud, who struggled with its concept faced as he was perhaps with another reality.

DuPont (1985), Bach (2006), and Shaw (2014), among many others, regard the presence of erotic forces as also a here-and-now need and desire to be regarded and experience themselves as loveworthy or being wanted and prized and draw attention to the idea of 'analytic love', a type love for the client by the therapist. They go so far as to say that no healing will take place unless the therapist in some way loves who the client is and that the client lives in the therapist's mind and can feel that love, and feel themselves as lovable. Quite separate from the transferential understandings, Ferenczi was perhaps the first psychoanalyst to observe this and made valiant efforts to love his clients better, and be a better mother to them than their original experience, in defiance of and opposition to his mentor, Sigmund Freud.

In supervision we reflected carefully to understand the developmental relational differences as much as was possible. However, it is finally understood and whatever it's root it is a real experience powerfully and passionately felt experienced and embodied be it infantile, of the past or the present (probably both).

Understanding and pondering in this way meant my supervisee was able to contain the embodied transference which inhabited him for a moment and accommodate its uncertainty and eventual meaning. It was his understanding that trust was not risk free but nevertheless seemed essential. By me, in turn, by not giving concrete answers and foreclosing on our mutual effort to reach a meaning was essential to reach the true meaning of his clients "legs wide open" embodied transference communication.

In thinking about this chapter, I revisited instances of the presence of the erotic and sexuality and my own embodied countertransference in my practice which I had taken to my own supervisor over the years and where through the strength of our supervisory relationship I had learned how to approach these issues clinically. As we reflected and remembered each one and I asked for his reflections and associations, we recaptured the obvious connection linking them all was the central involvement of a human body in connection with another human body, a fact so obvious as to be almost hiding in plain sight and that the presence of the erotic and sexuality is most often communicated by an embodied countertransference experience as the above story clearly reveals.

I describe some of my embodied countertransferential experiences here, disguised. They immediately illustrate the straightforwardness, embodied, centrality and rawness of the erotic and of our sexualities as they arise in clinical work despite all the complex and complicated obfuscating descriptions about the erotic and sexuality.

My eyes were unwillingly repeatedly and horrifyingly drawn to a client's crotch after he had asked to leave our session early to go for an appointment. I later learned that that appointment had resurrected the trauma of a wicked abuse of him as a little boy. My arousal in session with a bereaved man which led to his understanding of loss as he recalled the sex and passion of his wife and felt deep shame that what he missed most was her vagina. The man whose sexual proclivities were so revolting to me that I struggled to stay in the room as he lustfully indulged himself by describing in animated fashion his desire, concealing a deep self-hatred and disgust. Me spontaneously touching a client on departure who froze and objected, leading to an exploration of that rupture and awareness of their own forbidden desires to touch.

The poignant memory and personal struggle to agree to the request of a shy young woman risking all in asking me where her clitoris was so that she could guide her partner or indeed herself. The ache in my arms to reach out and gather in to me a lonely love-starved person weeping with me for the want of touch so much so as to break my heart. My erotic attraction to a new client the moment I set eyes on him. Looking forward with anticipation and enjoyment to seeing and gazing at a particularly beautiful client who nevertheless felt herself ugly beyond redemption.

So from my supervisory experience, I expect the erotic and sexuality to be felt most keenly as an embodied phenomenological experience rather than in any verbalised commented upon process for all the reasons I have discussed. Sexuality and the erotic is about bodies, the body, we might say, in relationship with itself and with another body also in relationship with itself, together. In supervision the embodied countertransference was captured in supervision by the somewhat cliched and outmoded idea nowadays of the parallel phenomenological process. But it is also one of a story retold, communicated through one body to another, and in the case of supervision it is also about another body. As in Susie Orbach's now famous observation, "There is... no such thing as a body, there is only a body in relationship to another body", I might respectfully use her idea to know that there is no such thing as a client or a supervisee, only a supervisee with a supervisor and a client with a therapist (Orbach, 2004, p. 28).

As well as the sometimes painful always passionate content of my stories above they also carried with them a deeper communication, they all conveyed a 'seeking'. I thought of re-connection with someone or something lost. For example loss and desire: of peace of mind, safety, childhood, trust, self-esteem, a beloved wife and marriage, freedom to touch, freedom to have pleasure, freedom to be appreciated, freedom to have attention, freedom to make an impact. What also accompanied them was a sense of hope.

I came to regard them all as about a loss, rupture, or interruption of attachment. The late Stephen Mitchell's relational views describe our sexualities as the place where "emotional connection and intimacy is sought, established, lost and regained" (Mitchell, 1988, p. 107).

Whether it was my own clinical experience or my paralleling experience in supervision they seemed to be searching with hope for a way to express, to communicate, the intensity of the experience of loss to regain it in some way, to go forward. They were most keenly felt and communicated through the erotic visceral force of the body. As perhaps only a body can communicate, feel, and understand such passions.

In Cornell's exquisite article *The Impassioned Body*, itself a love letter of sorts, he describes the losses which accompany any awakening of desire and hope and what is risked and lost when that risk is taken (Cornell, 2003, pp. 92–104). Cornell's ideas chime with Mitchell's views about sexuality and attachment above. In addition, his ideas differ and advance somewhat the ideas of a secure base attachment in the development of our sexual selves, that our sexualities also include vitality, passion, and some necessary transgression as components in the developmental dimensions of sexuality. The manner in which sexuality and erotic desires are welcomed or not and transmitted by caregivers about what might be forbidden, shameful, but nevertheless essential to a maturing sexuality determines the strength of what is risked and what is lost in seeking to make an erotic and sexual connection.

In taking that risk all of them expressed something of their individual experience of forbidden, shameful, and transgressive forces. It was to this place that I 'directed' my therapeutic and supervisory effort.

Ways and means

The liminal space and the transgressive edge

In all the examples I have given, both clinical and supervisory, I did not have a conscious behavioural 'treatment plan'. There are numerous ways to address sexuality and the erotic and what helps therapeutically in the same way as there is no one description or experience of sexuality. In my experience each situation is entirely unique so in that respect in the work I have described there was no treatment plan which fitted all. There are interesting parallels to be drawn with the ideas of queer theory about what is normative and what is performative in this approach. I did, though, have a 'direction of travel' which was embedded in my own theoretical approaches and ethical containing framework.

Rather than move away from the erotic and sexuality as they were made apparent in the therapeutic relationships and encounters I describe I moved towards them, however and whenever they became known to me. Coming close to Joseph Swartz and colleagues' ideas of understanding and addressing sexual and erotic desires in sessions the same as any other expressions of longings and feelings and not distinctive or special in any way. Sexuality and the erotic made 'normal, everyday' (Schwartz, 2007, p. 50).

As I hope I have shown, most transgressions and disturbances are unintentional and of course unconscious. One of the central supervisory challenges I found in matters of sexuality and erotic is to grow the capacity to understand and make the distinction between having erotic and loving feelings and putting those into inappropriate action, in other words not act them out nor to eroticise and therefore trivialise such a fundamental human connection. It is to have the capacity to understand the difference between what is a therapeutic, as opposed to non-therapeutic response to sexuality and the erotic in the consulting room.

With that broad approach in mind as a 'direction of travel' what made sense, as I have mentioned throughout this chapter, are the ideas of a liminal space and of the transgressive edge. The Liminal space is understood by me as a dynamic, a place that is on the way to somewhere else. The Latin root for liminal is threshold.

Deary's idea of "no longer/not yet" also captures a paradoxical liminal space of vulnerability and empowerment is entirely descriptive of the hidden dilemmas which were communicated in the work I described (Deary, 2017).

As does Laura Praglin. Using ideas from both Donald Winnicott and Martin Buber, she describes what both are portraying and which resonate with the idea of liminality. Winnicott's developmental approach describes an 'in-between', transitional space necessary for the development of healthy self-hood. Buber's approach, what he terms *das Zwischenmenschliche* is to do with community and the coming into being.

> This is a meeting-ground of potentiality and authenticity, located neither within the self nor in the world of political and economic affairs. In this space, one finds the most authentic and creative aspects of our personal and communal existence, including artistic, scientific and religious expression.
>
> (Praglin, 2006, p. 1)

A similar liminality was sought and found in the situations I describe by attending to our phenomenological experience, the 'potential space' therapeutically that is created between neither acting out nor ignoring what seems erotic and is captured by the liminal space idea. In all cases that effort was to 'create together' a new relational 'potential space' of the type referred to above and which I have described throughout this chapter. I see it as the potential relationship that can happen between the therapist and client, between supervisor and supervisee rather than an old repeated space and dynamic from which the erotic and sexuality can be addressed (in which ever manner is clinically appropriate, as best is understood). Within that fresh space addressing the transgressive edge first described by Novak (2014) and taken up in Cornell's writing (2015) and in Shadbolt (2017) was possible.

Novak describes respectful exploration as a central feature of the transgressive edge which transforms violation of a boundary into a freedom.

To Cornell similarly working at the transgressive edge "allows an exploration of boundaries rather than a violation of them" (Cornell, 2015, p. 71). Navigating the transgressive edge is to find a way through from the certainty of uncertainty to curiosity, in the presence of the forbidden, unsayable, and shameful. As in my supervisory example where abuse was so vividly communicated.

The transgressive edge in my examples were places where the most shame, potential transgression, and sometimes trauma were to be found. These were the very places when approached, like the idea of a 'good hurt', where healing was most achievable. It's the place of comfort. In finding a place to say to my supervisee that I couldn't imagine her hugging anyone is as close as I can imagine of that edge, given the nature of her hidden shame about her value as a person. Working at the transgressive edge, or to be more correct in the supervisory field transgressive edges, is a respectful accounting for boundaries, of enquiring of the others experience with curiosity and purpose to help them reach an articulation of what may be dissociated from and is forbidden.

Addressing that edge from within a respectful intersubjective relationship made it possible to neither act out nor remain silent, and as a natural consequence engaged with meaningfully, with a degree of courage to address ethically the presence of sexuality and erotic as part of the work.

Summary

In summary this chapter has been largely a personal reflection, an account of my thoughts, feelings, and practice, where instances of sexuality and the erotic have appeared in supervision and sometimes in my clinical practice. I have attempted to adopt an autoethnographic style.

In describing their presence in the supervisory relationship in this way my aim was to convey some of the multilayered challenges of recognition, acknowledgement, and action. These have been to do with overcoming and accommodating aspects of the forbidden, shameful, and transgressive 'forces' present in some way in all the examples. I described aspects of co-transferences, embodied and dissociated from by way of bringing the work alive and in that way I have regarded them as instances of attachment and loss. I have briefly mentioned psycho social aspects such as power setting the examples in that context. I have taken a relational view of practice matters, one which embraces principles of uncertainty, trust, and mutuality, and proposed a 'direction of travel'. The Liminal space and the transgressive edge are not offered as techniques or as methods of intervention but rather as examples of what seemed effective relational ways to address the disturbances I encountered towards an articulation of them, a moving towards rather than a moving away from them and in that way offering the provision and discovery of comfort.

References

Bach, S. (2006). *Analytic Love, Analytic Process*. Hillsdale, NJ: The Analytic Press.
Bond, T. (2006). Intimacy, risk and reciprocity in psychotherapy: Intricate ethical challenges. *Transactional Analysis Journal, 36*(2), 77–89.
Cornell, W.F. (2003). The impassioned body. Erotic vitality and disturbance. *British Gestalt Journal, 12*, 92–104.
Cornell, W.F. (2015). In *Somatic Experience in Psychoanalysis and Psychotherapy* (p. 71). Hove: Routledge.
Deary, V. (2017). One size doesn't fit all. *The Psychologist, 30*, 14–15.
Dupont, J. (1985). *The Clinical Diary of Sandor Ferenczi*. Hillsdale, NJ: The Analytic Press.
Lorde, A. (1993). The uses of the erotic: The erotic as power. In H. Abelove, M. A. Barale & D. M. Halperin (Eds.), *The Lesbian and Gay Studies Reader* (p. 339). London: Routledge.
Mitchell, S. A. (1988). Sex without drive (theory). In S. A. Mitchell (Ed.), *Relational Concepts in Psychoanalysis* (p. 107). Cambridge, MA: Harvard University Press.
Novak, E. (2014). When relief replaces grief. *Transactional Analysis Journal, 44*(4), 255–267.
Orbach, S. (2000). *The Impossibility of Sex* (p. 231). Touchstone, NY: Simon and Schuster.
Orbach, S. (2004). The body in clinical practice, part one: There's no such thing as a body. In K. White (Ed.), *Touch: Attachment and the Body* (pp. 17–34). London: Karnac.
Praglin, L. (2006) The Nature of the "In-Between" in D.W. Winnicott's Concept of Transitional Space and in Martin Buber's *das Zwischenmenschliche. Universitas, The University of Northern Iowa Journal of Research, Scholarship and Creative Activity, 2*(2), 1.
Probyn, E. (1997). Michel Foucault and the uses of sexuality. In A. Medhurst & S. R. Mundt (Eds.), *Lesbian and Gay Studies: A Critical Introduction* (pp. 133–145). London: Cassell.
Sacks, O. (2012). *Awakenings*. London: Picador.

Schwartz, J. (2007). Attachment and sexuality: What does our clinical experience tell us? In K. White & J. Schwatrz (Eds.), *Sexuality and Attachment in Clinical Practice* (p. 50). London: Karnac.

Shadbolt, C. (2017). Dancing in a different country: When the personal is professional. *Transactional Analysis Journal, 47*(4), 264–275.

Shadbolt, C. (2018). The sorrow of ghosts: The emergement of a traumatized ego state. *Transactional Analysis Journal, 48*(4), 293–307.

Shaw, D. (2014). *Traumatic Narcissism: Relational Systems of Subjugation*, electronic edition loc. 3495. Hove: Routledge.

2.3 Sexual orientation in the supervisory relationship
Exploring fears and fantasies when different sexual orientations are present in the client/therapist and/or supervisory dyad

Di Hodgson

Introduction

I have been contemplating how sexual orientation is discussed and handled in supervision for many years, both as a supervisor and supervisee. In researching for this chapter, I found little written about how sexual orientation is discussed in the supervisory relationship. Similarly I looked at programs for supervisory training and saw no references to the inclusion of sexual orientation as a topic for attention.

In this chapter I will set out some possible themes which I believe are not necessarily, or often enough, given the time and space for adequate exploration. I am framing this around our willingness to name and discuss our fears and fantasies. I am including several case examples, all of which are pseudonyms.

As supervisors we have a professional, and ethical responsibility for the well-being of our supervisees' and their clients. We always have the best interests of the client in mind, but how do we think about how these best interests are served when the client is gay or lesbian or one half of the supervisory dyad is gay or lesbian? I am choosing to use the terms gay and lesbian, even though there are many alternatives.

In preparing to write this chapter I spoke to several colleagues. Some interesting themes emerged. Overall most respondents reported that they liked that I was asking the question about how sexual orientation impacts the supervisory relationship. Most focussed on the impact of parallel processes between the supervisor/supervisee and supervisee/client. Their thoughts on what kinds of discussions each dyad can and do have being based partly on how open each feels that they can be with the other and the degree of receptivity they anticipate. They also identified the supervisor's capacity to deal with complex issues of disclosure and identity and the interpersonal and relational processes around these themes, including co-transference (Orange, 1995). I am using the concept of co-transference which focusses on the way in which both parties to the dyad influence what is discussed. Although it is not the focus of this chapter, several colleagues also pointed to the power imbalance of the supervisory relationship and how this might evoke erotic transference. What does seem relevant for this chapter, however, is how the boundary between the supervisory dyad may be experienced as somewhat less 'tight' than that between therapist and client and which may therefore influence whether or not sexual attraction is named and/or discussed between supervisor and supervisee, how it might go undisclosed or unacknowledged, and how that might be influencing the work with the client. The extent to which it is named may well be influenced by the respective sexual orientations of the supervisory dyad.

When I originally embarked on this task, I knew that I wanted to focus more on sexual orientation rather than the erotic. I have a preference for separating the two. Similarly, I prefer to separate sexuality and sexual orientation, with awareness that the words are often conflated or used interchangeably. They are not the same to me. Sexual orientation usually refers to a person's enduring pattern of relationships, attraction, and sexual encounters with someone of the same sex, and to a sense of personal and collective identity. Sexuality is how we express ourselves sexually, regardless of orientation. When the terms are conflated or used interchangeably the effect can be to put more emphasis on the sexual aspect of lesbian, gay and bisexual (LGB) people's lives, further embedding the idea that sex rather than the more complex aspects of relationships is the defining feature. When someone identifies as, or in reality does or says nothing and is therefore assumed to be, heterosexual, their sexual life is rarely a focus in the mind of the therapist unless it is concerns about their sexuality that has brought them to therapy.

A field perspective – the influence of the historical and current context

One of the core elements of Gestalt theory is the field theory of Lewin, and later Parlett (Parlett, 1993, 2005). Field theory shifts the focus from the interpersonal and intrapersonal to a social or societal perspective and influence. The field in this context means the multiple forces impacting on any given situation. It is the influence of this wider perspective that I believe is paramount to exploring the responsibilities of supervisors when different sexual orientations are present in the therapist/client and/or supervisor/supervisee dyad. Field theory recognises the phenomena as they appear in the here and now and how they change over time. The aspect of sexual orientation as a key element of the field has contemporaneous impact and has changed considerably over the past 30 years. Despite the massive changes, the field can readily be overlooked or dismissed. In Gestalt theory we can only understand others and ourselves in a context or field. However, in most psychotherapy there is a common understanding that our sense of self is formed in relationship to others and is influenced by the time and place of our birth. To some extent we must adjust to the environment in which we live and adjust the environment to the self. This adjustment is an interesting phenomenon when applied to sexual orientation (or any minority status for that matter), which I will explore in more detail later.

Although the theory is not described similarly in all modalities, there is some shared understanding of the principle of 'the paradoxical theory of change' (Beisser, 1970). This refers to the idea that change does not occur by trying to be what one is not, but rather growth occurs from identifying with what one is. Therefore any attempt to disown who we are, or aspects of who we are, are antithetical to the overarching aim of psychotherapy. Being able to identify with our ongoing existence is paramount. Therefore being able to identify with our sexual orientation existence in supervision will also support learning and growth, whereas any attempt in this relationship to disown or diminish aspects of ourselves is likely to stultify it.

One key aspect of a relational way of working is the ability to get as close as possible to the experience of the client which has the effect of confirming their very existence. For the clients who have experienced a lack of acceptance and confirmation of a major aspect of their identity and existence, that is, their sexual orientation, it is even more important that we consider how to support supervisees with how to do so.

A privilege of being heterosexual is having a sense of belonging at a field level. Belonging to the majority, the 'normal'. Every day their broad experience is confirmed in books, TV, news, etc.

Over the past 30 years attitudes and laws have changed. Depending on the respective ages of supervisor, supervisee, and client, if any of us identifies as gay or lesbian, we will have experienced these changes and the impact on our lives collectively and differently. Who we are and how we, have, and now, live in the world, will inevitably frame our ways of working. If we have personal experience, or multiple experiences, of being in an oppressed minority it will shape what we prioritise as worthy of, or in essential need of, attention. Some of what we need to learn in terms of how to support supervisees in working with clients of a different sexual orientation will also be present in the here and now of the supervisory relationship. It may be that our willingness to explore these dynamics as they present themselves in supervision will inform the work. The nuances of our different lived experience and how this has shaped and influenced our sense of identity and belonging will also shape and influence our approach to supervision. The client, and in turn the supervisee, will bring their past and their present to our meeting. As a supervisor I will also bring mine. We have a complex web of histories and relationships and expectations about how we will be met and received in our sexual and sexual orientation differences. In Gestalt, we prioritise the co-created nature of our contact. Therefore, in this chapter I am interested in how the supervisor dyad supports or avoids the explorations for this meeting.

As Gestaltists we focus on presence and on an openness to noticing what is happening between us. For supervisors to ask themselves questions such as "what happens to me as I hear from my supervisee? What captures my interest? What do I prioritise? What do I fear? What do I censor? What disturbs me? How am I oppressing others or myself?" will inform us. In supervision our starting point is often an exploration of how the therapist feels towards and is impacted by the client: this may be on many levels and layers, including their bodily response. It may be here that the beginnings of some complex phenomena may emerge. The impact of sameness and difference, of comfort and discomfort, of known and unknown, familiar and unfamiliar, shared and divided may emerge. The more capable and willing the therapist is to understand where they stand in the field of the client, the more able they are likely to be to meet their client, and similarly within the supervisory dyad. As supervisors are we alert to oppressive assumptions? For example, that a client's difficulties are as a result of their sexual orientation rather than the oppressive world in which they have lived and continue to live. Caution from the lesbian, gay, or bisexual client can easily be pathologised through a diagnostic and individualistic frame. I recall my first therapist saying that I was hypervigilant: I said, "I am lesbian, of course I am".

The impact of changing times and attitudes to sexual orientation

In this section I will continue the theme of the impact of the historical field and hopefully, invite discussion and exploration on the extent and impact of change.

Some 25 years ago I remember being in a supervision group and experiencing what I felt was a strong challenge about how my client knew about my sexual orientation. I remember being acutely aware that other group members had openly discussed with their clients the fact that they were married and/or had children. I realised over time that none of my heterosexual peers were ever asked about similar self-disclosures. The disclosures were there, but they typically went unnoticed in supervisor discussions, except, it seemed, by me. Of course, I realise we are not comparing apples with apples. There was, and still is, an assumption of heterosexuality. The impact of a client 'finding out' or being told about their therapist's different sexual orientation was, and still is, seen to be different. Given the societal changes in the past 25 years I am interested in whether and how these differences are experienced now. At the time I challenged my supervisor and I recall being met with reasons why self-disclosure might not be a good idea. Of course, there are many times when I do not overtly disclose my sexual orientation. For me though, there is a difference between not doing so because it seems irrelevant for the client or what has brought them to therapy, and what sounded to me like a suggestion that I should actively hide a major aspect of my identity. Was there an implication that who I am is somehow potentially harmful to the client? I wondered then, and still do, about what it would sound like if we suggested that the colour of a person's skin might be harmful.

At the time I was also on a committee of a significant psychotherapy training institute. We had recently set up an LGB support group, which also came in for some significant challenges in terms of the perceived necessity for, or even potential benefit of, specific support for this oppressed group. I have maintained my interest in how as a profession we acknowledge power and oppression in relation to sexual orientation and how we ensure that there is sufficient support.

When I wrote my doctoral thesis some ten years ago, I was interested in the impact of diversity on complaints against psychotherapists. An actual fear amongst several of my lesbian and gay colleagues was that they would be more at risk of a complaint than their heterosexual peers. The statistics available at that time did not make it possible for me to determine from the professional bodies whether that fear was a fantasy or based in reality. The fear was often expressed as one where if the therapeutic relationship broke down, the client might use the therapist's sexual orientation as something on which to hang their complaint. A later aspect of my research was a survey concerning who thought they would get a fair hearing in any formal complaint if such a situation were to arise. A fantasy and a fear amongst colleagues in a sexual minority group was that most panels would fail to understand the nuances and that their confidence in the procedures and processes was significantly lower than for their colleagues who inhabited the majority.

On a similar theme I co-wrote an article for *The Psychotherapist* (Harrison et al., 2009) entitled "Living on the edge of acceptance" with two colleagues. All three of us shared examples of complaints which had been discussed in supervision groups and which from our respective perspectives included elements of homophobia in the conscious or unconscious intentions of the complainant. We all had questions about how supported we would feel. "People need space and safety to explore issues of being discriminated against and oppressed". It is still true that coming out is a daily occurrence, fraught with potential pitfalls and exacerbated when there is insufficient support. "...when clients, by default, assume that we are heterosexual and the impact this has on our choice of therapeutic intervention" (ibid). As I wrote this chapter I regularly asked myself what has changed since then, what needs updating, and what is still worthy of contemplation and discussion. One of my concerns is that as time has passed there is more likelihood of a belief that things have changed for gay and lesbian people, but that the belief in the extent and positivity of these changes is held more strongly by the heterosexual majority rather than by those of us in the minority group.

As recently as in the last decade Daniel (2009), found that one in six psychotherapists in the UK believes homosexuality is a "condition" that can be changed through therapy. In his article about the enduring aspects of homophobia, Desmond (2016) also includes some sobering statistics. The very word homophobia was originally based on fear (Weinberg, 1971), though over years it has taken on other negative attitudes. In her article 'homo-erotic horror' Jacques (1998) states that 'living outside of the "moral majority" is psychologically stressful, life-threatening, and sometimes fatal'. Although this was written over 20 years ago I found it interesting to ask myself two of its questions: first, to what extent is this still an accurate descriptor for the experience of some people who live on the outside; second, to what extent does this describe the historical, if not the current, experience of some clients and some supervisees? Some of the psychological stressors are sometimes the result of a lack of awareness or dismissal of what it means to live on the outside. Although there is less blatant homophobia in the therapy world, as Desmond says, "homophobia endures" (ibid). It therefore follows that it is likely to endure in therapeutic and supervisory relationships. I am interested to explore what supports and challenges supervisors to help explore their own responses and those of their supervisees. Most writing on transference still prioritises heterosexual therapist/client relationships. As Mann said in 1997, do we still "beat a hasty retreat from the emergence of homo-erotic desire" (1997, p. 117). We need courage to step into the unknown, the unfamiliar, the unsayable. My concern with the current culture of 'acceptance' of homosexuality is that difficult feelings are less likely to be expressed. Even if we agree that there is less homophobia, we are still operating within a heteronormative frame; otherwise the very concept of 'coming out' would cease to exist. The concept of 'out' effectively means being outside of the norm. Those on the outside are used to carrying the weight of difference. Rather than us being different from one another, those in the minority often feel, or are invited to feel, that they are different from 'normal'. So the outsider does what they need to do to get by. They adapt, they silence themselves, they let small and large hurts go unchallenged.

Historically lesbians and gay men were known as 'mad, bad and dangerous to know'. Now homophobia is less overt, and I doubt these fears would be named. Though it is still hard to find a lesbian character in a drama who is not mad, bad, or dangerous to know, or who disappears from the story in rather unfortunate circumstances; we seem to have more than our share of tragic accidents. And attraction between same sex people has usually been characterised by a prejudice that we are less able to maintain appropriate boundaries than our heterosexual counterparts.

Two years ago, I accepted an invitation to co-write a chapter with a colleague for an anthology about gender and sexual diversity (Hodgson and Skye, 2016). We experienced a gamut of emotions in the sharing of our experiences and our struggles to write the chapter. It was at times, an enlightening, painful, and challenging experience. One aim was to describe all that we had felt was 'missed, missing and dismissed...' Both of us had had several therapeutic experiences and several supervisors. We shared experiences of how we had felt we had been overlooked. This begs interesting questions for me about the role of the supervisor and how we approach the therapeutic task. How come clients do not share experiences with their therapists? Especially those whose lives are outside the experience of the therapist or the 'norm'. What do-created conditions need to exist to enable the client to step into this particular vulnerability? What might the therapist do or not do early in the relationship that might trigger the client to be more forthcoming or more reticent? And how does the supervisor spot this dynamic? In my first significant therapeutic relationship I remember not being asked about children. I remember it because it stood out. I had the sense that my therapist jumped over it because she was uncomfortable in stepping into that territory with me. My response was a familiar one: in the way in which I had learned to live in a heteronormative world, I adapted to make her feel more comfortable and tacitly agreed that that was a subject best avoided. She also never mentioned sex or sexual attraction. Again, in my well-practiced adaptation, neither did I. Now I am interested in whether these missings were noticed or challenged by her supervisor. This is several years ago, and I would not be so amenable now. However, in my work as a trainer I see some of the underlying assumptions behind these examples still exist. Some attitudes have changed enormously. And some attitudes, fears and fantasies have stayed the same. I remain interested in how these types of fears remain, how they might inhibit discussion in supervision, and how the existence or lack of discussion around these themes informs or supports practice.

The challenges of discussing sexual orientation and the responsibilities and receptivity of the supervisor

I first want to set out some of the challenges of discussing sexual orientation, in the supervisory relationship. I am particularly interested in how supervisors and supervisees are able to name their fears and fantasies and how the supervisory relationship supports the exploration of these potentially challenging topics. I also want to explore how the fears and fantasies are potentially explored and experienced differently depending on the sexual orientation of the supervisor and supervisee. I am acutely aware that gender, religion, and other differences may also play a huge part, but that is not my focus in this chapter.

One potentially challenging area where either the supervisor or supervisee is gay or lesbian is the extent to which they are 'out' or is the extent to which the therapist is 'out' with their clients. The supervisor has a key role here. Not least in whether anyone in the supervision dyad or group thinks it is a good thing to be 'out'. Now most gay and lesbian colleagues have in my experience tussled with this question in great detail. We have tussled with what it means for ourselves, our families and friends, our colleagues, and our clients. What is often forgotten or outside of others' awareness is that 'coming out' is a daily occurrence rather than a one-off activity. I am not sure that my heterosexual colleagues have thought about their own sexual orientation to the same extent, and if they have it has not been evident in supervisory relationships that I have been involved with in the same way. In my experience thoughts and beliefs about this vary enormously amongst professional colleagues, and across different modalities.

Our attitudes to discussing sexual orientation, sexuality, and the erotic are important. Times have changed. Laws have changed. Attitudes have changed. And homophobia still exists. If we are to facilitate the exploration of fears of fantasies, we must regularly check and update our own attitudes and be willing to explore and challenge ourselves. It is easy in these apparently more liberal times to imagine that all is well and that no one has a problem with their own or anyone else's sexual orientation anymore, especially in a professional such as ours. Yet we also know that there is an ongoing challenge re conversion therapy. There are risks inherent in an attitude of benign non-judgementalism, that is, in falling into the trap of thinking, "I'm Ok with anyone's sexual orientation, so there's no problem". I fear that challenges and difficulties with our own or others' sexual orientation may now be more underground and may therefore pass below the radar of supervision. So, what are some of the challenges, fears, and fantasies we may need to explore? As supervisors how do we encourage and facilitate discussion? In supervision groups I have often been involved in discussions about whether it is good for a client for the therapist to be 'out'. I have rarely heard this discussed in relation to heterosexuality. Of course, it is not the same. Assumptions of clients will not be the same. Yet even the concept of 'out' is interesting to me. How did I come to be 'in'? Is it merely a feature of the heteronormative world in which I live that unless I make a statement, I am presumed heterosexual? How does that fit with so many years, policies, and laws on equality, diversity, and inclusion? How can we discuss with supervisees the potential merits and risks of being 'out' with their clients without exploring our own attitudes and prejudices? I am informed by my political stance, which is in line with my modality which puts some emphasis on authenticity. In my role as an organisational consultant, trainer, and supervisor I feel some responsibility to be 'out' or, more accurately for me, to not go along with any assumptions that I am 'in'. Even the question of whether being 'out' might be beneficial or not to the client might imply the potential for harm. I wonder whose fears and fantasies these are? Who gets to decide what is 'good' for the client? How do we create the atmosphere under which these discussions can take place? In the same way that we have therapy ourselves so that we have as much self-awareness as we can and a place to take our concerns when we feel provoked or disturbed by our clients, there is a parallel in supervision. There is still the risk of being 'damned' if you do and if you don't. How do we normalise these challenges without brushing them off?

When the supervisor challenges the therapist in sharing her orientation, whether she does so overtly or not, it reinforces the suggestion that our clients are somehow at risk from our homosexuality and that we are indeed dangerous if we are known. Clients often come to therapy because they want a better relationship with themselves. If we role model our own ease, self-acceptance, and self-love our client may learn these things for themselves. Similarly, if as supervisors we inadvertently imply that repression is preferable we overtly support a social prejudice. Gay men have suffered from criminality, lesbian women from invisibility. Therefore the courageous conversation is one where supervisors support therapist to explore their feelings, fears, and fantasies about homosexuality and desire. In therapy, we know that taboos need scrutiny. The apparently benign non-judgementalism that now pervades the discussion of sexual orientation may result in a lack of scrutiny.

I was working with a lesbian supervisee recently who was working with a heterosexual client. Her sexual orientation had not been a topic of conversation in the therapy, so the supervisee said she had no idea whether the client knew she was gay or if it was a matter of interest to her. It came up as a matter of interest in the supervision because the client had asked for a hug. Again, as the whole issue of touch in psychotherapy has been explored elsewhere at length, I will not repeat that here. However, I do believe the issue of touch has the potential to take on a whole other dimension when sexual orientation becomes part of the discussion about the relative pros and cons for the client. As well as a detailed exploration of what the request meant to the client, how it is connected to their presenting issue, the impact of key aspects of assessment and diagnosis, the potential benefits and risks inherent in accepting the request etc., was a whole other diversity lens about what it might mean to the client if they were to subsequently discover that their therapist was lesbian. I am old enough to have many examples in my life of people actively avoiding being in the same space as me. I don't recall ever actually asking why, but I imagine I was perceived as threatening or dangerous in some way, so I am influenced by my personal historical field as well as my professional role in relation to committees and complaints. The risks here from my perspective could be a repetition for the therapist of their sexual orientation being seen as dangerous or inappropriate and may leave the therapist feeling more vulnerable to a complaint as discussed above. I was curious that I felt some concern for my supervisee, while she did not or certainly did not to the same extent. The age gap is not massive, but it is different, and our different experiences of the impact of our respective histories significantly changed our concerns about the inherent risks. In that moment I wasn't at all sure whether my supervisee was being naive or I was being too cautious, or possibly both. What was important was our willingness to share and discuss our perspectives.

There is also the reverse situation of a lesbian client asking for a hug from a heterosexual therapist. If a heterosexual therapist chooses not to touch a lesbian client, when they might or would if the client were heterosexual, they risk reinforcing the suggestion that the client is indeed untouchable or dangerous in some way. The client misses out on the potential benefit of a particular kind of support which may have been lacking in their historical field and which may therefore have added meaning and potential harm or healing for the client, depending on how the therapist responds. It is important that the supervisor remains alert to these dynamics and is willing to explore their own attitudes and those of the therapist through this lens of difference.

This diversity lens and the different ways in which we experience this particular aspect of diversity is apparent to me very regularly. I recently attended an international conference in Europe. One of the keynote speakers gave an example to illustrate her key message, which focussed on a client who was exploring and potentially changing, how she identified herself in relation to sexual orientation. I found the example offensive and voyeuristic. My lesbian colleagues on the same table agreed. To our ears the example seemed gratuitous. Not only did we not see the relevance of the example to the theme of the keynote, there was something disturbing about how the client's sexual orientation was being explored. For example, how the role of her then husband was being described as if giving permission or consent for this woman to explore her sexual orientation and the extent to which he might also be an active participant in any such exploration and the therapist and the speaker seeming to find this acceptable and not worthy of examination. Heterosexual colleagues who were asked did not understand our concerns: another example of what is seen and what is missed and what is experienced differently though the lens of sexual orientation.

In my current supervision peer group, where I am not the only lesbian, I notice how much easier it is for me. There is an understanding of the complexities and nuances which are not shared by my heterosexual colleagues. Several weeks ago, a client shared with me her husband's fantasy that he would like her to have sex with him and another woman. I felt snagged. From one lens there is no reason at all why my client should adapt or censor what she says to spare my feelings. To do so would be antithetical to the whole purpose of the therapeutic space being somewhere where clients can openly express and discuss whatever is troubling them. What concerned me more was only my lesbian colleague understood why I would feel snagged by this example. Only she was willing to engage with the challenge of whether and how to handle my response and the extent to which it had anything to do with my client's broader presentation and difficulties.

This leads me to invite consideration about the responsibilities of supervisors and their receptivity to discussion regarding sexual orientation. Overall the supervisor needs to be alert to pain, power and privilege, projection, prejudice, and oppression. Clients need to feel seen and safe enough to address issues of difference and oppression within the therapeutic space. Similarly, supervisees need the same within the supervisory relationship. The example above has been both a typical and ongoing example of where I have felt the need to educate colleagues, therapists, supervisors etc. about the impact of being in this particular minority group. This might include awareness of the impact on mental health and risk factors of being in a minority.

The issue of whose responsibility it is to educate and the receptivity and willingness towards education on these themes is another interesting focus. About ten years ago I ran a workshop on sexual orientation and supervision at one of the UKCP conferences on supervision. I had hoped it would attract a board audience. It didn't. I had hoped that heterosexual people would come. They didn't. In 25 years of working in the field of equality and diversity it is more often those who have experienced oppression themselves that have the willingness and interest to explore. This leaves me wondering how we ensure that this topic, and in parallel other aspects of diversity, are given the attention they need.

One might think of the supervisory relationship as an attachment relationship creating a secure base in which to facilitate exploration. Sexual orientation may impact what Bowlby (1979) describes as the distinct aspects of both the quality and the strength of the supervisory relationship. If the strength and/or quality of the supervisory relationship is weakened by different sexual orientations or willingness to engage in conversations about them, this may have significant repercussions for the work with clients. This may be especially true if sexuality-related shame is evoked. Kearns and Daintry (2000) explore shame in the supervisory relationship at length and much of what they say in terms of the parallels can apply here. Shame as a feature of the supervisory relationship is likely to impact the therapist/client relationship.

Meeting on the bridge of difference – who carries the weight of difference, and how do we share responsibility for relational meeting?

A concern that I have had for many years is the extent to which clients should use their hard-earned cash to educate the therapist about what it means to inhabit a different and minority position in the world, when their therapist does not. Of course, there is a balance to be struck here. Everyone has their own particular history and experience and it is not for the therapist to make stereotypical assumptions. On the hand it is interesting to consider what the therapist thinks are their responsibilities in highlighting and learning some of the ground or context from which the client's experience emerges, both the historical and current influences. Often clients in a minority will take on the task of educating those in the majority. There is a parallel in supervision concerning whose responsibility it is for the supervisee to educate the supervisor, or the supervisor to educate the supervisee in order from them to work effectively. These two examples have different implications depending on who is in the power up position. It is not only about education though, to be effective as a therapist working with a someone from a different sexual identity, there is also a need for someone who can support you and take you fully into issues and help you see beyond where you are. The supervisor therefore needs to be alert to their own and their supervisees' blind spots.

I would like to think and hope that most trainings now encourage students to explore their own sexual orientation, sexuality, and beliefs about the extent to which their own or others' sexual identities are fixed. Similarly, their beliefs about what 'causes' sexual orientation/identity and for whom naming an identity does or does not matter. Being other than 'normal' results in attempts to explain. Over time there have been several studies and research into the 'causes' of homosexuality. As supervisors we need to be alert to how this frame can slip into the therapeutic relationship with therapists trying to figure out why someone is gay or lesbian, or assuming the client is interested in this question or that their difficulties must be in some way caused by their orientation. The fact that within the therapeutic dyad one person's sexual orientation has been scrutinised whilst the other's has not creates and adds to a power dynamic that reinforces the unequal outside of the therapy room.

Many modalities include phenomenological exploration. The question which flows from this might be – how do we support heterosexual therapists and heterosexual supervisors to enquire into "what was it like for you"? which would demonstrate an openness and willingness to explore how it was to grow up different and through some significant historical events, both positive and negative. Alongside this exploration we can encourage research into some of the history and map this against the age of the client, for example, what was it like to have lived through Section 28; the Aids crisis etc. In peer supervision with another lesbian, it is her first experience of this shared dynamic. We both have a sense of one another 'getting it'. The 'it' is understanding something of what it means to live a lifetime on the outside, to have been discriminated against and to have grown up with persecution and others' fears and fantasies.

Desmond (2017) makes what sounds to me like a very good suggestion that as therapists we 'try out' or 'try on' some aspects of what it might be like to live as a gay, lesbian, or bisexual person when in these so-called enlightened times homophobia is an enduring facet of life. Whilst a momentary experiment will in no way convey the depth and enormity of a lifetime's experience, a suggestion from a supervisor that a supervisee tries this out may not only provide genuinely useful insights into the world of the other, but the willingness to do so if shared in some form with the client will demonstrate a willingness to meet on the bridge of difference. It is perhaps that willingness to step towards, that will provide some healing from the hurts of the past.

To take this theme of willingness and receptivity further, I recall a client who said she came to me because she assumed, correctly, that I would have needed to examine my sexual orientation in some detail and with some discomfort. She felt more able to examine her own fears and fantasies precisely because of that fact. Kennedy (2009) suggests that therapists working with LGB clients must be willing to enquire into their sexual orientation on a regular basis and with a degree of depth which has inevitably been experienced by those in a sexual minority, as well as their attitudes to different sexual orientations. Desmond (ibid) adds the need to explore their openness to their own same sex attraction. I suggest it is the responsibility of the supervisor to support this ongoing reflexive enquiry.

These enquiries can also contribute to facilitating discussion on the extent to which supervision can be or become another heteronormative structure. In those initial conversations with colleagues about this chapter, a theme emerged concerning what might be projected onto the supervisor by the supervisee and in particular concerns about how their relationships with their clients could be perceived. This, together with how much the supervisee thinks the supervisor holds a lens of diversity, might influence what is and isn't brought to supervision: and how much the sexual orientation of the supervisor, if known, or named, might influence this. Mostly those I asked reflected on how little they had explored such possible projections in supervision. Confidence in the felt sense of the supervisor's receptivity was a key theme. That confidence coming from the perception of receptivity from the supervisor's openness and ease in exploring both their personal feelings around sexual orientation and sexuality as well as curiosity in the unique experience of the client. As Lynne Jacobs (2000) says, we need to examine our whiteness and how we contribute to racism. I would suggest that we also need to examine our heterosexuality and how it contributes to homophobia and heteronormativity.

One aspect of openness and potential difficulty is language. Language matters: as does how lesbian (I am choosing this descriptor in full awareness that it will not be liked by some people) supervisees and their clients choose to describe themselves, if indeed they do. Bearing in mind the power imbalance in both relationships it is important that the powerful one in the dyad does not get to choose the terms. The adaptation of generosity on the part of the person in the minority often leads them to accept the terms chosen. As discussed earlier those in the minority often adapt and carry the weight of responsibility to enable meeting by not challenging the more powerful and accepting something with which they are not entirely comfortable. I was recently at a conference and a colleague referred to my partner as my wife. I am not married and have no wish to be. I also dislike the patriarchal connotations of the term 'wife'. I imagine that my colleague was attempting to be inclusive, in its common rather than psychotherapeutic sense. This was not a relationship based on a differentiated power dynamic and still I let it go. I decided to prioritise the person's intentionality over my own experience of irritation and despondency as this feels like a whole new phase of coming out conversations where I feel tasked with challenging assumptions, this time based on the idea that as marriage is now on offer I should embrace it and be grateful. The supervisory challenge is therefore to be alert to this new phase of assumption-making and to explore with and support the supervisee in having and inviting conversations about language with their clients.

The need for, and benefit of, courageous conversations

In the example above I prioritised the feelings of my colleague. In a therapeutic or supervisory space this would not have been a good idea and I would have needed to be more courageous. All too often the potential for genuine understanding is lost because the therapist is focussed on demonstrating their accepting credentials at the expense of staying with the experience of the client. The latter only serves to reinforce the experience of being missed and the closing down of the dialogue. It can leave the client with an additional relational injury to process on top of the original one. From the therapist's perspective it is possible that this closing down may spring from fear: fear of giving offence, of getting it wrong, of being in unfamiliar territory, saying the wrong thing etc. From the client's perspective it is possible that it may be fear of being seen as hyper-sensitive, being ungrateful, etc. The cautious response also repeats the earlier injuries: the client adjusts to make the therapist feel better. Now ordinarily I would imagine that most supervisors are alert to the possibility of the client taking care of the therapist. I have heard this conversation often in groups of experienced supervisors and occasionally at viva panels when recordings of work have been played. I have less confidence in the possibility of this dynamic being seen in relation to supervision as the adaptation is a phenomenon that exists everywhere and maintains the power of heteronormativity. As supervisors we must also be on the lookout for the problem then being made into the 'hyper-sensitivity' or 'paranoia' of the person in the minority rather than another example of missing, or fear, or caution by the therapist.

The willingness of the therapist to enquire into the experiences of their LGB clients requires walking a sensitive but not overly cautious path. It takes courage to enter into unfamiliar dialogues where the risks of offence feel palpable. The supervisor can support the therapist to tread a path of genuine interest rather than voyeurism and to enquire into how their interest is actually experienced by the client as the intention to do one may be experienced as the other. An example is a supervisee who was concerned that her 'active curiosity' (Polster, 1985) might be perceived as intrusive and consequently felt reluctant to enquire into her client's experience. It is the support to navigate rather than avoid this relational challenge that will be needed.

Depending on the therapeutic goals and contract, this might also include the courage of the supervisor and the willingness of the therapist to talk together about what they have not shared. What was in the co-created dynamic of their relationship which made it more or less possible? As a supervisor, do we look for what is missing, or what is missed, or what is dismissed by the therapist? Does the supervisor need to be courageous to support the therapist to step into the unknown, to challenge themselves? Not only to ask what has not been asked, but to ask themselves why they did not? Then to reflect on responses, and perhaps to name how much is fear of the unknown, or highlighting the differences, of the implicit and explicit privilege and oppression.

We need to support supervisees to in turn support their clients to use words and language which they choose rather than that which continues the adaptation of making the therapist feel better. The adaptation can easily go unnoticed since the person in the minority may be doing so in or out of awareness but certainly with plenty of practice, and the therapist may not be alert to the potential for the adaptation and transferentially may respond in the expected way, reinforcing a familiar and unhelpful pattern. When I ask supervisees "how does your (gay or lesbian) client like to describe themselves regarding their sexual orientation?", the question has rarely been asked. The therapist decides and the client goes along with it. It takes courage to ask and courage to name the possible, and even likely, adaptation of the client so that the client gets to choose. As supervisors we may need to explore with our supervisees their visceral responses to descriptions which have historical and difficult connotations. Mostly we understand the potential power of naming our experience in words that have meaning for us, hence sometimes inviting clients for whom English is not their first language to use their mother tongue. There are parallels here.

Most psychotherapists would agree that in the psychotherapeutic relationship, the erotic is gender neutral, in the same way that any transferential feelings tend to be gender neutral.

As I was writing this piece, I had a very helpful and insightful conversation with a colleague. What happened between us is what I would like to happen more often in supervision: somehow, we create an atmosphere where both parties can allow their thoughts, feelings, reactions, and responses to flow freely. We both acknowledged the rarity and need for such conversations, so I will share the themes which emerged here. There are so many sexuality and gender permutations, but I will use the one we discussed to highlight the key themes. I am aware that they may be further complicated by religious beliefs, but that is not something I will focus on here.

We embarked on a conversation about what feelings are evoked when we discuss the potential attraction between heterosexual women and men, heterosexual women and gay men, lesbian women and gay men, lesbian women and heterosexual men, heterosexual men and lesbian woman, lesbian women and lesbian women, gay men and gay men, gay men and heterosexual men, heterosexual men and heterosexual men. In which of these permutations do we find it acceptable to discuss attraction? Which evoke fantasies; which evoke fears?

We were both aware of the metaphorical voices of our mother's as we spoke. We were both engaged in the conversation and aware of the loudness of our respective mother's disapproving voices. This led us to focus even more on the need for the supervisor to normalise these challenging feelings to reduce the potential for shame (without question reduced by the naming of this potential by both of us), to regulate anxiety and again to create an atmosphere in which difference can be held and enquired into. The themes were: who is allowed to fantasise about whom, and who fears naming those fantasies.

I described a situation in which a heterosexual colleague had expressed with amazement and some disgruntlement that a lesbian colleague had said she had not found her attractive. I felt a familiar feeling of offence. I don't find the woman attractive either. This sparked a fascinating dialogue. The woman concerned is known to my colleague. So, my colleague's view was that the woman is attractive, and she knows she is attractive. So, we named the possibility that reciprocal attraction by the lesbian may have been repressed. This might be described as internalised homophobia. In his article, Desmond (ibid), challenges the very concept of internalised homophobia as a function of the field. I shared my perspective and response, that is, that for a heterosexual woman to imagine that she is universally attractive to all lesbians is arrogant. My colleague asked what might be being repressed by me. So I sat with her question – did I have a fear of owning some attraction? Did I fear that if I didn't, I would be seen as having internalised homophobia? Was I in danger of not being able to win either way again?

We continued our conversation into how we own our attractiveness and attractions. Do I not find this heterosexual woman attractive because she is attractive through a heterosexual lens, that is, in a way that would be obvious to a heterosexual man and that is therefore seen by heterosexual women through the same attraction lens, that is, do heterosexual women think they are attractive because they conform to a heterosexual norm of what constitutes attractive? Is it more Ok for a heterosexual man or woman to own and name that they find another heterosexual woman attractive? Now, what happens to our fears and fantasies if we move things around a bit? What if the person in question were a lesbian? Would it be similarly Ok for both heterosexual men and women to own and name their attraction? Our discussion took us onto considering whether women are easier about sexuality and sexual orientation than men. And especially same sex attraction. Is it more Ok to discuss attraction between women than men? Certainly, the relationship between gay men and heterosexual women is very different from heterosexual men and lesbian women. How often might we hear a male heterosexual supervisee name their attraction for another man though?

Our conclusion was that conversation such as we had had happen hardly ever, and even more rarely in supervision. Therefore, as supervisors we need the space to name our fears and fantasies. We need to allow these conversations to emerge with support so that censoring does not get in the way of genuine exploration and reflection. We need the support to sit with some difficult questions. We also need to be heard and not pathologised when our experience is different from the heteronormative.

I had a recent example of a supervision session which included exploring the relationship between the heterosexual male therapist and an openly gay client. The therapist had not considered possible erotic transference. I noticed my bodily hesitation before doing so. I was more aware of feeling cautious than I ordinarily would with other gender dynamics. Instead of dismissing this caution I shared it with the supervisee, and it led to an interesting conversation about the field and relational dynamics between men of different sexual orientations. In another example, I was recently in a process group at an international conference. None of the group had previously met. At our penultimate meeting of four, one man named his caution with me. He was concerned about causing offence by asking me some questions: I thought he was courageous to name his caution. I was genuinely sad that he was cautious with me, and I noticed my wish to name my experience of the polar opposite of how I have been threatened so from another lens I welcomed his caution. I felt courageous in naming my wish for his interest even if that risked offence, because to be ignored is to be further marginalised. If we feel that we can only enquire into the experience of another when we can predict the certainty or guarantee of response will are likely to be silent. It is this balance of caution and courage that is needed. We must avoid living at the polarities of the imaginary overly thick or overly thin skin. If we can trust our capacity to manage ruptures in other aspects of the therapeutic relationship, then why not this one.

Conclusion

Yontef (1996) describes three aspects of supervision: administrative, educational, and consultative. The consultative aspect of supervision requires our understanding of particular clients with their particular issues. Our role as supervisor is to enable and facilitate the supervisee to gain a multi-dimensional knowledge and awareness of their clients. In this chapter I hope that I have identified some of the responsibilities of the supervisor to educate the supervisee in the best interests of the client, and to be alert to the opposite, that is, that the client educates the therapist.

In summary, there are many potential responsibilities for the supervisor when differing sexual orientations are present in the therapeutic and/or supervision dyads. Our motivation in writing the chapter "women desiring women" (ibid) was in part to share our thoughts and feelings about what we would want therapists to know; what is not asked; what is feared to share; what is missed from assessment; what is assumed; and what is taken for granted. I would now add the need to look for blind spots, heteronormative practice, homoerotic horror, and disclosure, and to investigate the historical and current field. We must remain alert to what goes under the radar of the therapy; what might be missed, missing, and dismissed that passes for acceptance; what goes under the radar of the supervisor; and how the supervisor's own attitudes might reinforce heterosexism and heteronormativity.

References

Beisser, A. R. (1970). The paradoxical theory of change. In J. Fagan and I. Shepherd (eds.), *Gestalt Therapy Now* (pp. 77–80). Palo Alto, CA: Science and Behaviour.

Bowlby, J. (1979). *The Making and Breaking of Affectional Bonds*. London: Routledge.

Daniel, J. (2009). The Gay Cure. *Therapy Today*, 20, 8, pp. 10–14.

Desmond, B. (2016). "Homophobia endures in our time of changing attitudes: a field perspective". *British Gestalt Journal*. Vol. 25, No. 2, 42–52.

Harrison, H., Hodgson, D., and Howdin, J. (2009). "Living on the edge of acceptance". *The Psychotherapist*, No. 41, 47–49.

Hodgson, D. and Skye, E. (2016). Women desiring women: reflections on the field. In P. Karian (ed.), *Critical & Experiential: Dimensions in Gender and Sexual Diversity* (pp. 193–205). Hampshire: Resonance Publications.

Jacobs, L. (2000). "For whites only". *British Gestalt Journal*. Vol. 9, No. 1, 3–14.

Jacques, G. (1998). "Homo-erotic horror". *British Gestalt Journal*. Vol. 7, No. 1, 18–23.

Kearns, A. and Daintry, P. (2000). "Shame in the supervisory relationship: living with the enemy". *British Gestalt Journal*. Vol. 9, No. 1, 28–38.

Kennedy, D. (2009). An excess of certainty: the gospel, the church, the Gestalt therapist and homosexuality. *British Gestalt Journal*, Vol. 18, No. 2, pp. 48–57.

Lewin, K. (1952). *Field Theory in Social Science*. London: Tavistock.

Mann, D. (1997). *Psychotherapy: An Erotic Relationship*. London and New York: Routledge.

Orange, D. (1995). *Emotional Understanding: Studies in Psychoanalytical Epistemology* (1st edn). New York: Guildford.

Parlett, M. (1993). "Towards a more Lewinian Gestalt therapy". *British Gestalt Journal*. Vol. 2, No. 2, 115–120.

Parlett, M. (2005). Contemporary gestalt therapy: field theory. In Woldt, A. and Toman, S. (eds.), *Gestalt Therapy: History, Theory and Practice* (pp. 41–64). Thousand Oaks, CA: Sage publications.

Polster, E. (1985). "Imprisoned in the present". *Gestalt Journal*. Vol. 8, No. 1, 5–22.

Yontef, G. (1996). "Gestalt supervision". *British Gestalt Journal*. Vol. 2, No. 2, 92–102.

2.4 Editor's Summary and reflection on sexual attraction and orientation in supervision

Biljana van Rijn

Introduction

Clinical supervision is one of the key support mechanisms in psychotherapy. Although Part 2 has a primary focus on supervision, references to it are present throughout this book and demonstrate its significance in psychotherapy practice overall, and in relation to working with sexuality.

Commitment to supervision starts early in the professional life of the practitioner. Psychotherapy students engage in clinical supervision from the beginning of their practice and continue to use it, in different formats, throughout their working lives. Professional bodies like UKCP (United Kingdom Council for Psychotherapy) and BACP (British Association for Counselling and Psychotherapy) require supervision as a condition of registration for individual practitioners. Although supervision is becoming more common in other helping professions, such as in the fields of mental health, teaching, and social work, it has been a source of mentoring and support for psychotherapists throughout the history. In terms of therapist development, supervision is a source of teaching, modelling, and exploration. It is of particular relevance to our subject that is also expected by the professionals to have a role in maintaining ethical practice.

As a psychotherapist and a supervisor I have experienced both sides of the supervisory relationship for many years. I have found my own supervision helpful in dealing with issues of sexual attraction over the years, and have encouraged my supervisees to explore and voice it in our work together. Separation between the supervision material and personal psychotherapy in this is not always clear. At any time, personal and professional contents intersect and overlap during supervision making the boundary between the two permeable. This is perhaps more complex in the areas of sexual identity and sexual attraction. They seem to belong firmly to the personal domain and we often need to make a conscious step to reflect on these experiences within the professional context. The required levels of reflection are also related to the type of the therapeutic practice. Different theoretical orientations engage in varied levels of personal exploration, and depth of personal exploration required in relational supervision is high. Relational therapeutic practice requires high levels of reflection and the use of self, in order to work with the intersubjective process, and this is mirrored in the supervision. The authors of the three chapters in this section each give a specific focus on relational supervisory practice.

In the first chapter (2.1 Hunt and Sills, 'The supervisory dimension') the authors start from a broad and familiar theoretical supervision framework for working with sexuality and sexual attraction, framing their thinking within the Proctor's theory (Proctor, 1988). They demonstrate how the different functions of supervision, formulated by Proctor as 'Restorative' (supportive), 'Formative' (developing skills), and 'Normative' (boundaries of ethical and professional practice), each have a role in addressing the themes of sexuality and sexual attraction. The authors also highlight a range of perspectives in supervision by referring to the Hawkins and Shohet seven-eyed model of supervision (Hawkins and Shohet, 2012). This model offers a layered focus on different relational dynamics in supervision encompassing a range of relational systems, and gives a scope for a whole range of perspectives and interventions. The chapter by Carole Shadbolt (2.2 'The disturbance and comfort of forbidden conversations (sexuality and erotic forces in relational psychotherapy supervision)') delves into the subject of the impact of the erotic material in supervision and through the reflective case material demonstrates the practice of relational supervision. The chapter by Di Hodgson (2.3 'Sexual orientation in the supervisory relationship: exploring fears and fantasies when different sexual orientations are present in the client/therapist and/or supervisory dyad') adds another dimension to the supervisory process. She reflects on the intersection of the personal and the societal when the supervisor or the supervisee identifies as gay or lesbian. She emphasises raising awareness of the impact of assumptions and prejudice and their meaning for the individual.

The following is a summary and my reflection on some of the common themes related to relational supervisory practice in working with sexuality, which each author develops in their own way.

The supervisory frame

Supervisory, like the therapeutic, frame relates to the metaphorical container in which the work takes place. This container is built over time by the impact of the interweaving practical and emotional boundaries between the supervisor and the supervisee. They consist of agreements about how and where the work takes place; spoken and unspoken agreements about its scope, aims, and limitations; and agreements about levels of confidentiality (Sills, 2006). Supervision contexts vary. Supervision can take place in the private, consultative setting. The supervisor might have a role in the assessment of training and practice teaching (training supervision) or have a role within the psychotherapy service in ensuring ethical practice for clients within a service. Supervision can take place individually or in a group. It can take a format of individual presentations, or group discussions, exercises and reflections on the group process. All of this determines the aims, the scope, and the levels of confidentiality available within the supervisory frame. Just as the practice of psychotherapy combines the personal and the professional selves of the practitioner, the effective practice of supervision encompasses both. One of the boundaries of the supervisory frame is that, even though it required engagement in personal reflection, this does not equate with psychotherapy, a boundary between 'teach and treat' that Carole Shadbolt refers to. This boundary could be difficult to distinguish when experiencing and working with sexual attraction. Aspects of the sexual, vital, and erotic intertwine our different selves in a way that is often difficult to verbalise and has a potential to bring up feelings of shame, as all of our authors have identified. In that context, the frame of the supervisory relationship as a strong and secure container, 'Finding the words to say it' (Hunt and Sills, 112), that can sustain uncertainty and foster trust and mutuality, becomes particularly important.

Relational supervision practice

The way in which supervisors and supervisees both contribute to and impact the experience in supervision, as well as psychotherapy, is another theme that flows through all three chapters.

All of the authors work as humanistic relational supervisors combining integrative and humanistic approaches like Transactional Analysis and Gestalt psychotherapy, with a psychodynamic focus on exploring the unconscious and the intersubjective (Orange et al., 1997, Stolorow, 2013, Stolorow et al., 1987) to describe the shared experience in supervision. Concepts of co-creation (Summers and Tudor, 2000, 2014) and field theory (Lewin, 1951), more commonly referred to in humanistic approaches, are also used here to describe this shared development of meaning and experience, which also includes the socio-political context. Moving beyond the supervisory dyad, the impact of the socio-political context on the co-creation of meaning is particularly highlighted in the Chapter 2.3. In this chapter Di Hodgson addresses how the societal norms and ways of relating impact the personal experience in supervision in constructive and unconstructive ways. A lack of reflection, or a lack of the supervisor's awareness of diversity could influence whether supervision becomes a place of trust and safety, where difficult subjects could be voiced.

Intersubjectivity in relational supervision requires the supervisor to be willing to reflect on their own experiences and raise the subject of the erotic. This involves an expectation that their own feelings would be evoked. Shadbolt (Chapter 2.2) talks about this as a willingness to engage in the 'disturbance' and uncertainty brought up by the dynamics of sexuality and the erotic, and gives a beautiful case illustration of this process.

Uncovering the hidden

The hidden in the context of supervision relates to the material psychotherapists consciously hide from their supervisors, often due to shame, fears that they would be judged or penalised, and due to the asymmetric nature of the supervisory role. Di Hodgson's chapter also shows how a lack of a 'diversity lens' by the supervisor can also lead to silencing. Material that is hidden, that remains unspoken also relates to the unconscious experiences and feelings operating beyond our reflective and verbal abilities and awareness. The unconscious material becomes evoked in the intersubjective process between the therapist and the client and is experienced in supervision within a parallel transferential process. The authors give case vignettes for consciously and unconsciously hidden experiences, and illustrate the complex and multilayered nature of supervision and the overlap between the professional and the personal in supervision.

This complexity of the unconscious and the material that is actively hidden limits the scope of the normative function of supervision. The literature suggests that most of the transgressions emerge due to therapists' rationalisations and personal and developmental factors (Celenza, 1998; Gabbard and Lester, 1995). Supervisors can only attend to what they know about and are therefore limited as gatekeepers of ethical practice. This highlights the importance of being alert to what could be hidden, consciously and unconsciously. Shadbolt's case vignette (Chapter 2.2) gives a vivid example of transgression (an inappropriate hug) hidden from the supervisor due to the therapist's feelings of shame. The material was accessed through the vehicle of the relational supervisory practice, and became accessible to both the normative and restorative supervisory functions. Once the 'hidden' is accessible and spoken about, supervision can realistically support ethical practice.

The case vignettes in all three chapters give vivid and clear illustrations of the experiences by supervisors and supervisees, although none of the authors gives concrete suggestions or sets of supervision instructions. This is significant. Relational supervision practice emerges though interaction and co-creation, and is unique to the individual experience. In that context, a supervisor's role is not about giving words to the therapist to address their client. Once the supervisor and the therapist are engaged in the reflective process, the words and actions they choose to use to address the issue need to remain their own, emerging as they do from the intersubjective process with their supervisees.

Embodiment

Following on from the theme of uncovering the hidden, and reflecting on the experiences described by the authors, many supervisees report not feeling safe to voice those experiences to their supervisors. Our feelings of sexual attraction and our sexual orientations are rooted in the deep sense of our private personal identity, not always integrated within our professional selves. This is a challenge in using clinical supervision as a space for exploration, and yet, we need to explore its impact in supervision in order to develop the therapeutic work, as well as to identify and work with ruptures and potential transgressions.

The experiences of sexuality and our sexual orientations are embodied and visceral. Even when conscious and not hidden, they are not necessarily verbal. Feelings of attraction and disgust, fleeting images, and sensory experiences, in this context, all become avenues for exploration in supervision. However, supervisors might need to take an active role in exploring and inquiring into these experiences. The authors give examples of attending to the body posture and the nuance of expression, their own visceral experiences, as well the metaphors they and their supervisees use in communication with one another. The active role by the supervisor in their own reflection and sharing and enquiring with their supervisee has a potential to create the environment where the exploration can happen freely and without shame.

Societal perspectives and power

All three chapters in this section refer to the wider societal context, although Di Hodgson, in her chapter (2.3), addresses this theme in depth, particularly in relation to different sexual orientations. She gives numerous examples of the potential for silencing and shaming, as well as misattuning, when the supervisor lacks, what she terms a 'diversity lens'. Within the socio-political context in which heterosexuality is a norm, and prejudice is only gradually acknowledged and addressed within the field of psychotherapeutic practice, supervision can become another heteronormative structure, damaging to the individual. All authors have addressed some of the power issues between the supervisor and the supervisee contained within the nature of the role, as well as its normative aspects.

The normative function of supervision means that the supervisor sometimes has role in ensuring the standards of clinical practice, particularly in the case of training supervision, or supervision within services. In training supervision this means that the supervisor could involve the training organisation and potentially stop the student from practising. This could be similar in organisations. Even within a consultative setting, the supervisor might need to reach out to the professional ethical bodies. Even if that is not the case, the supervisor is usually a more experienced professional with a wealth of knowledge and understanding. These aspects of the supervisor's role contribute to making the supervisory frame a safe container, where a therapist can explore and find support in working with the material they find challenging (restorative and formative functions). However, when the therapist is struggling with disturbing personal material of sexual attraction and desire, which may be partially hidden from their own awareness, the supervisor becomes someone with enormous potential for shaming and punishment. Although a supervisor's power to stop a qualified therapist from practicing is limited, there is a sufficient power differential to impact the process of supervision. Supervisors' are, of course, also human and have limited awareness and unresolved issues of their own which can contribute to the ruptures. A sense of humility and willingness to explore this are as important in the supervisory relationship, as they are in psychotherapy.

Practice points

The three chapters follow on well from one another, providing a framework for working with sexual attraction and focussing on sexual identity. All authors give suggestions and examples of good practice in supervision, arising from the process of relational supervision, with intersubjectivity and co-creation as the focal theme. Their aim is to address layers of personal meaning and professional meaning in the experience of sexual attraction, and sexual orientation.

Starting from the same perspective, and in order to give an additional focus to good practice, I will highlight some of the supervision strategies:

- Allowing the space to name the therapist's fears and fantasies. This might involve fears about the nature of the work with the client, as well as fears and fantasies about the supervisor. This work needs to take place within a supervisory frame with a range of agreements about the nature of the relationship, its scope, and boundaries (Sills, 2006).
- Finding 'the words to say it' (Chapter 2.1, Hunt and Sills). In working with sexual attraction, the supervisor might need to explore of the unconscious, embodied and non-verbal material. This involves the openness to exploring the supervisor's own experience and willingness to engage in working with their own edge of awareness, even when that experience may be disturbing.
- The supervisor needs to hear the supervisee without pathologising. Feelings of shame and the fear of judgement are easily evoked in working with the material of the erotic. They can be deeply wounding, and do not contribute to the development of safe practice.
- Awareness of the societal power and prejudice is essential in enabling effective and supportive supervision in working with the material of the erotic. Prejudice about gay and lesbian sexual orientations, and transgender identities is present in the society and can be easily evoked and experienced in supervision. Working with the material of sexual attraction within the context of heteronormative society, with a binary view of gender, adds complexity for lesbian, gay, and transgender therapists. Supervisors need to be mindful of their power within this asymmetric professional relationship as well as their own identity and how that might limit or enhance their understanding of the therapist's experience.

- Normative functions of supervision involve awareness of boundaries and ethical practice. This might involve engaging other professionals to prevent or deal with transgressions and violations against clients.

The way these aims could translate into practice is individual and varies in each supervisory relationship. The broad suggestions we can offer relate to needing to be proactive in bringing up and enquiring into the hidden, the non-verbal and the unconscious material. Sexuality is ever present in human relationships and needs to be reflected on in supervision, alongside other core human experiences, although this is often more challenging because of the societal inhibitions and dynamics. Alongside being proactive, there is also a need to be patient, accepting, and willing to engage. This requires the supervisor to be willing to attend to unsettling experiences, their own psychological process, as well as prejudices.

References

Celenza, A. (1998) Precursors to therapist sexual misconduct: Preliminary findings. *Psychoanalytic Psychology*, 15, 378–395.

Gabbard, G. O. and Lester, E. P. (1995) *Boundaries and Boundary Violations in Psychoanalysis*, Arlington, VA, American Psychiatric Publishing, Inc.

Hawkins, P. and Shohet, R. (2012) *Supervision in the Helping Professions*, Buckingham and Philadelphia, PA, Open University Press.

Lewin, K. (1951) *Field Theory in Social Science: Selected Theoretical Papers* (Edited by D. Cartwright), Oxford, Harpers.

Orange, D., Atwood, G. E. and Stolorow, R. D. (1997) *Working Intersubjectively: Contextualism in Psychoanalytic Practice*, Mahwah, NJ, The Analytic Press.

Proctor, B. (1988) Supervision: A co-operative exercise in accountability. In Marken, M. and Payne, M. (Eds.) *Enabling and Ensuring Supervision in Practice*, Leicester, National Youth Bureau.

Sills, C. (Ed.) (2006) *Contracts in Counselling and Psychotherapy*, 2nd ed., Thousand Oaks, CA, Sage Publications, Inc.

Stolorow, R. D. (2013) Intersubjective-systems theory: A phenomenological-contextualist psychoanalytic perspective. *Psychoanalytic Dialogues*, 23, 383–389.

Stolorow, R. D., Brandchaft, B. and Atwood, G. E. (1987) *Psychoanalytic Treatment: An Intersubjective Approach*, Hillsdale, NJ and Hove, Analytic Press.

Summers, G. and Tudor, K. (2000) Cocreative transactional analysis. *Transactional Analysis Journal*, 30, 24–40.

Summers, G. and Tudor, K. (2014) Co-creative transactional analysis. In *Co-creative Transactional Analysis: Papers, Responses, Dialogues, and Developments*, London, Karnac Books, 1–28.

Part 3
Ethics
Preventing and dealing with transgressions

3.1 Sexual transgressions and transgressing gender and sexuality
Steven B. Smith

Introduction

As I address the issue of sexual transgressions, I am mindful that this can take the form of a therapist committing a boundary violation by engaging in sexual relations with their client. While much has been written and researched on this breach of public trust, which calls into question our ethical and professional standing, I am also concerned about transgressing our clients uniquely, evolving, intersecting identities, relating to, for the purposes of this chapter, to gender and sexuality. This last point becomes particularly striking when we consider that while heteronormative views on gender and sexuality have 'shifted markedly in the last few decades ... [with] ... people [becoming] more aware of the various identities and practices that are possible in all these areas' (Richards and Barker, 2013, p. 2), there has also been an unprecedented and growing polarisation on these matters, leading to 'culture wars' as to what constitutes normativity on the issue of identity, on multiple levels. On this last point, it is deeply concerning to note that police recorded that hate crimes in England and Wales rose from 42,255 to 94,098 between 2012/13 and 2017/18 (Home Office, 2018). Of the 94,098 cases reported, 76% relate to race, 12% to sexual orientation, 9% to religion, 8% to disability, and 2% to transgender issues. While these increases are thought to be the result of considerable improvements in police protocols and procedures in recording such information, there are nevertheless significant spikes in reported hate crimes around the EU Referendum in 2016 and the terrorist attacks of 2017. So, as practitioners, while we may be consciously committed to being inclusive and celebratory of difference and diversity in our clinical practice, we are not immune from the impact of these 'cultural wars' within our own society at the explicit and implicit or unconscious levels of communication. This makes it even more incumbent upon us to be informed and vigilant regarding the growing field of identity politics, along with a willingness and openness to explore our own biases, conscious or otherwise.

When clients disclose their sexual fantasies or reveal the sexual acts that they engage in with other consenting adult(s) the challenge, as I see it, is to be curious with our clients as to how these excitations and happenings may be enhancing or thwarting their human growth and development. Simultaneously, we need to non-defensively monitor as to how these fantasies and practices might impinge upon our own personal values that, if unmonitored, could potentially put at risk our ethical and professional responsibilities. As we wrestle with such complex, deeply personal, and delicate matters as gender and sexuality, we need to be aware, therefore, of our own sexual preferences. Critically, this will also involve scrutinising our subsequent biases that ultimately involve personal 'permissions' and 'taboos' that have been culturally mediated through our unique familial, societal, political, and religious contexts. Such explorations can help us to hold fast to our ethical obligation to be a cause for good (beneficence) in our clients' lives as they share and discuss the intersecting intricacies of their genders and sexualities. In this way, we can hopefully guard against becoming a source of harm (maleficence) to our clients on these deeply personal matters.

In this chapter, I will begin by providing a brief overview of my integrative framework to date that I lightly hold in mind when working with my clients' sexual material. Then, I will briefly reflect upon sexual transgressions in terms of sexual boundary violations, before exploring in detail the equally salient issue of transgressing our clients uniquely, evolving, intersecting identities, relating to gender and sexuality. Here, I will be arguing that due care and attention is called for regarding the power imbalance within the therapeutic relationship that is unavoidably stacked in our 'favour' as practitioners. Hence, we need to sensitively explore and discuss issues of gender and sexuality in a respectful and collaborative manner, both within the relational dyad between therapist and client, and in the interpersonal flow between supervisor, therapist, and client. In order to enliven the issue at hand, I will highlight two case examples to illustrate the importance of fostering an integrative and humanistic stance to guard against pathologising our clients' gender and sexuality, particularly when such material 'falls outside' of our own sexual desires, fantasies, and experiences. With the exception of my supervisee (who kindly gave me permission to reflect upon his material), all other aspects of these two clinical vignettes are composites of different clients to safeguard client confidentiality; without, I hope, compromising the rich learning to be potentially gained from these examples. I hope that these cases will help to deepen our awareness and further calibrate our relational capacity to manage the ethical and professional challenges that relate to working with our clients' sexual material, so that we do not unwittingly commit acts of transgression, whether explicitly or implicitly, against our clients uniquely, evolving identities.

A brief overview of my integrative stance

My integrative framework arises out of the conviction that no one psychotherapy modality holds exclusive truth claims regarding the human condition. Hence, several perspectives, even seemingly paradoxical or contradictory ones, can be simultaneously considered when encountering the human condition. However, the challenge here is to locate an overarching theory or organising theme(s) to consistently and coherently integrate various psychological concepts from different modalities. In effect, it is important to reduce, overcome, and creatively manage the natural tensions that will emerge from this process to avoid conceptual and clinical confusion. Such tensions arise when considering such issues as the structure of the self (human nature), what drives us (human motivation), what helps us to thrive and strive (human function) and what causes human suffering (human dysfunction); and, importantly, what needs to happen within the therapeutic relationship to work through the client's presenting issues.

Erskine rightly contends that for an integrative approach to be truly integrative, rather than an *ad hoc* process (eclectic), we must 'separate those concepts and ideas that are not theoretically consistent to form a cohesive core of constructs that inform and guide our therapeutic practice' (1997, p. 21). As I consider the overarching theory or central thread that I utilise to integrate diverse concepts from the field of psychotherapy, it is the theme of relationships that comes to the fore. Indeed, research has repeatedly highlighted that a key component for good psychotherapeutic outcomes is the efficacious quality of the co-created, psychotherapeutic relationship between therapist and client (Wampold and Imel, 2015). Hence, I hold 'in mind the generative (optimal), causative (traumatic), and curative (restorative) impact that human relationships can afford' (Smith, 2015, p. 238). Consequently, this central theme supports me to integrate concepts from developmental psychoanalysis, humanistic and psychoanalytic notions of relationality, and transpersonal perspectives. Collectively, these vantage points help me to consider my client's unaddressed developmental deficits and traumas, current relational struggles and spiritual longings as these emerge as figure and ground within the vicissitudes of the therapeutic relationship; and, in particular, how these issues interconnect with my clients' gender and sexuality.

These three vantage points can be likened to Rowan's image of the Three-Headed Goddess of Hinduism, with 'one face looking back to childhood and the repression and hang-ups of the past; one face looking into the present, the existential now; the other face looking forward to spirituality and the divine' (ibid, 2008, p. 6). The chronological and spatial categories of past, present, and future can be linked to the terms aetiological, dialogical, and teleological, respectively. An aetiological viewpoint relates to a *cause and effect* perception in terms of how the past is casting a shadow upon the present moment. In contrast, a teleological perspective looks for a spiritual appreciation as to how the future might be influencing the client to become their fullest self; this is about *purpose*, rather than cause and effect. Finally, the dialogical outlook relates to the *power of the present moment*: how the self-other dichotomy can be transcended through intimate meeting and communication within the therapeutic relationship that renews the self of the client (and arguably, the therapist) (Hermans and Dimaggio, 2004).

Ultimately, the aim of holding these multiple perspectives is to guard against the risk of committing conceptual oppression, whereby a client is forced into a singular viewpoint in a reductive or transgressive manner; particularly as this relates to the deeply personal and delicate issue of organising one's own gender and sexuality. For example, if the aetiological face looking back to childhood is championed as *the truth*, in a reified fashion, we can become wedded to a causative link, whereby the *why* is exclusively searched for to make sense of the human condition. As soon as someone asks the question 'What causes "homosexuality?"', by definition they are relying on an aetiological explanation that leans towards pathologising a person's sexual orientation (Richards and Barker, 2013). I have yet to hear a person earnestly asking, 'What causes heterosexuality?' unless this has been mooted as a subversive question to circumvent the inherent bias that the previous question on 'homosexuality' could carry. Also, asking a question as to what causes 'homosexuality' could be revealing the underlying heteronormative bias of a straight person posing such a question or potentially an indication of internalised homophobia, if asked by a gay person. Similarly, if a client in their mid-40s is suddenly faced with the realisation that they can no longer identify with their hitherto perceived cisgender, then solely pursuing the teleological face of the Three-Headed Goddess of Hinduism to create spiritual meaning and purpose out of such an existential crisis could be a way of spiritually bypassing (Welwood, 2007) their emotional distress and confusion, that such an awareness might herald.

Finally, I continue to hold fast to Stolorow, Brandchaft and Atwood's (1987) timeless warning with conscious intent, as much as is humanly possible, whereby they have cautioned against the dangers as to what is deemed or considered to be 'true'. Here, I am mindful of a handful of synonyms that can be associated with the word 'true' such as factual, correct, accurate, right, and so forth. 'Such dangers lie in the fact that judgement about what is "really true" about the analyst and what is distortion of that "truth" are ordinarily left solely to the discretion of the analyst – hardly a disinterested party' (ibid, 1987, p. 35). While this quote is directly critiquing and commenting upon the power imbalance favouring the analyst in their interpretation of the patient's transference, it nevertheless feels relevant as we encounter our clients' uniquely, evolving, intersections of gender and sexuality. Likewise, Stern's (2010) postulation that all understanding is context dependent, and that therapist and client are called to be partners in thought, co-creating a narrative to make sense of the patient's unformulated experiences, is both respectful and timely for our subject at hand. Notwithstanding, that alongside this relational posture to work with issues of gender and sexuality, I also hold a humanistic regard, and reverence, for the client's homeostatic mechanisms or 'inner healer' that is also a key constituent part of the journey towards, change, growth, and healing (Norcross and Lambert, 2011). These timeless and timely reminders, along with the client's role in their restorative journey towards self-acceptance and wholeness, further calibrate my intent to strive to be cause for good when working with issues of gender and sexuality.

Having now explicated my integrative framework, I now briefly turn to an exploration of sexual boundary violations committed against clients, before addressing the less addressed violations against a client's sexual preferences and proclivities.

Violations against a client's sexual boundaries

The United Kingdom Council for Psychotherapy (UKCP) updated their Code of Ethics and Professional Practice for registered UKCP psychotherapists in October 2019. In this document, under the subheading, *Best Interests of Your Clients*, it states that practitioners must:

1   Act in your client's best interests.
2   Treat clients with respect.
3   Respect your client's autonomy.
4   Not have sexual contact or sexual relationships with clients.
5   Not exploit or abuse your relationship with clients (current or past) for any purpose, including your emotional, sexual, or financial gain.

Further ethical codes are cited, but for our purposes these five points emphatically underscore the beneficent stance that we need to adopt and embody as therapists. This is essential, so that within the therapeutic dyad we aspire to be a cause for good in the client's life and not a source of harm. Critically, honouring and maintaining the aforementioned professional and ethical boundaries are designed to keep the client-therapist dyad safe as delicate and sensitive material arises in their uniquely evolving, co-created, therapeutic relationship. While these ethical and professional codes are laudable and necessary, sadly, they do not involve the simple task of subscribing to them in a manualised or formulaic fashion. No manner of rote learning, regarding the UKCP Code of Ethics and Professional Practice, will prevent explicit, sexual transgressions in respect of boundary violations. Rather, unconscious dynamics are always at play (Gabbard and Lester, 2003) that require a robust capacity for honest reflexivity (Bager-Charleson, 2010), along with a supportive and challenging supervisory relationship within which to process more challenging aspects of ourselves (and our clients), as practitioners. These personal and professional qualities and resources are indispensable to call upon in delicate and complex moments of exchange within the therapeutic relationship, especially as they relate to erotic transference and countertransference dynamics that can emerge in the in-between (Kearns and Smith, 2007).

The explicit professional and ethical reference not to commit sexual boundary violations set out in points 4 and 5 above, have been rigorously addressed by Glen Gabbard over many years. He has researched and reviewed explicit sexual transgressions within psychoanalysis in an earnest attempt to identify and distil the salient dynamics that can lead a psychoanalyst to sexually violate their patient's boundaries. When considering these dynamics, he articulates a particular set of characteristics that can single-handedly or collectively, predispose a psychoanalyst to transgress their patient's sexual boundaries. These include: psychosis (which is extremely rare), such as a manic-episode, wherein the psychoanalyst loses their ethical and professional boundaries; a life of predatory psychopathy (usually male) in existence prior to qualifying as a psychoanalyst; and features of lovesickness, masochistic surrender, and narcissistic vulnerability (Gabbard, 2016). Sexually explicit breaches involving the violation and exploitation of vulnerable clients are not, of course, the sole domain of psychoanalysis. As humanistic and integrative psychotherapists we need only consider the following quote:

> There is a thin line between altruistic wishes to help our patients and omnipotent strivings to heal them. We must avoid the quasi-delusional conviction that only we are capable of helping a patient and that it is only our unique personhood ... that is useful. We must even accept that, in our limits as analysts, we must lose some patients. This recognition might help us avoid masochistic surrender scenarios in which we sacrifice ourselves in a blind and grandiose effort to save another person.
>
> (ibid, 2016, p. 70)

To my mind, Glen Gabbard's words have a universal and sobering application to psychotherapists from all modalities, calling us to humility about the tininess of our role in the therapeutic dyad (Smith, 2015). While most therapists would publicly agree that our professional duty is to respect and honour our clients' sexual boundaries as inviolable, I am correspondingly concerned about the ways in which we can harm our clients, as they explore and self-disclose their sexual preferences and practices, which I now address.

Adam: "should I be worried?"

Adam came to see me a few years ago for individual psychotherapy. He was a white, 26-year-old Caucasian man, who was raised in a middle-class family. He was the youngest of three children. His older sister and brother were both married, each with a young child. Adam lived in a house share with his long-term friends from University. He was a very likeable and sociable young man, who reported that his mother was a caring and emotionally available person and that his father, while caring, was a little absent. Adam held down a job in finance in a leading private hospital and reported that there were good career opportunities within his place of work. He described his sexual orientation as heterosexual. After several weeks of reflecting upon tensions within the workplace, he disclosed that while he enjoyed sex with women on a fairly regular basis and identified as heterosexual, he would from time to time have masturbatory fantasies about having sex with a man, and he would also consummate this sexual desire by having sex with men on an occasional basis. He followed up this disclosure with "Should I be worried?" In my reactive counter-transference (Clarkson, 1995) my immediate, emotional and visceral response to his question was one of surprise because clearly, he did not phenomenologically embody any sense of anxiety as I sat with him. As we explored this further it became apparent that his mother and father, and some of his male and female friends had become polarised in response to his disclosure. Some people were worried (his mother and some male and female friends) that he was denying either a repressed gay identity or at least a bisexual one. Interestingly, his father did not have a problem with this disclosure, along with numerous male and female friends.

Kahr, on reflecting upon the relationship between sexual fantasies and orgasm, notes that a tension may exist between these two points that creates a deep sense of discomfort, even conflict, in the patient. He goes on:

> I have come to refer to this tension in human psychology as the 'Masturbatory Paradox', the fact that, as a result of our fantasies, we experience paradoxically, pleasure in our genitals and our bodies, but often, simultaneously, disquiet in our minds.
>
> (ibid, 2007, p. 11)

Adam, was not only having occasional masturbatory sexual fantasies about men but following this through from time to time, in an embodied and sensuous way, without any disquiet in his own mind. This was clearly being communicated by his immediate context via his mother and some of his friends, which caused us to be curious and somewhat intrigued.

Over several weeks in my personal supervision, we initially wondered aloud together whether Adam's sexual proclivity was an unconscious response to his father being caring but somewhat distant. I recalled Siegel (1996) reflecting on an American patient of Heinz Kohut's who had regular sexual contact with women but occasionally had sex with men in the locker room at his local gym. The patient's engagement in performing fellatio on other men was interpreted as a compensatory act for an unavailable father, with the penis of the other man becoming a symbolic substitute for the lack of an unmet idealising self-object need in respect of the father. I remember at the time as a trainee psychotherapist finding this aetiological perspective somewhat reductive and potentially harmful, if not pathologising. While my supervisor agreed with my concerns we nevertheless decided to tentatively wonder aloud with Adam about his relationship with his father, apropos, his sexual desire that he occasionally enjoyed in his masturbatory fantasies and consummated in actuality with other men.

In the next session I broached this issue with some apprehension. To my surprise, Adam was open and curious to engage with this line of enquiry. He noted with me that while his father had been somewhat distant, he had indeed had good male bonds with his male friends both at school and at university and onwards since that time. Here, Wachtel's (2008) critique of a purely aetiological stance came to mind. Simply put, this approach can all too readily locate a wound from the developmental past and then link this to the patient's present anxiety and current relational struggles in a simplistic cause and effect manner. In this process, what gets overlooked are the subsequent, relational experiences that are contextually negotiated that can further exacerbate the original injury to the self or indeed heal or transform the initial wound through successive reparative and restorative experiences. As a way of combating against this developmental determinism, Wachtel (2008) has made a persuasive plea to rename relational psychotherapy as *contextual* psychotherapy to labour this very important point. In other words, we are constantly being shaped by multiple relational experiences facilitated within particular contexts that can support us to heal and thrive and strive in the aftermath of a relational injury to our unique sense of self; and indeed, the opposite can also be so whereby the existing relational injury to our sense of self is further reinforced through successive dyadic, triadic, or group experiences.

Being mindful not to be a cause of harm (maleficence), I listened carefully to Adam's narrative about the strong male bonds he had experienced up until the present time. Through reflection-in-action (Schön, 1983), and as a way of staying close to Adam's unique subjectivity and experiences, I invited him to phenomenologically explore with me as to what the qualitative difference was for him when he had sex with men compared to sex with women. Adam shared that his sexual experiences with women were often intimate and receptive, whereas his sexual experiences with men had a sense of combat and warmth that was both bonding and affirming. In the co-transference (Orange, 1995), I felt that Adam needed something more from me, something of myself, as a comparatively older man which was perhaps missing from his relationship with his father, especially in terms of closeness. So, in that moment I moved away from a place of knowing and safety, using this as a springboard to gently move towards a relational stance of not-knowing and risk. I shared with him that as somebody who identified as a bisexual man in my previous relationships, both with men and women, my emotional intimacy and sexual intimacy prefigured highly, in an interwoven fashion; and furthermore, that I was struggling to make sense of how he clearly identified as heterosexual but nevertheless enjoyed intermittent sexual fantasies of having sex with men and effectuating his sexual desire with a man on some occasions. Adam was clearly touched that I had taken a risk and stepped forward in our therapeutic relationship in this way. As a result of taking this risk at the intimate edge of our exchange (Ehrenberg, 1992) the following conversation unfolded between us:

ADAM: "Well, for me I do emotionally love women, emotionally and sexually as a straight man. But with men, its different, I enjoy their maleness and it celebrates my maleness".

STEVEN: "So, it celebrates and confirms your maleness".
ADAM: "Yes, you know, a bit like 'Broke Back Mountain', the movie?"
STEVEN: "Oh! The Double!"
ADAM: "Sorry, what?"

At this point I explained in everyday language the transpersonal or *purposive* nature of Adam's sexual desire and sexual relations with men. Walker (1976) conceptualises the archetype of the Double to celebrate same-sex relationships. Here, he adds his concept of the Double to complement the archetypes of anima and animus, and hereby create a more holistic schema to understand the diverse manifestations of human sexuality. Traditionally, within Jungian analysis the man's anima is the anthropomorphic feminine soul image and the woman's animus is the anthropomorphic masculine soul image – both unconscious opposites to that of physical maleness and femaleness – that play an important part in the individuation process of psychological growth and spiritual development. Jung, contended that: 'Wherever an impassioned, almost magical relationship exists between the sexes, it is invariably a question of a projected soul-image' (1921/1971, para. 809). In other words, romantic and sexual relationships occur when a man and a woman unconsciously project their soul image onto the opposite gender as a means of finding the middle ground between the feminine and masculine opposites within themselves. This process aids personal integration of these life forces and enhances each person's individuation process across the life cycle. Post-Jungian analysts (Samuels, 1985; Schaverien, 2003) have quite rightly critiqued these contra-sexual binaries between men and women as outdated modes of making sense of gender and sexuality for the modern mind.

While these critiques are admirable and much needed, the ramification of this legacy has been, nevertheless, to explain same-sex desire as the result of a man over-identifying with his anima (feminine) that compels him to seek out male sexual partners; and, in a similar fashion, a woman who over-identifies with her animus (masculine) propels her to seek out female sexual partners. In effect, contra-sexuality is unwittingly purporting that if a man is seeking out same-sex erotic pleasure with another man he is doing so because he is psychologically over-identifying with his femininity (anima). Likewise, if a woman is seeking out same-sex erotic pleasure with another woman she is doing so because she is psychologically over-identifying with her masculinity (animus). What is apparent from this outdated reading is that if a man is seeking out sexual pleasure with another man he is more like a woman and if a woman is seeking out sexual pleasure with another woman she is more like a man. The homophobic undercurrents to this theorising are all too apparent.

While these conceptualisations are endeavouring to make sense of heterosexual (opposite-sex) attraction and desire in terms of psychological growth (individuation) and human development, whereby the man and woman gradually find the middle ground between their feminine and masculine qualities within themselves, these ideas have nevertheless relegated same-sex sexual relationships outside of the canon of normativity; thereby making them abnormal and unhelpful for the purposes of human growth and psychological development. Hopcke (1989), however, is quick to point out that in practice Carl Jung was far more compassionate in his analysis of 'homosexual' men and women, compared to his theorising on same-sex sexual attraction. As a way of countering a pathological reading of same-sex desire as a result of contra-sexuality, Walker (1976) adds the notion of the Double. Here, what he is proposing is that soulful and intensely warm close bonds between two men and between two women (or groups of men and women for that matter), whether platonic or sexual, is a result of the projection of the Double (i.e., male-to-male and female-to-female bonding) that can be both affirming and confirming of one's maleness or femaleness, respectively. In this way, in my mind, he is integrating contra-sexuality (sexual attraction and desire for the opposite) and the Double (sexual attraction and desire for the same) to craft a more nuanced and complex continuum between opposite-sex and same-sex attraction, ranging from straight, bisexual, and gay configurations of sexual relationships, and how these various, multiple manifestations of relationships are encounters and experiences that can enhance the individual's and couple's human growth and psychological development across the life cycle.

The dialogical encounters based on the contra-sexuality and the Double strengthened Adam's sense of self and further calibrated his pre-existing self-acceptance of himself regarding how he organised his gender and sexual relations regardless of his mother and friends concerns. As I end my reflections on Adam, I am mindful of Richards and Barker (2013) who make the important distinction between *identity* and *doing*. They write:

> A man may have sex with another man (practice) and define as something other than gay or bisexual (identity). For this reason, sexual health professionals have terms such as *MSM* (men who have sex with men) and *MSMW* (men who have sex with men and women) as these terms do not denote identity, but simply practice.
>
> (ibid, 2013, p. 4 – italics in the original)

Looking back, clearly for Adam, he was a heterosexual man whose sexual proclivities could be described as MSM that honours his unique way of organising and presenting his gender and sexuality both in a meaningful and authentic way. As a result of my psychotherapeutic journey with Adam I learned a great deal about holding my theories lightly and considering multiple perspectives through our intimate co-created dialogue, so as not to cause harm to his uniquely emerging gender and sexuality.

Timothy: "I want to be penetrated by a Lady Boy"

My supervisee Simon presented his client Timothy in supervision over several months. Simon was in his mid-50s and prior to becoming a psychotherapist he had an illustrious and impressive career in the arts and television media. He had worked both as a theatre director and then as a theatre manager. He had retrained during this latter stage of his career to qualify and work as a full-time psychotherapist. He described his sexual orientation as bisexual and was currently living with his long-term male partner. As I hope to demonstrate, these details are salient regarding the dynamics that eventually became constellated in the parallel process between Timothy, Simon, and myself. In the early stages of the work Simon experienced his client Timothy as somewhat aloof. Timothy was highly intellectualising, cold, and distant, with a modicum of superiority to match – possibly as an unconscious way of creating interpersonal distance. Timothy was in his early 40s and was a successful director within a leading advertising agency. He would attend the gym every day and was well groomed and presented, sporting the latest designer wear. He clearly took pride in his appearance. As the process of therapy unfolded, Timothy reported that while he could be brutal at work and perceived himself as a successful alpha male who in his own words was "living the dream", he nevertheless felt deeply isolated and alone. He reported that he had successive brief relationships with the latest 'girlfriend'. His girlfriends were invariably attractive and successful, but he would always end these so-called relationships within approximately three months.

As I sat with my felt sense of Timothy through Simon's presentation of his client, I was mindful of how gender rigidity, just as much as gender confusion, can be a cause of intrapersonal and interpersonal anxiety for some people, leading to a deep sense of loneliness and alienation. Indeed:

> Some people have rigid assumptions about what it means to be a man or a woman and become very distressed trying to match up to these, while others might flexibly engage with *masculinity* or *femininity*, and others find different ways of conceptualising gender which are more congruent.
>
> (Richards and Barker, 2013, p. 2 – italics in the original)

After sitting with this visceral sense of rigidity and isolation in the parallel process, I asked Simon to describe how he was experiencing Timothy in the in-between of their relationship. Simon replied, "Impenetrable!" This profoundly resonated with me, and I shared with my supervisee how lopsided his client felt in organising his gender and how Timothy felt so cut-off from his feelings. Indeed, I did not feel any sense of *joie de vie* in Timothy's life whatsoever. This led us to consider Mitchell's (2000) appreciation and articulation of Hans Loewald's understanding as to what constitutes human function and human dysfunction. This is one possible theory of mind that we considered together at this point in our supervisory relationship. For Loewald a healthy mind ties together, in a unifying way, experiences that seemingly appear separate and disconnected. To my mind this is about psychic integration within oneself and the world around us. This integrating or unifying process of the mind involves a centrifugal and centripetal motion whereby the mind moves between the centre of experience (centrifugal) and away from the centre of experience (centripetal) in a reciprocal and flexible manner. In simple terms, this means that an individual can seamlessly move between self and other, fantasy and reality, and past and present that brings a richness to that person's psychic life (inner world) and their intersubjective relationships (outer world). In sharp contrast, according to Loewald, psychopathology or human suffering transpires when this dynamic interplay becomes imbalanced. In an ongoing centrifugal state of mind lodged in the centre of experience psychosis occurs undermining the 'adaptive, normative distinctions between inside and outside, self and other, actuality and fantasy, past and present' (Mitchell, 2000, p. 4). When in a constant centripetal state of mind dislodged from the centre of experience the mind has travelled so far from its original unity that neurosis or anxiety emerges, with 'inside and outside becoming separate, impermeable domains; self and other are experienced in isolation from each other, actuality is disconnected from fantasy; and the past has become remote from a shallow, passionless present' (ibid, p. 4).

This understanding helped us to appreciate Timothy's impenetrable nature with compassion, regarding his inability to move between self and other, fantasy and reality, and his past and present. Sometime later, Simon brought to supervision that Timothy had disclosed that he would often watch Lady Boy porn in the evening after a long day at work. He had revealed, "I would like to be penetrated by a Lady Boy in real life". He also shared that this uplifted his spirits, and he was worried that he might become addicted to porn. While this gratified me in that at last there was some semblance of fantasy, desire, and longing in Timothy's world, I also sensed that Simon was agitated and upset. As we discussed this revelation Simon disclosed that in his group supervision, where he had shared this information two weeks earlier, the word *perversion* had been used by a fellow supervisee to describe Timothy's sexual fantasy and pornographic choice. Simon was shocked by this sweeping statement. This also triggered Simon's story (and my own to some extent) regarding bullying and abusive language being used to pathologise him during his formative teenage years and as a young adult man. We took time to process this in our supervisory relationship with a great deal of tenderness, kind-heartedness, and reflection. On this term perversion Kahr writes:

> Admittedly, the term 'perversion' often rankles, and many regard this label as outmoded and judgemental. But in contemporary psychoanalytic discourse, mental health professionals use the diagnosis 'perversion' in

a very specific way. We would define perversion as the wish to cause harm to oneself or to another, a wish so strong that it evokes sexual pleasure in the 'perpetrator'.

(ibid, 2007, p. 232)

Dimen (2001) argues that such a term still has some theoretical credibility and clinical leverage as long it is considered as a co-constructed meaning-making aspect of the therapeutic relationship, rather than a prescription or proclamation from the analyst. While this may be an honourable attempt to redeem the term *perversion*, it nevertheless brings us back to the beginning of our discussion regarding the inherent power imbalance that is always at play and how the analyst or therapist is 'hardly a disinterested party' (Stolorow, Brandchaft and Atwood, 1987, p. 35); no matter how vociferous we are about being consciously committed to beneficence on behalf of our clients.

In the parallel process, it was equally important not to be induced into a splitting process which Simon had encountered in his group supervision. So together we critiqued the word perversion and instead endeavoured to hold a 'both-and' stance by honouring the generative (Lady Boy porn lifted Timothy's spirits) and destructive (Timothy was worried that he might become addicted to porn) components to his client's fantasies and desire. What had not gone unnoticed by either of us was Timothy's impenetrable nature and his longing to be anally penetrated by a Lady Boy. What was the archetypal or purposive nature of this emergence in Timothy's life that might help to reinvigorate his centrifugal and centripetal dynamic? In tandem with this way of thinking we also considered the archetype of androgyny. Androgyny comes from *andro* (male) and *gyne* (female) signifying the integration of masculine and feminine qualities. While these terms are problematic as to what constitutes masculine and feminine qualities as noted above in our discussion earlier, we nevertheless found it helpful to consider what Timothy was trying to integrate within himself and in his relationships, in order to realign his head and heart and soul; in other words, his opposites within – whatever that might mean to Timothy. Reflecting and writing on androgyny, Singer (2000) notes that:

> The archetype of androgyny appears in us as an innate sense of primordial cosmic unity, having existed in oneness or wholeness before any separation was made. The human psyche is witness to the primordial unity; therefore, the psyche is the vehicle through which we can attain awareness of the awe-inspiring totality.

(ibid, 2000, p. 5)

Clearly, a Lady Boy is a physical amalgamation of male and female attributes, whether this is a result of birth or surgical procedures: what would commonly be referred to as a hermaphrodite. Whereas androgyny is about psychological integration of masculine and feminine opposites within. So, in supervision we wondered what a Lady Boy symbolised to Timothy about his own inner landscape and what it would mean psychologically, as well as sexually, to be penetrated by a Lady Boy. Simon reports that his line of enquiry and exploration has been fruitful to date in their weekly sessions. Simon's unerring compassion, curiosity, and acceptance has had a profound impact upon his client. Here, the dialogical nature of their deepening therapeutic relationship was transcending the self-other dichotomy of Timothy's world, gradually renewing his sense of self and indeed that of Simon (Hermans and Dimaggio, 2004).

To date, Timothy's porn consumption has significantly decreased to once or twice a week and he is beginning to engage with others with a somewhat delicate and tenuous sense of growing intimacy. He has now candidly spoken with one male friend (who until recently had been more like an acquaintance) and his father about his sexual fantasies, longings, and desires. They have responded with warmth, curiosity, and acceptance which has allayed Timothy's anxiety or Masturbatory Paradox (Kahr, 2007). These interactions alongside his therapeutic relationship with Simon have softened Timothy's demeanour and his way of relating with himself and others; including, much to the relief of his work colleagues, his team at work. This is clearly a journey still in process that Simon and Timothy continue to embark upon. Significantly, by holding an aetiological (*cause and effect*), dialogical (*the power of the present moment*), and teleological (*purpose*) stance, Simon has been supported to hold multiple truths to tease out Timothy's shoots of psychological growth, while compassionately monitoring his propensity to retreat into a lopsided, passionless, and centripetal mind set. His sexual passion to have sex with a Lady Boy has seemingly been ignited by his homeostatic mechanisms (Norcross and Lambert, 2011) or inner healer (Smith, 2015) to address his hitherto imbalanced intrapersonal and interpersonal world.

Conclusion

In this discussion, I have reflected upon sexual transgressions both in terms of sexual violations against clients' sexual boundaries and the potentiality for us as therapists to transgress our clients uniquely evolving sense of gender and sexuality. Culturally, we are in a seismic shift as to how people define their essence and/or socially construct and organise their intersections as unique human beings. Gender and human sexuality are no exception. Unsurprisingly, the current zeitgeist regarding the proliferation of multiple ways that people can organise and define themselves is resulting in 'culture wars' as to what constitutes and what is deemed acceptable as normal or normative. While our ethical and professional frames of reference demand that we are a source for good and avoid harming our clients as they explore such issues as sex, sexuality, and gender, we are nevertheless part of the macrocosm that can all too unwittingly infiltrate the microcosm of the therapeutic consulting room. Due vigilance, honest reflexivity, and robust supervision are necessary to mitigate against such implicit or unconscious dynamics permeating our therapeutic practice. This is even more poignant given the power differential that sits with us as therapists and particularly pertinent when clients bring sexual fantasies and sexual practices with other consenting adults that are outside of our own sexual preferences, proclivities, and experiences.

References

Bager-Charleson, S. (2010) *Reflective Practice in Counselling and Psychotherapy.* London: Sage Publications Ltd.

Clarkson, P. (1995) *The Therapeutic Relationship.* London: Whurr Publications.

Dimen, M. (2001) Perversion is us. Eight notes. *Psychoanalytic Dialogues*, 11(6): 825–861.

Ehrenberg, D.E. (1992) *The Intimate Edge: Extending the Reach of Psychoanalytic Interaction.* London: W. W. Norton & Company.

Erskine, R.G. (1997) *Theories and Methods of an Integrative Transactional Analysis: A Volume of Selected Articles.* San Francisco: Transactional Analysis Press.

Gabbard, G.O. (2016) *Boundaries and Boundary Violations in Psychoanalysis* (2nd Edition). Arlington, VA: American Psychiatric Association Publishing.

Gabbard, G.O. and Lester, E.P. (2003) *Boundaries and Boundary Violations in Psychoanalysis.* Arlington, VA: American Psychiatric Association Publishing.

Hermans, J.M. and Dimaggio, G. (2004) *The Dialogical Self in Psychotherapy.* New York: Brunner-Routledge.

Home Office (2018) *Hate Crime, England and Wales, 2017/18* (statistical bulletin 20/18). London: HMSO. Available at: https://assets.publishing.service.gov.uk/government/uploads/system/uploads/attachment_data/ ile/748598/hate-crime-1718-hosb2018.pdf [Accessed: 19 October 2019].

Hopcke, R. (1989) *Jung, Jungians and Homosexuality.* London: Shambhala.

Jung, C.G. (1921/1971) Psychological types, CW 6. In: C.G. Jung (1953–1983), *Collected Works*, eds. Sir H. Read, M. Fordham, G. Adler and W. McGuire, 20 vols. London: Routledge & Keegan Paul, abbreviated as CW in all references to individual essays and books.

Kahr, B. (2007) *Sex and the Psyche: The Truth about Our Most Secret Fantasies.* London: Penguin Books.

Kearns, A. and Smith, S.B. (2007). Love and hate in the in-between. In: Kearns, A. (Ed.) *The Mirror Crack'd.* London: Karnac, pp. 61–88.

Mitchell, S.A. (2000) *Relationality: From Attachment to Intersubjectivity.* New York: The Analytic Press.

Norcross, J.C. and Lambert, M.J. (2011) Evidence-based therapy relationships. In: Norcross, J.C. (Ed.) *Psychotherapy Relationships that Work: Evidence-Based Responsiveness* (2nd Edition). New York: Oxford University Press, pp. 3–21.

Orange, D.M. (1995) *Emotional Understanding: Studies in Psychoanalytic Epistemology.* New York: The Guilford Press.

Richards, C. and Barker, M. (2013) *Sexuality & Gender: For Mental Health Professionals – A Practical Guide.* London: Sage Publications.

Rowan, J. (2008) *The Transpersonal: Psychotherapy and Counselling* (2nd Edition). London: Routledge.

Samuels, A. (1985) *Jung and the Post-Jungians*. London: Routledge.

Schaverien, J. (2003) The psychological feminine and contra-sexuality in analytical psychology. In: Withers, R. (Ed.) *Controversies in Analytical Psychology*. Hove: Brunner-Routledge, pp. 282–292.

Schön, D.A. (1983) *The Reflective Practitioner: How Professionals Think in Action*. New York: Basic Books.

Siegel, A.M. (1996) *Heinz Kohut and the Psychology of the Self*. Hove: Routledge.

Singer, J. (2000) *Androgyny: The Opposites Within*. York Beach, ME: Nicolas-Hays.

Smith, S.B. (2015) The ontological nature of change: critical connections between the humanistic psychotherapies and Jungian analysis, past, present and future. *Self & Society*, 43(3): 237–247.

Stern, D.B. (2010) *Partners in Thought: Working with Unformulated Experience, Dissociation, and Enactment*. Hove: Routledge.

Stolorow, R.D., Brandchaft, B. and Atwood, G.E. (1987) *Psychoanalytic Treatment: An Intersubjective Approach*. Hillsdale, NJ: The Analytic Press.

United Kingdom Council for Psychotherapy (2019) *UKCP Codes of Ethics and Professional Practice*. London: UKCP. Available at: www.psychotherapy.org.uk/wp-content/uploads/2019/06/UKCP-Code-of-Ethics-and-Professional-Practice-2019.pdf [Accessed: 19 October 2019].

Wachtel, P.L. (2008) *Relational Theory and the Practice of Psychotherapy*. London: Guilford Press.

Walker, M. (1976) *The Double: An Archetypal Configuration*. Available at: http://uranianpsych.org/articles/The%20Double.pdf [Accessed: 7th September 2017].

Wampold, B.E. and Imel, Z.E. (2015) *The Great Psychotherapy Debate: The Evidence for What Makes Psychotherapy Work* (2nd Edition). New York: Routledge.

Welwood, J. (2007) *Perfect Love, Imperfect Relationships: Healing the Wound of the Heart*. Boston, MA: Shambala Publications, Inc.

3.2 Firefighting

Managing sexual ruptures and transgressions within counselling and psychotherapy services

Biljana van Rijn

Introduction

This chapter focusses on sexual transgressions and boundary infringements from the perspective of counselling and psychotherapy organisations. I draw on my experience of managing a large low-cost counselling and psychotherapy community service, which is also a training clinic; experiences of colleagues within the statutory and voluntary sector; and literature on the subject.

Sexuality and sexual attraction naturally emerge in human interaction and we can assume that they will be present within the intimate and supportive environments of counselling and psychotherapy. Where therapy takes place in organisations they will emerge in a variety of ways, not necessarily resulting in abusive transgressions, but still having an impact on the therapeutic process.

An example of this was a call I received from a male client who stopped therapy after a couple of months and asked whether he could change to a different therapist. When I inquired into his reasons, he told me that he couldn't work with this therapist because she was 'too attractive, like a model'. He felt distracted and unable to talk to her about this, or any of his presenting issues and wanted to see someone 'less attractive'. He was certain that she noticed his feelings and his discomfort, but did not say anything. This contributed to his embarrassment and unwillingness broach the subject with her.

On another occasion, a therapist wanted to stop working with the client because he felt attracted to her. He did not have any intentions of acting on this feelings and wanted to protect both the client and himself, and act professionally. He spoke about it in supervision and the supervisor recommended the ending.

Both cases were well intentioned. A lack of therapeutic dialogue meant that the therapy was curtailed, and ended prematurely, although it did not lead to harm. Ideally, issues like this could be more effectively addressed within the setting of the therapist's personal therapy and supervision. This did not happen in either of these cases and the impact of sexual attraction led to premature endings with clients. Clinical managers, however, rarely have an opportunity to address these issues gradually. We mostly become aware of difficulties when something goes wrong, when there might be too late to intervene, or when there are therapeutic ruptures and transgressions, and we are called upon to contain the process and reduce harm.

My aim as a manager in this context would normally be to create and support an open and engaged organisational environment, focussed on harm prevention and fostering of ethical practice, and on ensuring client safety. In this chapter, I would like to share some of my thinking and experience with you as a reader and invite you to reflect of your experiences.

Professional standards and literature on boundary violations and transgressions in psychotherapy

Sexual boundaries of the relationships between therapists and clients are, at first sight, very clear. Some ethical codes state this overtly:

> 1.3 The psychotherapist undertakes not to abuse or exploit the relationship they have with their clients, current or past, for any purpose, including the psychotherapist's sexual, emotional or financial gain.
>
> (UKCP, 2017, p. 3)

Others, like British Association for Counselling and Psychotherapy (2018), invite an in-depth reflection on ethical principles, values, and standards of good practice, which also stress the importance of clarity about the boundaries of the therapeutic relationship.

Although all therapists know that sexual abuse and exploitation of clients are unethical, it is possible for boundary infractions to become more graduated and complex within the intimacy and intensity of the therapeutic relationship.

Research literature in this area is limited, but there is a growing awareness of sexual transgressions in the helping professions. One of the early examples is a paper published in 1999, which examined the accepted complaints directed at Social Workers in the USA, a group of professionals with similar boundaries and challenges to psychotherapy (Strom-Gottfried, 1999). The researchers found that 72.7% of these cases involved some form of sexual violation. The majority of the claimants in this study were female (77.5%). This is similar to a later figure of 80% derived from a wider pool of mental health practitioners (Alpert and Steinberg, 2017). More specific figures for psychotherapists estimate that 2.5% of female and 9.4% of male psychotherapists have engaged in sexual contact with their clients, and 87% experienced sexual attraction towards clients (Pope et al., 1986, 2006). This normalises the feelings of sexual attraction, and potentially shows that only in small number of cases those feelings lead to inappropriate behaviours. However, the same figures viewed from a different perspective, also show that nearly one in ten male therapists, and a smaller number of female therapists, engage in sexual contact with their clients. This raises a note of alarm. How is it that, despite the training, knowledge, and the professional ethical codes, there are so many therapists who abuse privileges of the therapeutic process?

Violations in mental health professions, reported in other publications, included a range of behaviours, such as sex as treatment (sometimes by using techniques interpreted as sexual by the clients, such as holding), sex during treatment, sexual assault or harassment, or sex with a client's partner.

How do boundary violations occur?

Within the field of psychotherapy, there is a range of papers particularly within the psychoanalytic literature giving insight into the phenomenon of boundary violations and transgressions such as (Alpert and Steinberg, 2017; Celenza, 1998, 2017; Mann, 2015). The authors expressed their hope that studying these phenomena would help to reduce enactments and protect client. I share that hope.

The psychotherapy literature shows that enactments by psychotherapists happen, irrespective of their education, status, or experience (Gabbard, 2017), in different types of treatment (Alpert and Steinberg, 2017) and in different mental health settings. This raises questions about what might predispose therapists to engage in sexual contact with client. A psychoanalytic paper by Celenza (1998) presented some preliminary findings on the predisposing factors and highlighted individual internal difficulties such as: long-standing and unresolved problems with self-esteem, sexualisation of early (pregenital) needs, restricted awareness of fantasy, experience of covert boundary transgressions by a parental figure, unresolved anger towards authority figures, intolerance of negative transference, and defensive transformation of countertransference hate into countertransference love. Gabbard (2017) and Mann (2015) focussed more on the mechanisms by which therapists' circumvented their knowledge, experience, and professional standards, primary of which was rationalisation. Their writing shows a range of rationalisations by the therapists which include: statements about the supposed helpfulness of the sexual relationship to the client; the expressed feelings of love for the client (a 'special relationship'); views on the informed choice clients exercised when they engaged in a sexual relationship with the therapist as consenting adults; and the assumed lack of harm. None of these arguments acknowledge that a therapeutic relationship is asymmetric in terms of power and responsibility. It therefore comes as no surprise that Pope and Vetter (1991), in a systematic survey of clients, found that 90% of clients who reported having sex with their therapist during treatment found it harmful. This survey, and a further study by Blechner (2017), found that 80% of clients who reported having sex with their therapist after the treatment also found it harmful. Harm is further exacerbated when we know that clients who are most at risk from sexual abuse by their therapists are those who have a history of sexual abuse in childhood (Alpert and Steinberg, 2017). The paper by Alpert and Steinberg does not go into the reasons for this, but some of the similar factors reported by Celenza (1998) in relation to transgressors could be of relevance. Clients with a history of sexual abuse usually suffer from long-standing problems with self-esteem and have often experienced sexualisation of their early developmental needs and covert boundary transgressions by an authority figure. Added to that is the impact of trauma, which makes this client group particularly vulnerable.

Preventing abuse and dealing with transgressions is complicated by difficulties in recognising that the problem is occurring, as well as the silencing in the professional community (Alpert and Steinberg, 2017; Brüggemann et al., 2012; Gabbard, 2017). Although there is a typology of transgressors developed by Gabbard and Lester (1995), which includes categories such as predatory psychopathic and psychotic therapists, as well as the literature on the background of predisposing factors (Celenza, 1998), the majority or therapists who breach sexual boundaries are likely to be isolated practitioners in personal distress, believing they are in love with the patients, trying to 'save' them or engaging in other rationalisations for their behaviour. The abuse is much more likely to emerge gradually, as a slippery slope of boundary infringements, than as a sudden violent assault.

Psychotherapy is an intimate emotional and confidential process. Although profoundly different to our usual social experiences, it is also familiar and could resemble an emotionally close and private intimate relationship. It is perhaps not surprising in that context, that the majority of the reported complaints in this area relate to private practice where therapists work in a degree of isolation. However, the literature tells us that the victims often don't want to report the abuser. All too frequently they blame themselves for the transgressions and are blamed for them by the professionals (Alpert and Steinberg, 2017; Brüggemann et al., 2012). Sadly, this might suggest that the real scope of the transgressions is larger than we know.

Although there is no specific literature or research on violations within counselling and psychotherapy services (as different from the private practice settings), there is no reason to think that the findings in the literature above are not transferable to a range of contexts and it is, therefore, essential to reflect on good practice and safety in these environments.

Counselling and psychotherapy services

Counselling and psychotherapy services in the UK are hugely varied in terms of their size, setting, and resources.

Statutory services are often situated within the NHS, with large numbers of staff, structured professional hierarchy, and a range of organisational policies and procedures. Depending on the type of service, and the population they serve, statutory services usually offer shorter-term therapy, unless they specialize in specific presenting problems (such as trauma or personality disorders). Although these services have more professional support available, they generally deal with large client populations with multiple and complex needs and experience stresses arising from working in large organisations. Personal distress and burnout are factors in reduced competency and increased vulnerability by the therapists which put them at increased risks of ethical breaches and enactments (Barnett, 2014; O'Connor, 2001). An advantage of these services in the UK are the well-established management structures and policies and procedures designed to prevent harm. Although this could be supportive to therapists and clients, it does not always help clients to take a step of disclosing the abuse. The intensity of monitoring and a fear of being misunderstood and blamed could also make the therapists risk-averse and reluctant to engage in the reflection of issues like sexuality.

Community services and counselling provision in educational establishments are far more varied in size and resources. In many community service, there is only a small number of professional staff and the majority of the service is provided by the therapists in training. Some might operate with a single part-time member of staff who manages the service with a support of a voluntary board. Others could be much larger. Although the community-based organisations generally operate with far more limited resources than the statutory services, they frequently work with clients with complex needs, referred to them by the statutory services because they need longer-term treatment, but have presentations not deemed sufficiently severe to require tertiary or crisis services. In the contexts of community services, therapist vulnerability could stem from their lack of knowledge and experience (Barnett, 2014), or from personal vulnerabilities which trainees bring into the training and practice settings (Johnson et al., 2008). To illustrate this, I can quote from the experience of the service I manage. According to our evaluation data for 2017/2018 approximately 70% of all clients who attended the service reported with traumatic symptoms. These symptoms, measured by the NHS approved measure IES-r (Beck et al., 2008), showed that over 50% of these clients experienced symptoms of trauma that were high enough to suppress the immune system, even ten years after the traumatic event (Kawamura et al., 2001). This highlights the reality faced by inexperienced therapists, who are starting their training practise by working with a very vulnerable group of clients, as well as the potential challenges this presents to clinical managers and supervisors in these settings.

Challenges in organisations

According to Blechner (2017) and Gabbard (2017), the majority of therapists who abuse their clients through sexual violations, do so despite training and knowledge of the ethical codes, often at times of personal vulnerability and by engaging in rationalisations for their behaviour. Rationalisations could be partially explained by the feelings of shame and anxiety about inappropriate behaviours. Shame is a private experience, and likely to result in secrecy. When we know that clients do not always raise their concerns about sexual transgressions, sometimes for reasons related to other experiences of sexual abuse, we can recognise the importance and responsibility of organisations to recognise transgressive behaviours and address them. Taking this responsibility is not a simple matter. It is a challenge for any organisation to prevent harm by addressing something hidden from view. In order to do that, we need to consider all available avenues.

Supervision is one the professional arenas where potential sexual transgressions by the therapist might emerge. Most counselling organisations have a provision for clinical supervision. Where therapists are trainees, the in-house supervision as well as external training supervision are a requirement for the therapists. Services that employ qualified therapists also have a provision for clinical supervision, provided in-house or by the external supervisors. In both types of services managers also provide supervision or consultation focussed on management issues related to the caseload, performance-related issues, and personal support. They sometimes provide clinical supervision as well.

Another professional arena that can be helpful to therapists in challenging their journey into sexual transgressions is personal psychotherapy. Personal psychotherapy is often not a requirement for qualified practitioners, but is mandatory for psychotherapy students in training.

Although service managers have an overall responsibility and oversight within organisations it is important to recognise that prevention of harm requires involvement of the whole organisation as well as management and professional structures to support dealing with it.

The following two case vignettes will illustrate some of the relevant themes in different types of organisations, followed by my reflection on each case and a summary of the management themes.

Case vignette 1: mutual attraction

In the counselling service which offered a limited duration of psychotherapy, a female trainee in her mid-30s, Janna, has been referred a client with addiction problems.

The client, Edi, was an attractive man in his 20s who had just completed his in-patient rehabilitation programme for addiction. He still lived in a hostel and aimed to use counselling for support while he was establishing and adapting to his new life in the community.

Edi's family of origin was dysfunctional. Both of his parents were addicted to heroin and had a chaotic lifestyle. Edi was neglected, and physically and sexually abused until he was taken away from his family and fostered. He started using heroin in his teens, eventually becoming homeless. He went into a rehab after a spell in prison.

Janna started her psychotherapy training after a range of stressful life events. She was made redundant from her job, and the marriage to her long-term partner ended with his affair, only a year after they married. Counselling helped her through this period and she decided to change career and become a counsellor. She was living with her parents after the divorce.

Janna was delighted to have a new client. She liked Edi. They had a good rapport and she was looking forward to seeing him each week. She found him very attractive but felt very uneasy and tried not to think about those feelings.

Edi idealized Janna. She physically reminded him of his ex-girlfriend and he felt a sense of excitement at the thought that she was waiting for him every week and was deeply interested in his feelings and well-being. He arrived to the centre early, trying to catch a glimpse of her coming in, trying to guess which car belonged to her, and daydreamed about having her as his girlfriend.

Janna noticed that he was always arriving early for his appointments and started inviting him into the session before their agreed starting time. She was working in the evenings and eventually changed his appointment to her last. She usually bumped into him as she was leaving the building and they would often spend a few minutes chatting to each other. She started wondering whether it would be ok to have a drink with him.

Throughout this time Janna had regular clinical supervision and personal psychotherapy but didn't talk about her feelings towards Edi. She rationalised the experience as having a particularly good rapport. Eventually, the receptionist noticed that they were both still talking outside when she locked up the building at the end of the day and informed the clinical manager. The manager talked to both the therapist and the client separately.

Edi was keen to reassure the manager that Janna didn't do anything wrong and that he was the one who had feelings for her and wanted more than a counselling relationship. However, he also acknowledged that he really wanted her to like him, and didn't talk about the troubling feelings and concerns with her. During the conversation, he said that he wasn't sure about going back into counselling with her. He was referred to a different therapist.

In the conversation with the manager, Janna started to recognize how far her feelings for Edi have gone beyond the therapeutic concern and empathy, and the gradual slipping of boundaries. She felt shocked by her behaviour, as if suddenly waking up from a trance. She now recognised the need to talk this through in her supervision and personal psychotherapy.

Reflection on the case

In cases where therapeutic boundaries were infringed, the external behaviours, such as timing and duration of the appointments are frequently one of the visible signals of overinvolvement, potentially leading to boundary violations.

Once recognized, there is the often delicate task of containing the enactment and supporting the therapist and the client without shaming. In this case vignette, it could be sufficient to talk to the therapist and the client, re-establish boundaries and direct the therapist to address these issues in supervision and personal therapy.

Where the therapist is still in training, the tutor would also need to be involved, as an additional support and challenge. Most counselling organisations that work with trainees have input into the formative assessment process within the training establishment, formally through providing placement reports, and informally through regular contact and reviews. Clinical managers could be reluctant to use this route, partly because they wished to protect the therapist, partly because they might feel uninvolved with the training process.

However, the role of practice assessment cannot be overlooked in supporting the development of individual therapists and needs to involve assessment of fitness to practice, and protection of clients. Assessment of competence to practice during training can be complex and ambiguous process (Johnson et al., 2008) and practice placements have a gatekeeping role in it, as well as being places of learning and development.

As addressed in Chapters 2.1–2.3 of this book, supervision has a significant role in addressing issues of working with sexuality in therapeutic practice, and it is helpful to have a trusting and collaborative relationship with the supervisors to support safe practice.

Trainee therapists are particularly vulnerable to feelings of shame in their practice and the levels of disclosure tend to depend on the levels of trust in the supervisory relationship. Janna didn't initially talk about her feelings for Edi in supervision, and hardly brought the case into the sessions. Her supervisor was external to her placement organisation, but with an agreement of open communication regarding the practice of supervisees. Once the clinical manager was involved, and contacted the supervisor, this opened up the exploration in supervision about the impact of the boundary infringement on the work with Edi. During this exploration, Janna recognized how the magical feeling of falling in love with her, much like his previous use of heroin, numbed Edi from feeling the pain of loss of both his parents and the impact of addiction on his life. An enactment in a relationship with her had a potential to replicate the pattern with untrustworthy parental figures, even to the point of it being stopped by someone in authority. Although intensely painful, talking about this in supervision over several appointments, helped Janna to reflect and recognize the gradual and entrancing dynamic of entering into a transferential process, and its impact on both of them. As a trainee, she didn't have a clear sense of what a sexual boundary infringement could entail and that it didn't necessarily have to involve a full sexual act.

It is apparent in this case vignette that Janna's personal circumstances were a part of the enactment with her client, and this highlighted the importance of her own psychotherapy.

A majority of therapists in training in the UK, particularly those who study humanistic, relational, and psychodynamic approaches, engage in regular personal therapy throughout their training. The fact that it is normally a confidential process which runs in parallel to training is helpful in addressing deep personal feelings that arise during placement practice and training. As a psychotherapist, I have often worked with clients like Janna, who developed intense feelings of sexual attraction to their clients and colluded with them. Therapists are ordinary human beings and like Janna, those feelings and boundary infringements related to them, are more likely when they feel vulnerable. Exploration of these feelings in personal psychotherapy has a potential to support the practitioner in facing the feelings and exploring them within the safety of the confidential therapeutic environment. However, therapists often need to overcome feelings of shame and the internal self-deception in order to use this space effectively. Used well, and in addition to clinical supervision, personal psychotherapy is essential in prevention of sexual enactments in psychotherapy and the protection of clients. Although the psychotherapy is confidential, an intervention by the clinical manager, like the one in this case vignette, can facilitate the therapist's awareness and the ability to use it.

Case vignette 2: crossing the boundaries

Ian worked as a psychotherapist in a busy NHS service specializing in working with victims of sexual abuse. Majority of his clients experienced abuse in childhood as well as in their adult life. The service offered long-term outpatient individual psychotherapy, alongside group treatments. The work at the service has always been stressful and the clients frequently presented with symptoms of self-harm and suicidal ideation and behaviour. Ian was also going through a difficult period in his personal life. His relationship with his long-term partner was ending, and he developed a habit of working long hours in order to postpone having to go to an empty home. He had no therapeutic support at this time and felt that he could not afford it.

The clinical manager valued Ian's experience, his warmth, and his commitment to working with clients who often struggled to trust him. Recently, the service experienced funding cuts which meant that it became impossible to replace staff who left and the remaining therapists had to take up more clinical work. The manager was also overworked and struggling to fulfil her duties as a supervisor. Within her role, she had often dealt with various levels of complaints but was surprised to receive a complaint from a young female patient who was receiving therapy from Ian. She said that Ian was spending too much time focussing on the details of her sexual abuse and that she knew that he was sexually aroused by it. He touched her and offered to physically hold her during therapy. In her subsequent conversation with Ian, he acknowledged that he asked the patient to talk about her sexual abuse in graphic detail, with a belief (contrary to his previous experience and practice) that this would be beneficial to her. He said that he felt very fond of her and desperately sad about the abuse she experienced. He talked about the importance of touch and his understanding how it was important in the healing process. Ian felt that he wanted to hold this client and firmly believed that his touch would be soothing. He was incredulous about her complaint, particularly as he hugged her after each session believing that she appreciated the contact (despite knowing that she never asked for it). He felt certainty in his assessment and continued to defend his actions during the conversation with the manager. Despite the evidence to the contrary, he continued to believe that he was best placed to understand this client. The manager discovered that, although Ian attended the in-house group supervision, he didn't discuss the work with this client with his supervisor.

In this case, the client's complaint was upheld within the service. With her consent, she was referred to another therapist and supported in considering using an external professional ethical complaints procedure. She eventually decided to raise an ethical complaint and the service conducted a disciplinary procedure against Ian. As a result of both actions, he was stopped from working with other clients for a period of time and was mandated to an intensive period of supervision and psychotherapy, which gradually helped him to move away from his defensiveness and recognise the harmfulness of his behaviour, as well as his own vulnerability. He eventually returned to practice after a long period of rehabilitation.

Reflection

This case vignette is an example of an experienced therapist who engaged in boundary infringements and created a rationalisations for his own harmful behaviour. How did this happen?

The case above illustrates a situation all too common in our busy services, where staff and management become increasingly stressed and burnt out, and the space for reflection and support in supervision that could prevent an enactment disappears in the overall business.

Pairing vulnerable clients and needy therapists potentially creates an environment where fluctuations in the individual fitness to practice are not addressed with damaging consequences. In this case, the clinical manager had a particular role in recognising the impact of the pressured work environment and the additional level of personal stress Ian was experiencing. In this environment, the therapist's natural warmth and commitment might have been a factor in his overinvolvement and harmful behaviour, when he was going through a painful personal experience and was in need of touch and closeness himself.

Supervision for qualified and experienced therapists is usually a requirement by the professional bodies but its importance is not always recognised by the services, particularly at times of increased stress and workload. Sometimes, managers expect therapists to initiate supervision, and the boundaries between the management and the clinical supervision are not clear. However, times when we are not functioning at our best, are usually not the times when we are aware of our needs. In these situations, it is the role of the clinical manager to ensure regular access to supervision, and a possibility of a referral for individual psychotherapy.

Summary of management themes

Both cases demonstrate some of the themes in dealing with sexual transgressions and boundary infringements in organisations. I would like to summarise them as *developing awareness, containment*, and *collaboration*.

Developing awareness in both cases related to paying attention to the environment of the organisation and behaviours related to boundaries. This could be very different depending on the organisation and change over time.

Within the service where Janna practised, it was important to be aware of the relative inexperience of the therapists and their additional support needs. Obstacles to developing awareness of potential transgressions, in Ian's organisation, had some of the different elements and related to the stressful work environment and the absence of the usual areas of staff support.

Containment relates to working with both the therapists and their clients who were involved in the transgression, ensuring safety, and supporting rehabilitation and redress for the client. For therapists involved in transgressions, there may be a need for a referral to the professional bodies responsible for ethical conduct, prior to rehabilitation. In working with clients, it is always too important to address their individual needs, provide safety, and provide support. Clients may have a complex relationship with the abuser, and a mix of conflicting feelings towards them. The process of ensuring psychological safety may not be simple but always needs to involve consultation and involvement in the decision-making process.

Collaboration, as reflected in both case vignettes, shows that managers need to. at the least, be able to have an involvement with clinical supervisors and training programmes, where appropriate. Clear three-handed contracts about sharing information, and roles with external and internal supervisors, and with the training programmes are particularly helpful.

I will further elaborate these themes in the discussion.

Discussion

This chapter illustrates that professional rules are not in themselves sufficient in dealing with and preventing sexual transgressions and infringements.

Although sexual exploitation has always been prohibited within psychotherapy, professional codes have changed emphasis over time and increased the role of reflection over the rules. This is not surprising, given how easy it seems to be to create a justification to non-adherence to the rules.

Over time, there have also been differences in how the profession viewed different boundaries. For example, although physical touch could lead to sexual enactments and become abusive even when the therapist did not intend it as sexual, views on it in humanistic psychotherapies have changed over time. When I trained as a psychotherapist in the 1980s, physical contact, such as hugging and holding clients, was seen as appropriate and therapeutic, and I experienced both. Increased awareness of the depth of feeling this could arouse and a potential for harm has changed this practice, which is now far less common or accepted. There are also still differing opinions within the profession of psychotherapy on whether it might be possible to engage in a sexual relationship with a client after the end of treatment. My position on this, based on my experience as well as the literature, is that this is never appropriate, and constituted an abuse of power. However, as feelings of sexuality and sexual attraction are both powerful and widespread in social interactions, our focus as professionals needs to be on working with them safely and openly and preventing boundary infractions and harm.

The literature on the subject shows the importance of preventing sexual abuse and exploitation of clients, and suggests that this is not happening sufficiently (Blechner, 2017). In this retrospective paper on sexual boundary violation, Gabbard (2017) writes:

> My growing pessimism has emerged from the recognition of the numerous ways that individual clinicians can rationalize why their situation is somehow different from others, the failure to utilize consultation of supervision, and the inability of institutions to see what's in front of their eyes.
>
> (p. 151)

This is a sobering reflection from one of the prominent authors on the subject, which stresses the importance of tackling the complex problem of sexual transgressions in psychotherapy from different practice perspectives.

However, in order to remain open and non-blaming, we also need to adopt a stance of personal humility and reflection, and in that spirit, I would like to offer a reflection on some of my personal experiences.

We are all vulnerable some of the time

I have dealt with cases similar to these case vignettes and many others over a number of years. I also experienced sexual attraction in therapeutic relationships and worked with supervisees who have. Because of that, I recognise the intensity, secrecy, and deep shame within those experiences as well as their complexity and variety. As a psychotherapist, I have found support and challenge primarily in my own supervision and psychotherapy, which helped me voice and navigate these issues over the period of my training, as well as throughout my career. Although this is an ongoing practice theme, I now appreciate the richness of the material they bring to the therapeutic process and endeavour to engage my supervisees in exploration. However, most of the hardest challenges for me happened while I was a trainee. At those times, dealing with sexual attraction in addition to the rest of the learning and stress of in-depth psychotherapy training, brought up feelings of incompetence, shame, and fear. The subject was not addressed as a part of the training curriculum, which made my feelings more intense, as I believed that my peers didn't have to struggle with them.

As a clinical manager, I have often felt frustrated by the limitations of my role. Addressing these issues has often felt like 'firefighting'. I have found most help in recognising difficulties early from non-clinical staff who were on the ground and in regular contact with clients and therapists and were often the first to notice small shifts in boundaries and unusual actions. Those could be related to changes to the schedule, increased contact between the therapist and a client, and the ways the communication flows within the organisation. They have been an invaluable resource in creating safety and an early warning system in flagging up difficulties.

Preventing harm

The previous text gives some suggestion about helpful practices in the prevention of harm in counselling and psychotherapy organisations. I would like to summarise them, as they are ultimately our main aim in area of sexual transgressions.

The literature highlights some of the precursors to engaging in sexual boundary infringements and violations. Awareness of and attention to external boundary violations are an important organisational signal and could be viewed as 'red flags' (Strom-Gottfried, 1999). Some of them have been illustrated in the previous text and include:

- Changes to the therapeutic frame, such as extended sessions, changes to the schedule enabling increased contact to favoured clients, offering additional sessions, external contact, not charging, exchanging gifts or favours, socialising etc. These and other similar behaviours, once noticed can show a pattern of apparent and obvious breaches of the therapeutic frame. Awareness of these behaviours can support clinical mangers in intervening early on the slippery slope of boundary infringements and preventing harm and abuse.
- Attention to the additional stressors within the service environment. For example, working in an environment where therapists are seeing too many clients and working excessive hours impacting on their work-life

balance, might also make them more vulnerable to experiencing contact with some clients as a fulfilment of their social needs.
- Attention to the individual staff. Assessment of someone's fitness to practice means that managers need to have a way of knowing and recognising that their staff are experiencing difficulties in coping, or are going through a period of personal crisis. Fitness to practice fluctuates in all clinical environments, and therapists in crisis are no better than any other profession in recognising that they are struggling. Many therapists, in my experience, have a highly developed sense of responsibility and find it hard to let go of their role as helpers.

Collaboration with other professionals can help in recognising the 'red flags'. This could include supervisors, practice tutors (with trainees) and, indirectly, psychotherapists, by enabling access to personal psychotherapy. This collaboration could be highly supportive to the therapist and facilitate the process of psychological containment and support, essential to prevention.

Other members of staff in the organisation could be another source of support. One of the advantages of having therapy within an organisation for clients often lies in having access to more people on the ground, in contrast to seeing a sole practitioner in private practice. Finding a sympathetic ear while talking informally to an administrator or a receptionist is often supportive to clients, who might question whether something they experienced is a 'normal' practice or just help them to share an experience they are unsure of. These conversations could bring potential ethical problems to light and lead to useful preventative work with both the therapist and the client. For example, being told that a particular therapist often extended the appointments, helped me to open up an exploratory dialogue with them, and supported them in holding the frame.

Clinical managers could enhance this informal process greatly by ensuring that the more formal and confidential supportive structures, like supervision, are used in this way, and that management supervision is used, as well as clinical supervision. Clinical supervision in many organisations is provided by supervisors who are external to the organisation and perform a consultative function. In those cases, it is important to attend to the contract with the supervisor which clearly stipulates the material which is confidential, as well as the limits to confidentiality and channels of communication within the management structure. Clarity and levels of open communication which enables members of staff to talk to one another and raise questions can only flourish in an environment which has clear boundaries but is not punitive.

Training issues: assessing 'psychological fitness'

Training issues are related to prevention of harm but have some distinctive features that I would like to highlight. Work and life stress can affect anyone's fitness to practice and this may lead an individual therapist to gradual increase in boundary infractions and sexual enactments with clients. However, we also need to address this issue also from the perspective of starting to practice and the responsibilities of training organisations. The assessment of competency to practice can be particularly complex in psychotherapy training, and a paper by Barnett (2014) discusses this from the position of assessing professional competence during psychologist training in the USA. Johnson, one of the authors in this paper, also wrote in 2008 that his perception was that training programmes could be too lenient in assessing practice (Johnson et al., 2008).

In the UK, where training, placement practice, and supervision, normally take place in different settings, the assessment of competence to practice is even more challenging. It is not uncommon for psychotherapy students to enter training motivated by various and distressing personal experiences and history (Bager-Charleson et al., 2010), or have experience of mental health issues. This could support them in developing empathy and patience in working with their clients. At times, it could also add to their personal vulnerability. Psychotherapy training programmes are often life-changing for students and involve a great deal of personal exploration. Tutors' assessment role combines the summative assessment of academic and professional achievements, as well as a formative assessment of personal readiness and competence. Johnson commentary in the Barnett paper (2014) highlighted the assessment of 'moral character' (honesty and integrity), as well as 'psychological fitness', defined as emotional and mental stability and robustness. This is not easy to assess within a context of a training programme, and tutors need to rely on supervision and placement reports, as well trust that the required personal psychotherapy is sufficiently effective for individual students. As supervision normally relies on the therapist to bring in the material, and personal psychotherapy is confidential, difficulties that are potentially shameful and prone to rationalisations such as sexual transgressions are often most likely to first become apparent in placement practice.

Involving placement organisations in the assessment of practice is not practically easy, particularly where it takes place separately from a training institution. However, overcoming those difficulties could be very rewarding. I have found that having three-way conversations with tutors and supervisors, helped me to build a much fuller picture of individual students. In those cases, we usually found that we all noticed the same (problematic) process or behaviour, but were not aware of the extent of it, or the impact it had in different contexts. Based on our discussions, it was much easier to develop a planned response that would take into account client's needs, as well as the student's. However, this is difficult to achieve in day to day practice and I do not underestimate the time it takes to have such dialogues. In my experience they have only happened when I was aware that there was a problem, which sadly limits the scope of the prevention.

When harm has already happened: dealing with cases of sexual boundary violations

Preventative and supportive functions within the counselling organisations need to go hand in hand with client protection. Where sexual violations take place, client protection always needs to take a priority. A part of that involves dealing with complaints within the organisation, but in some cases, it also involves reporting the abuser to the ethical and professional bodies, and/or police, in cases of violent abuse and rape.

Dealing with sexual abuse and boundary violations usually starts within organisations and relies on their complaints and disciplinary policies and procedures, which all services are required to have. However, we know that in the area of sexual exploitation clients often might need help in initiating the complaint process. Sometimes this is the case because of the dynamic of the seductive transferential relationship with the abuser, where the clients feel 'special' and 'chosen' by the idealised therapist. The experience could also become overwhelming and re-traumatising if clients have experienced abuse in the past, and they may find it difficult to engage with the complaints process without support.

In addition to these potential obstacles to addressing transgressions, some of the organisational complaints procedures might seem forbidding and inaccessible to clients. Organisational procedures support the process of conducting objective hearings and aim to protect an organisation against vexatious complaints, as well as provide safety and redress for the client. That may well be best practice in many circumstances. However, clients might also need support in taking action, and this sometimes means that the manager might need to take a lead in starting the formal (disciplinary) process, even if the client hasn't made a complaint. In one of the cases I am aware of, it was only after the abusive therapist was disciplined, and a professional complaint upheld that the client felt able to talk about and acknowledge the abuse.

Where violations have occurred, they may need to be reported to the broader professional body, as well as dealt with internally within the organisation (UKCP, BACP, HCPC, or BPS, within the UK), in order to ensure good ethical standards within the profession and prevent the abusers from continuing their practice without acknowledgement, reparation, or engagement in a process of rehabilitation.

Once the incident is reported it would normally be the role of an ethical professional body to instigate the formal processes, respond, and engage with both the client and the therapist. Where the client does not wish to involve the professional body or raise an ethical complaint, services have different options. They may raise an ethical complaint as an organisation, and/or conduct an internal disciplinary procedure. This may be a complex choice to make and often relies on an assessment of the severity of the transgression and therapist's willingness to engage in reflection and rehabilitation. However, salutary and much-publicised cases from other helping professions, where abusers have been allowed to continue abusing vulnerable clients for years, might suggest that internal communities might not always be best placed to make such assessments. I would suggest that it is usually advisable to involve independent ethical bodies in this process.

Final words

Although examples I have used are mostly summaries and do not represent individual clients or therapists, I hope sharing some of my experiences and reflections could go some way to supporting other managers of clinical organisations in opening up discussions and finding ways of preventing and dealing with sexual infringements and boundary violations in our field. I am concerned that the problem of transgressions and exploitation could be much larger in our profession than we know. We owe our clients, and ourselves, a duty to address it.

References

Alpert, J. L., & Steinberg, A. (2017). Sexual boundary violations: A century of violations and a time to analyze. *Psychoanalytic Psychology, 34*(2), 144–150. doi:10.1037/pap0000094.

Bager-Charleson, S., Chatterjee, S. G., Critchley, P., Lauchlan, S., McGrath, S., & Thorpe, F. (2010). *Why Therapists Choose to Become Therapists: A Practice-Based Inquiry.* London: Karnac Books.

Barnett, J. E. (2014). Sexual feelings and behaviors in the psychotherapy relationship: An ethics perspective. *Journal of Clinical Psychology, 70*(2), 170–181. doi:10.1002/jclp.22068.

Beck, J. G., Grant, D. M., Read, J. P., Clapp, J. D., Coffey, S. F., Miller, L. M., & Palyo, S. A. (2008). The impact of event scale-revised: Psychometric properties in a sample of motor vehicle accident survivors. *Journal of anxiety disorders, 22*(2), 187–198. doi:10.1016/j.janxdis.2007.02.007.

Blechner, M. J. (2017). Dissociation among psychoanalysts about sexual boundary violations. In J. Petrucelli & S. Schoen (Eds.), *Unknowable, Unspeakable, and Unsprung: Psychoanalytic Perspectives on Truth, Scandal, Secrets, and Lies* (pp. 171–180). New York: Routledge/Taylor & Francis Group.

British Association for Counselling and Psychotherapy. (2018). Ethical framework for the counselling professions. From BACP www.bacp.co.uk/events-and-resources/ethics-and-standards/ethical-framework-for-the-counselling-professions/.

Brüggemann, A. J., Wijma, B., & Swahnberg, K. (2012). Patients' silence following healthcare staff's ethical transgressions. *Nursing Ethics, 19*(6), 750–763. doi:10.1177/0969733011423294.

Celenza, A. (1998). Precursors to therapist sexual misconduct: Preliminary findings. *Psychoanalytic Psychology, 15*(3), 378–395. doi:10.1037/0736-9735.15.3.378.

Celenza, A. (2017). Lessons on or about the couch: What sexual boundary transgressions can teach us about everyday practice. *Psychoanalytic Psychology, 34*(2), 157–162. doi:10.1037/pap0000095.

Gabbard, G. O. (2017). Sexual boundary violations in psychoanalysis: A 30-year retrospective. *Psychoanalytic Psychology, 34*(2), 151–156. doi:10.1037/pap0000079.

Gabbard, G. O., & Lester, E. P. (1995). *Boundaries and Boundary Violations in Psychoanalysis*. Arlington, VA: American Psychiatric Publishing, Inc.

Johnson, W. B., Elman, N. S., Forrest, L., Robiner, W. N., Rodolfa, E., & Schaffer, J. B. (2008). Addressing professional competence problems in trainees: Some ethical considerations. *Professional Psychology: Research and Practice, 39*(6), 589–599. doi:10.1037/a0014264.

Kawamura, N., Kim, Y., & Asukai, N. (2001). Suppression of cellular immunity in men with a past history of posttraumatic stress disorder. *The American Journal of Psychiatry, 158*(3), 484–486. doi:10.1176/appi.ajp.158.3.484.

Mann, D. (2015). 'Turning a blind eye' on sexual abuse, boundary violations and therapeutic practice. *Psychodynamic Practice: Individuals, Groups and Organisations, 21*(2), 126–146. doi:10.1080/14753634.2015.1020123.

O'Connor, M. F. (2001). On the etiology and effective management of professional distress and impairment among psychologists. *Professional Psychology: Research and Practice, 32*(4), 345–350. doi:10.1037/0735-7028.32.4.345.

Pope, K. S., & Vetter, V. A. (1991). Prior therapist-patient sexual involvement among patients seen by psychologists. *Psychotherapy: Theory, Research, Practice, Training, 28*(3), 429–438. doi:10.1037/0033-3204.28.3.429.

Pope, K. S., Keith-Spiegel, P., & Tabachnick, B. G. (1986). Sexual attraction to clients: The human therapist and the (sometimes) inhuman training system. *American Psychologist, 41*(2), 147–158. doi:10.1037/0003-066X.41.2.147.

Pope, K. S., Keith-Spiegel, P., & Tabachnick, B. G. (2006). Sexual attraction to clients: The human therapist and the (sometimes) inhuman training system. *Training and Education in Professional Psychology, S*(2), 96–111. doi:10.1037/1931-3918.S.2.96.

Strom-Gottfried, K. (1999). Professional boundaries: An analysis of violations by social workers. *Families in Society, 80*(5), 439–449. doi:10.1606/1044-3894.1473.

UKCP (2017). Ethical principles and code of professional conduct. From UKCP www.psychotherapy.org.uk/wp-content/uploads/2017/11/UKCP-Ethical-Principles-and-Code-of-Professional-Conduct.pdf.

3.3 An ethical container for erotic confusion

Sue Eusden

In this chapter I consider some of the ethical issues relating to sex and sexuality inside the psychotherapy profession.

I briefly explore the history of sexual transgression in psychotherapy and contextualise erotic confusion as an ordinary, inevitable experience in the therapy room, requiring welcoming rather than fear, and creativity rather than shame. I describe how ethics codes can lead to therapists being more frightened than curious, closing down on opportunities for engaging with clients. Rules and regulations don't reach easily into this kind of work.

Drawing on case material I explore consent and contracting, and offer the framework of an ethical compass to help navigate the risks and uncertainties needed for ethical containment when working with erotic confusion in psychotherapy.

In the beginning...

The largest sexual organ is often considered to be the brain since a lot of sex takes place in the mind. In 2007 Brett Kahr, a Freudian analyst, researched sexual fantasies, collecting and cataloguing 19,000 fantasies from the UK and 4,000 from America. His analysis is based on 18,000 respondents to an internet questionnaire and 132 in-depth face-to-face interviews. He discovered that the vast majority of those who responded to his survey do not fantasise about the person they are having sex with, but with someone other. The mind is the organ of the erotic, and a private place where sex and sexuality are free to play.

Each of us have grown in relationships to individuals, families, groups, and cultures. All this happens within a political complexity that usually both sustains and constrains growth. Our erotic life, our sexualities, and gender roles are contextualised and shaped in this landscape which can both ignite and inhibit the imagination. What is permissive and what is transgressive are personal points of navigation for each of us. The link between our private self and our public self is an interesting and complex area. It is often the confusion between the two that brings people into psychotherapy.

In therapy we are primarily working with the imagination. Clients bring their struggles to seek understanding and usually a solution of some kind, perhaps a change in their lives. Sometimes there has been a collapse of the imagination and what was feared has become real, what they most dread has happened in their lives, often 'again'! Sometimes the imagination has gotten tangled up in itself, confused, way-laid perhaps, clinging to some aspect of history. The past and historic traumas and transgressions can have a tight grip on the psyche. The distinction between memory and imagination can be hard to fathom.

Freud (1912) wrote of how transference is to carry across experience from the past into the present. Erotic transference is perhaps, an overlap of memory and imagination. Nick Cave evokes this potent cocktail in his writing:

> ... the imagination, that wildest of erogenous zones, where intense, obsessive yearning can be like a roaring in the heart and the loins both. The imagination becomes both the 'safe space' and the 'un-safe space', a strange blend of almost religious rigour and total abandonment, where everything rises to the starry heavens, even as it goes to hell.
>
> (Cave, 2019)

The attention of the therapist, the intimate nature of a face-to-face encounter and the directness of the dialogue can stir both archaic and current longings and sexual desires. In working with these we are working with the imagination of the client and the imagination of the therapist. This is the creativity in psychotherapy. It is where creativity and destruction run as close bed fellows. As Cave writes, we rise and fall at the same time. How we mind these tensions is partly about who we are as therapists, our personhood; how we seek help from our profession (supervisors, colleagues, etc.) and the theories that help us navigate unknown water to bring an illusion of knowingness to novel terrain.

History and tensions of sexual transgressions

> ... those who do not study the history of boundary violations may be condemned to reenact it with their own patients.
>
> (Gabbard & Lester, 1995, p. 70)

Codes of ethics are clear that the power and responsibility are with the therapist to attend to their duty of care; to do no harm; and to not exploit their clients sexually, financially, or otherwise. Sexual conduct between therapist and client is unethical due to the power imbalance that permeates all aspects of the relationship, and because research has demonstrated that this form of sexual conduct has ramifications for clients in the form of psychological damage (Koocher and Keith-Spiegel, 2008; Pope, 2001). Some ethics codes are explicit about this aspect of the relationship being prohibited, others are more vague.

At the beginning of psychoanalysis Freud struggled to clarify whether transference love was similar or different from love outside the therapy room, remaining somewhat equivocal (Gabbard, 1994; Schafer, 1993), lending an air of ambiguity that still clouds the profession today.

Some of our original leaders and thinkers have had sexual relationships with their clients. Gabbard (1994) cites Carl Jung, Otto Rank, Margaret Mahler, Karen Horney, and Frieda Fromm-Reichmann as examples of analysts who had sexual relationships with their patients. The question is whether these were 'labour pains accompanying the birth of a new field' (Gabbard and Lester, 1995, p. 3) or whether this is ongoing practice in our profession.

Subsequent years have demonstrated that sexual relationships between client and therapist are an Achilles' heel of the profession. In 2017 Gabbard wrote a 30-year retrospective, reflecting on his experiences of working directly with those who have crossed sexual boundaries with clients. He says:

> Despite my efforts and those of others to bring sexual boundary violations into the light of day and encourage prevention through seminars, regular consultation, and institutional awareness and reporting, sexual transgressions with patients continue to occur on a regular basis, often among analysts and therapists who are well-regarded, thoroughly familiar with the risks and dynamics of boundary issues, and well educated.
> (2017, p. 151)

I have spent many years involved in ethical complaints from different perspectives. I have worked on ethics committees, dealing with complaints from clients, supervisees and trainees of psychotherapy institutes. I have also consulted to a significant number of people who have been referred because they have had a complaint made against them. I have also listened to many clients, supervisees, and clients of supervisees telling of inappropriate sexual behaviours from therapists, past and present. This includes sexual relationships with clients. These are mainly experiences that have never been reported, complaints not made. Stories that leave scars and shame in those who have been objectified in relationships that should have been trusting and part of their healing rather than further trauma.

Whilst those complained about are held to account for their actions to ethics committees others transgress without professional consequence. A few professionals do report themselves. I believe that ethics committees only see a small percentage of such boundary violations and that most go unreported.

One question that seems to emerge from the history of transgressions is whether good therapists slide from their ethical perch or whether they are sociopaths/narcissists-in-waiting. Whilst such a binary is too simplistic, it seeks to wonder about the difference between therapists who might act as predators and those who are fallible, perhaps without enough training, supervision, or ethical structure. This binary seeks to 'know' who will transgress and who will not. Binaries can provide certainties, so we know which side of the line we are on.

Patricia Keith-Spiegel, in her seminal book *Red Flags in Psychotherapy* (2014) writes:

> The stereotype of unethical psychotherapists inspires images of unsavoury characters misusing, abusing, or harming vulnerable clients. In my experience, however, most psychotherapists charged with professional misconduct were neither sociopaths nor purposely exploitative, nor did they ever set out to commit an ethical violation.
>
> (2014, p. 1)

Gabbard (2017) agrees, arguing for a less binary approach to understanding those who violate boundaries with clients and that it is oversimplified to suggest there is one group of reasonably ethical practitioners and another group of purely unethical.

Ray Little, writing on the management of erotic/sexual countertransference reactions says:

> When therapeutic boundaries are transgressed/violated, it is frequently because the therapist has not considered his or her countertransference sufficiently and believes that his or her erotic/sexual reaction is real rather than understanding it as an illusion and part of a therapeutic process.
>
> (2018, p. 224)

Sexual boundary violation is a collapse of the imagination into the concrete, equating the symbol with the symbolised.

Gabbard reports feeling increasingly pessimistic about our capacity to prevent such transgressions, stating his recognition of the numerous ways that individual clinicians can rationalise why their situation is unique, the failure to use consultation or supervision effectively, and the inability of institutions to see what is in plain sight. He concludes that the prevention of boundary violations depends largely on a professionals' commitment to put the client's needs before those of the therapist. He agrees with the need for ongoing education and consultation with a trusted colleague, but is clear that we can all be masters of self-deception and as such none of us are exempt from the potential of crossing this line.

This begs the question as to whether writing, such as this book, can influence and help people interrupt a transgression and find the therapeutic edge of the work, or reflect during or afterwards to understand the powerful nature of such enactments.

For the purposes of this chapter I am going to continue with hope and belief that any of us are vulnerable to enacting erotic and sexualised transferences and that professional support through reading, supervision, learning can help us stay alert and awake and give us ways to understand the dynamics, whilst our ethical commitments hold us steady enough through such magnetic storms. We need to keep expanding our ways to think about sex and sexuality and understand how these show up in the therapy room and the therapeutic relationship.

As an educator, the show must go on. However, the wider history of sexual transgressions shows us that education is only one part of the project. Professional accountability through ethics committees will be another and each needs to compliment the other. As a profession we need to let go of the illusion that sexual violation will be a thing of the past, part of our history that we can stop altogether. This is not to support it, but to recognise that psychotherapy as a profession is no different to every other walk of life, where power can be abused and the vulnerable exploited.

The fact that such abuse happens should not limit or define the experience of sex and sexuality in the therapeutic relationship. We need to keep our imaginations alive, not from a place of fear but from a position of curiosity with responsibility. Finding out how to allow, explore, and help another person with their experiences of sex and sexuality is a vital project involving the therapist's own subjectivity and erotic vitality as well as erotic vulnerabilities.

We are always working with sex and sexuality in the consulting room. They are ever present, both implicitly and explicitly. I believe that practitioners need an ethical container, which can be developed, shaped, and strengthened through personal therapy, reflective practice, and honest supervisory relationships, risking opening our intimate settings to care-full scrutiny. This is what is necessary to provide curious spaces and safe relationships for exploration, discovery, and growth, whatever that looks like for the client.

Ethics, power, and enactments

Ethics committees are focussed on protection of the client, practitioner, and profession. In a formal complaint the subtle dynamics at play are eclipsed and a judgment call is required. In this chapter I am interested in where codes, rules, and regulations don't reach but potentially where boundary violations begin and how enactments, and particularly the subtly of erotic enactments, can be fairly elusive to any adversarial conduct process.

One of the functions of a code of ethics is to account for the power dynamics or asymmetry inherent in the practitioner-client relationship. This has led to ethics codes being largely conceptualised and developed within a one-person and a one-and-a half-person psychological frame. However, the cutting edge of contemporary relational psychotherapy explores mutual regulation between humans. There is a shift from thinking about projective identification (Bion, 1967) to mutual inductive identification (Ringstrom, 2010). There is also a significant shift to authentic relating and, as described by Stern (2004), an acknowledgment of "moment[s] of meeting" (p. 244) that may result in deep intra-psychic change. This understanding of what works in therapeutic relationships involves an awareness that both parties must be available for change. So, a contemporary ethical challenge for us is discerning how we account for the reality of mutuality while also tending to asymmetrical power dynamics. In working with a theory of enactments, bilateral on-going mutual influencing, and inductive identification, we enter a two-person frame (Stark, 1999).

Most codes do not account for the subtlety and depth of unconscious, two-person psychological dynamics inherent in working with sex and sexuality and the edges of disturbance evoked that are central in many psychotherapeutic practices. Care, power dynamics, and intimate settings of two people in a room together are highly evocative and can arouse our history and current desires around love and lust as well as trust and betrayal. The therapy room is ripe for evoking and exploring these issues and are ignored at the therapeutic couples' peril.

Gabbard (1994) argues that intense erotic transference is one of the most powerful and challenging phenomena in clinical work. Powerful longings for love and for sexual gratification are likely to elicit enactments in the therapeutic setting that interfere with the therapist's ability to maintain a dual state of awareness in which he or she is both a participant in and an observer of the immediate experience with the patient. These enactments occur on a continuum from frank love affairs between patient and analyst to subtle forms of partial transference gratification. Moreover, the two primary elements in the manifest content of erotic transference, love and lust, may be dissociated from one another and may produce significantly different reactions in the therapist.

Erotic confusion – getting into trouble!

I believe such enactments are a potentially vital part of our work in that they bring the process alive. It is in such expressions that we show what we cannot tell and discover experiences and stories that were not otherwise available to the work. However, such times in therapy need to be deeply underpinned by ethical thinking and questioning on the part of the therapist. In working with people who bring their states of arousal, distress, and dissociation into the room, therapists need to be willing to be recruited into the unconscious world of the client. Jody Davies writes:

> The analyst becomes the magnet that draws out the reenactment of unconsciously internalised systems of self and object and the architect of the transitional arena where such self and object experiences become free to play and reconfigure themselves in more harmonious ways.
> (Davies, 1994, p. 157)

I find her ideas of the therapist as magnet and architect useful, but extend this to understand the dyad as a mutual magnetic field where the erotic forces pull and repulse the therapeutic couple. The responsibility of the therapist, therefore, as well as being a good architect is to have a strong architecture to contain such dynamic possibilities that may emerge.

Wallin argues for the inevitability and desirability of enactments, describing them as potential 'collusions' and 'collisions' (Wallin, 2015). However, as these fragmentary self-states try to enter into the human conversation, they may evoke ethical disorganisation (Eusden, 2011) in the therapist, who also has their own multiple self-states. This is when minding the gap between positive therapeutic intention and unconscious participation in an enactment becomes critical.

I suggest, in a way, we are holding, internally, the following attitude towards the work:

> As we meet, we are likely to get into trouble together. I anticipate this and am prepared through my training, my own therapy and supervision. I have a strong and flexible architecture to contain the magnetic pulls that may arise in our work together. The difference is that when trouble arises here we seek ways to bring it to our attention so we can learn from and resolve it together, and differently to how trouble has ended before. Rather than act it out in ways that might be old and harmful, the hope is we will find new solutions to old confusions and hurts.

The frame of enactments means the therapeutic dyad will often need to get into trouble in order to experience it live, learn about it, and navigate a novel way forward. The idea of an ethical container is that the therapist is a safe pair of hands in this trouble. That they know and take care of their own 'trouble' and do not need their clients to be involved in it! We use our personal learning of our own trouble as a kind of set of muscles, familiar and strong enough to bend into different contortions and configurations and stay creative.

We also know that unconscious processes are bigger than us and happen outside of our awareness. Part of the architecture of an ethical container is having a 'surround sound' of supervision and consultation. It is through supervision and reflective practice that we can potentially catch the edges of these enactments, if we can keep our eyes open, and are prepared to have them opened, we can seek to mind the gaps between our intentions and impacts (Eusden, 2011). I think of this as ethical containment and as necessary in working with sex and sexuality.

Minding the gap

Lucy, a heterosexual therapist responded to a text from a lesbian client, about a change of appointment, ending it with a kiss. A mistake for sure. A confusion of an informal mode of communication in a formal role, sure, but also a lack of care and attention. No harm was intended, yet betrayal was experienced. Something was now 'out', that had not been previously known, an enactment. A gap had appeared between Lucy's intention and impact.

The client was outraged and protested. Lucy was shocked at her own exposure and provided a myriad of apologies. Shame collapsed her imagination and sent her into flights of terror. Her profuse apologies aimed to shield her shame. In wanting to plug the gap the erotic vitality in the 'mistake' was potentially lost. Fortunately the client maintained her protest until the therapist was able to open her eyes and ears.

Lucy reluctantly dragged her shame to her supervisor who supported her to explore the meaning in the mistake, rather than her overwhelming fear of any consequences. The supervisor was able to use her imagination differently and daringly. Gently they examined the dynamic like a curious object; they walked around it and began to play with the text kiss, her shame, and the clients' experiences of betrayal and her protest. Together they began to discover new ways of understanding the event, to bring their minds to the gap and mine any rich underground seams.

The client's history of early sexual intrusion by a family member was mixed with the therapist's anxious attachment pattern of over-caring and smothering. This magnetic collision became visible with the kiss.

The therapist was able to return to the client with a different understanding of her duty of care. It was not to foreclose on the mistake, but to open up to it and explore the client's experience about what this intrusion had felt like. Rather than define the kiss as a breach of ethics they were able to re-imagine the exchange as a curious incident, full of depth and unknown characters. In so doing the two learned together how to make use of experiences of being done-to, to keep them alive in the imagination, even when it is painful.

The client found more potency in her expressing and engaging with her protest and the therapist learned to attend to her anxious needs to gratify as a matter for her own therapy, rather than her client's therapy.

A therapist's understanding of their duty of care can often lead to foreclosure rather than exploration. With Lucy, the urgent apology was her attempt to attend to her duty of care. If we do not become interested in where the breaches of trust, fairness, and beneficence occur, then we miss the subtlety of what ethics codes offer us, and we risk using them as a shield to protect ourselves rather than a platform for understanding the unconscious dynamics at force.

The gaps that need minding are

> the co-created transitional space and experiences in which the therapist and client are free to reenact, create context and meaning, and ultimately re-create/transform in newly configured forms the central organizing relational matrices of the patient's and perhaps the therapist's early life.
>
> (Davies & Frawley, 1992, p. 12)

The reality is that this approach involves ethical risks if one enters the transitional space and ethical risks if one does not.

The paradox here is that ethics codes invite best practice, yet best practice in this work involves the willingness to make mistakes, be engaged in ruptures, and involved in enactments. Practitioners are measured and judged within their professional frameworks and communities with codes that are inconsistent with current thinking about how humans relate and how therapeutic change occurs. For example, over emphasising safety in the work can discount the need for risk. Authentic relating within the psychotherapeutic frame can be tricky, and therapists may avoid important therapeutic risks, as McGrath (1994) suggested, if their fear of complaints becomes the foreground.

Navigation of ethical tensions

Patricia Keith-Spiegel (2014) describes a useful set of 'red flags' in psychotherapy. These are gathered from her years of working with ethics cases.

- A desire for a different relationship from client/therapist
- Rationalising the acceptability of a contemplated boundary crossing or deviation from standard practice
- Concerns about personal ambition and financial gain
- Needs for enhancing one's own self-esteem
- Expecting the client to fulfil your personal or social needs
- Fear of being rejected or client terminating therapy for financial or other reasons
- Negative feelings towards a client
- Signs that the client is the more powerful individual in the relationship
- Personal life contaminating professional performance
- Belief that you are exempt from the above or not discussing the above for fear of being judged.

She provides a comprehensive list of alerts, all of which highlight ethical tensions which can link with sex and sexuality and erotic confusion. The desire for a different relationship and how either therapist or client might imagine something more, or different and then might begin to fantasise about this, or rationalise a boundary crossing.

Recently a supervisee started to make herself more available to a client as he began to get more in touch with the pain and abject poverty of care in his history. He emailed her with stirring words and erotic desires. The therapist was concerned about his potential for suicide (even though they had assessed this as minimal). She felt both outside of her competency, and that she should be more available to him, doing so outside her usual practice hours. The enactment of offering him something she could not sustain, based on her own fears and feelings of inadequacy, was a perfect collusion and repeat of his early history of promises and abandonment, and her history of having to please her father and work it all out on her own. Catching the enactment early meant she could open up the experiences with the client, exploring his needs and fears, rather than being preoccupied with her own. She was able to use her architecture of support to enquire into the magnetic forces between them, rather than be pulled around by them. In holding steady he was able to find grief and compassion rather than the familiar disappointment and depression.

To develop ethics codes and good practices relevant to a two-person approach, we need to utilise contemporary theories of mind and intersubjectivity. I believe we need to help practitioners consider relational methods of working with the unconscious so that mistakes, ruptures, and enactments in the therapy are understood as useful and used in the service of learning and growth. A significant factor in doing this is to foster supervisory relationships where we feel free to take our confusion, mistakes, shame, and terrors. This is how we resource our ethical containers to work with erotic confusion.

Developing an ethical container

Theoretical and practice frames which help us develop and deepen ways to listen and understand clients are essential structures in a therapist's architecture. Sex and sexuality are often expressed and communicated in coded forms. We cannot see or know what is being expressed. The language is often through the body, gestures, sub-symbolic communications. Therefore, ways to embrace erotic enactments and confusion are necessary. Ethical tensions are to be welcomed and navigated, rather than closed down on and defended against. Red flags are to be waved for telegraphing the need for help. Signalling is important and finding ways to decode, demystify, and reach the confusions inherent in sexuality is a core aspect of clinical work.

In order to work with enactments in this way there are two frames I find helpful. The first is that of contracting and consent. I outline how creating exploratory contracts with clients can help to open flexible and mutual agreements for any confusion to have space and where issues of consent can be explored rather than assumed. Secondly I expand on a model of care and risk in working with enactments and ethics. It is a form of ethical compass to track and explore interventions and interpretations.

Exploratory contracts

Research suggests that it is a client's level of involvement in therapy and their capacity to make use of therapeutic relationship are among the strongest predictors of outcomes (Cooper, 2008; Duncan et al., 2004). Bordin (1979) conceptualised the collaborative relationship between therapist and client as having three main components:

1   Their agreement of the goals of therapy
2   Their consensus on the tasks of therapy
3   The existence of a positive affective bond between therapist and client, with mutual trust, acceptance and confidence.

All therapy work has some form of explicit contract between therapist and client. Some are minimal and focussed around the business and administration of the relationship; money, time, venue, and cancellation details. Others might also have a more treatment focussed contract too, which might explicate the goals and tasks of the work. Charlotte Sills described the difference between hard and soft therapeutic contracts, saying, "The exploratory contract may be suitable when clients have neither understanding nor clarity other than a need to feel better; they need to go on an inner journey in a relationship with a trusted other" (Sills, 2011, p. 137).

When working with sex and sexuality a considerable amount is expressed in the implicit and unconscious exchanges that go on between therapist and client. Therefore an exploratory contract offers a mutual commitment to discovery that involves the client actively in their own therapy and acknowledges the different roles in the relationship. It starts the relationship with a dialogue and clarity about how what unfolds will be valued and explored.

I often talk with my clients about being a companion in adventure, or a co-investigator/detective. My metaphor varies and is generally informed by the client's capacity for curiosity and play. As therapists we are not taking on passengers to deliver to a pre-determined destination, but fellow explorers, intent on discovery. I believe therapy is a conversation or exchange you've never had before, a novel experience witnessed and shared.

I am interested in emphasising the mutuality in the encounter and sharing one of the paradoxes of psychotherapy – 'how do you make it safe enough to explore what is not safe to explore?' I do not assume that it is me that will 'make it safe', but trust we will learn together the challenges and possibilities of this. Most of the people I have worked with have a history where the person who was supposed to protect and keep things safe and steady was either not able to do so, or was the direct source of threat. This configuration is re-stimulated when people come into therapy and I think it is important to find a way to contract that invites exploration rather than adaptation.

Minding the gap between the client's goals and the therapist's goals is an early navigation point, an informative exercise in mutuality and a crucial task in the establishment of a working alliance. The collisions, collusions, and confusions that can emerge give us some early warning signs of the journey ahead.

The exploratory contract becomes part of the strong container to withstand the weather of enactments (Eusden, 2011; Eusden and Pierini, 2015; Novak, 2015; Shadbolt, 2012; Stuthridge, 2012) and stormy times in the work. I explore commitment to the work and build a contract to contain attention to the therapeutic relationship as a compass that can help us learn together how to help them towards their desired goal.

In my view the ethics of such a contract is that the therapist contracts to be interested in the client's life, not the other way around. Exploratory contracts mean the therapist explores with the client's experiences in and of the therapeutic exchange, but the therapist's personal explorations need to stay private. Dreams, feeling, and fantasies need to be talked through in consultation with a supervisor, no matter how mature a practitioner. Self-disclosure needs to be clearly considered and in the service of helping the client in their life.

A therapist who over discloses their own private life, even minimally, may invite a client into becoming interested in the therapists' life, rather than their own. All clients will know something of the therapist's private life which will be revealed by where they practice, what car they drive, clothes they wear etc. It is the more directed, in-session disclosures to be awake to. Such disclosures may direct a client's attention on the therapist's private life. This is particularly the risk for clients with a capacity to get lost in other's experience as a defence against connecting with their own. This is also the risk for therapist who are over-reliant on their clients for their narcissistic needs and recognition. This can be how the client begins to take care of the therapist, or gratify the therapist in small, maybe subtle ways. It can invite a powerful transferential dynamic and set the stage for enactments.

The job of the therapist is to be interested in the client's sexuality, not them sexually. The job of the client is to be interested in their own sexuality, not the therapist's. How these two jobs get entangled can be the source of fruitful understanding through enactment work or enactments too far and boundary violations. Exploratory contracts can help contain the entanglement providing there is a strong ethical container in the therapist.

Rosie approached a lesbian therapist who was kink aware. She said she wanted telephone sessions only. She did not want to 'see' the therapist and was very specific in her request to speak about her story, seeming to want to take control of who spoke. The therapist was unsure and concerned but agreed on the basis that they would meet twice a week in this way, that she had a connection with the Rosie's psychiatrist, and they would review how this experience was as they went along. A broad exploratory contract in which the therapist was open to experience the way the client needed to *show* her story.

Rosie's story was full of sexual abuse as a child, being taken away by her father, used by his friends, and then returned to the mother like some used-up rag when she was of marriageable age and of no interest anymore as a sexual object. She described her longing to be raped so that her experiences of early abuse could rise above the radar. Everything that had happened to her had happened in the dark. She fantasised that a 'real' rape would make it all visible somehow. When this eventually happened it did not achieve her aims, just added to her pain. She sought refuge in BDSM sex. She found Doms who re-enacted the abuse with her, leaving her full of want and dread but no nearer to relief or help. After one gruelling BDSM session she realised that her history was being repeated and decided to seek help from a therapist.

The therapist listened by phone for many sessions. Any intervention she made was dismissed, and Rosie pushed on relentlessly telling her story. The therapist was exhausted, used up, and filled with graphic details that were hard for her to process. She knew that she had placed herself in a bind with this contract and decided to sit through it, noticing the pain and tending to herself carefully. The two had become enmeshed in a sadomasochistic dance. The question the therapist brought to supervision was 'How do I use this to help her find a more productive mutual relationship?'

In discussing the case in supervision she recognised the repetition of the abuser/abused that she was hearing about. Jessica Benjamin (1995) writes of the 'doer/done-to' dynamic that gets enacted. The therapist felt 'done-to' by the client. She used the experience to learn and think about what Rosie was showing her that could not be conveyed in words. Their exploratory contract allowed something to be opened that could then be attended to with the client and in the relationship. She knew she had contracted to work this way but had also not quite known what she was consenting to. In catching and then exploring this as the next stage with Rosie, the two of them were able to begin to meet face to face and explore an intersubjective relationship, learning to discover the edges of doing-to and being done-to together in a more mutually respectful way. Rosie continued to prefer BDSM sex but began to find more feeling of control and agency inside it. Her choices of sexual expression did not need to change, but her experiences inside them were transformed. An important aspect of working with people is to be aware of our own preferences and prejudices in relation to sex and sexuality, and not need to impose these on others but be curious from the inside of others' experiences and preferences, and hold these with respect for difference and diversity of human sexual expression and preference.

Covering consent

A key aspect to an exploratory contract is that it provides a container for the unknown to emerge. It says, 'we don't know what will happen', and frequently with issues of sex, sexuality, and gender issues of power and consent are figural. An exploratory contract starts a relationship by aiming to say open and free from assumptions. However, we must not assume consent, but more look to be informed of what the issues are. What is the client consenting to? What are the subtle variations around consent? Where does consent, with this person, begin and end? Can they articulate their consent? What are the conditions under which consent become difficult? How can we increase our clients' agency when there is an imbalance of power? It may be the whole purpose of the therapy is to enable the client to find and know their own capacity to fully consent in their own life.

Consent rests on the idea that we have access to what we want or might seek. This can be problematic for many coming to therapy and it is important that therapists are acutely attuned to consent as a process rather than one single decision. This is even more vital where power dynamics and particularly sexual power dynamics are in play. Dr Meg-John Barker (2019), speaking at a Confer conference on Working with Sexuality, argues that consent is more explored by those in marginalised sexualities and sexual practices and potentially less explored in heteronormative sex. Therapists may need to pay extra attention to issues of consent if it has not been part of their own exploration of power, privilege, and vulnerability. Some camouflage their 'no' sometimes by saying, 'yes', and consent is intricately woven around issues of gender, sexuality, and power. These are ever prevalent in the therapy room, as outside it.

A therapist, working with a client who had been referred following a breakdown of trust with a previous therapist said somewhat casually that they had 'covered the issues of consent' related to contacting her GP. She was wondering why the client had emailed to cancel the next session saying she did not think she was ready to trust another therapist. Consent is a thorny bush, full of assumptions. Believing you have it 'covered' by asking one question is problematic. If a person does not have a history of their consent being sought and respected, they may not know how to give it, or respect it in others. A history of compliance makes it difficult to know what consent is. The exploratory contract offers a place where consent can be explored, considered and known, rather than 'covered' and hence 'covered-up' and complied with on both sides.

Jennifer, an experienced therapist, was working with a client, Molly. Both women have a history of sexual abuse. Molly from outside the family of origin and Jennifer from inside.

Molly was presenting as dissociated during the session and saying very little, finding it hard to engage. Jennifer had started to sit next to her client, on the sofa, moving out of her usual therapist's seat to sit close to her. She was drawing on body therapy techniques she had learned and had decided to make this move, in part, as she was not sure what else to do.

She consulted with a male supervisor at a psychotherapy training event about this move and left the consultation feeling shame and that she had done something bad. It had been a 'curbside consultation' (Gabbard, 2017) in that he was not her regular supervisor, but it had been an opportunistic moment in the training and there was no plan for further consultation. She did not talk about her shame with him, but planned to amend her practice with the client to adapt to what she imagined he had thought, that she should get back in her own seat. She was organised by a dynamic of power and historic shame. However, she had a strong enough ethical container to also know her imagination had been shut down and that she needed more help.

She brought her confusion to me, her regular supervisor. We explored the issue of consent. How did she pay attention to clues that the client was consenting or not? The supervisee repeated the phrase, out of her awareness, many times: "We talked about it". I asked about this sentence and what she meant and how she was using it. I commented that I learned nothing more about the client when she used this sentence, I only had an experience of things being closed or covered up, and that this sentence was the end of the story. Then she spotted her shame, realising she had felt humiliation in front of the male supervisor, and was anticipating the same with me. She was using the phrase like she was ticking a box of ethic compliance: "I have consent to touch this client because we have talked about it". I suggested that talking about anything did not guarantee consent. She agreed and knew the truth of this from her own history.

We spoke of how to support an enquiry into the client's experience that opens channels of possibility, rather than defines them. Language is such an important aspect of this and can be experienced as a weapon, or prison. Questions that ask the client what they want are loaded with unspoken assumptions that a client can firstly identify what they want and secondly feel free to express this to the other. Those who have been groomed know the difficulty of this.

Exploratory contracts are a way to investigate both conscious and unconscious material. Consent is complex and mobile and a core ethical tension to navigate with care. What cannot be spoken about will emerge unbidden and becomes the enactment dimension of the treatment. The therapist and client need to find the tension between living it, but not acting it out. Therapists need to be willing to be drawn into their client's world, whilst not needing to draw the client into their world. How we think ethically at this edge is fundamentally not covered by rules and codes, but by strengthening and expanding our own sense of ethical containment for the work.

Dare/care model

In our increasingly paranoid and litigious culture, admitting to a mistake or an unethical behaviour is hard to contemplate for therapists, and the 'therapist's honour' can become a defence. To be accused of acting unethically carries intense shame and is often felt as an attack on a therapist's professional integrity. It can touch on our most vulnerable narcissistic wounding, arousing our defences and can inhibit our thinking and productive meaning making. It can make us risk averse, or blind to the assumptions we might make in our understanding of 'duty of care'.

In her seminal paper, McGrath (1994) described a method of applying moral principles to ethical dilemmas. She highlighted two difficulties that may emerge as therapists apply ethical guidelines:

> First, therapists may confuse intentionality with good ethical practice, that is, they may assume that because they do not intend to hurt or

exploit their clients that their clinical work must be ethical. Second, the fear of legal or professional liability may lead therapists to be so cautious that the potency of the clinical work is impaired, and the client is not offered the best possible treatment.

(p. 8)

McGrath proposed the use of moral principles to navigate ethical complexity. However, while such principles may offer an excellent framework for thinking about our work, this idea assumes that we can be conscious enough to articulate and manage ethical dilemmas. The focus is on the practitioner as potentially objective rather than as immersed in a mutual process of subjectivity.

McGrath hinted at the implicit in her writing, but I think this needs to be explored further in order to expand our frame to account for the intersubjective and implicit relational knowing that is foundational to our current understanding of what goes on between people in the consulting room. This led to my development of an ethical compass as a necessary tool, that will support our exploration of the client's and therapist's internal and external worlds.

The compass is a quadrant model (Figure 3.3.1), drawing on Kohlrieser's (2012) links between caring and daring and Karpman's (1968) Drama Triangle which describes three roles (Rescuer, Persecutor, and Victim) that we can inhabit, particularly at times of difficulty.

The ethical principles in the top right quadrant are drawn from McGrath (1994). The North/South axis runs from High Dare to Low Dare and the West/East axis runs from Low Care to High Care. This allows me to wonder and wander in the transference/countertransferential matrix and ask self-supervisory questions. Am I coasting in the countertransference (Hirsch, 2008) by perhaps taking a high care, but low dare/risk position? Hence am I potentially in a Rescuer role? Or am I taking risks without equivalent care? Might I be in a Persecutor role? Where might the client be? When one of us is in a low care/low dare position, what does that invite in the other? How might these roles be complementary in our scripts and how might this help me/us orientate towards an ethically rooted tension of risk and care? How might my way of being or interventions nudge us into the North East quadrant? I may invite the client and I to use this explicitly to monitor risk and support both inside and outside the therapy room. This way we can track power, risk, trust, and enactments and, with an exploratory contract, build a dialogue and relationship that can be lost and found and grow from experience. The top right quadrant of High Dare High Care is perhaps the aspiration one to aim into, but risk and support must always be rooted in ethical attention and orientated with COMPASSion. Everything contributes to the goal of discovery.

I will give some brief examples of each quadrant.

An ethical container for erotic confusion 211

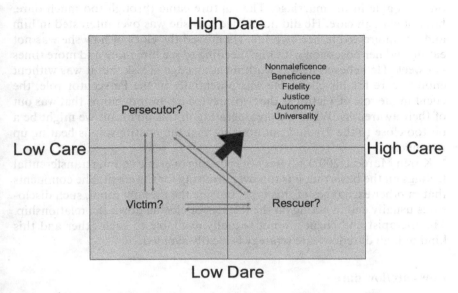

Figure 3.3.1 The ethical compass: high dare – high care (Eusden, 2018).

High care/low dare

Commonly this is where the therapist frame is more focussed around a maternal-type care-taking (Cornell and Bonds-White, 2001) rather than engaging with them in helping them consider what care means to them in their own life. The kind of care the therapist 'provides' may frequently Rescue a client rather than help them consider their own risks and losses. Here the therapeutic pair can coast in a supportive relationship that never quite gets close enough to the fire to grow resilience from risk.

Indi, a therapist who grew up in an atmosphere of domestic violence and terror and was subsequently sexually abused by her first therapist, tends to over identify with women who are the victims of domestic violence or sexual transgression. She keeps risks minimal as she is frightened of her own potential for power over the client. Paradoxically this maintains her power over her clients because she sees them as victims and denies her own vulnerability. Her learning edge in supervision and reflective practice is to stay vigilant to her desire to Rescue women with whom her sexuality and history may overlap.

High dare/low care

Kelvin (therapist) took risks with Maggie (client). Risks of self-disclosure, of over interest in her in the session, disclosing his feelings for her and his own struggle in his marriage. The rupture came through too much dare, but not enough care. He did not notice how she was over interested in him and not interested in her own life. He missed the clues of how she was not eating and her obsession with him, needing to see him more and more times per week. He believed he was working at an edge of risk, but it was without enough care for his client. He was potentially in the Persecutor role, the client in the role of Victim as the two enacted a power dynamic that was out of their awareness. When we are operating in this quadrant we might be a bit too close to the fire and not noticing that the relationship is heating up too much.

Karen Maroda (2002) advises not speaking of erotic countertransferential feelings on the basis that it is too over arousing for the client. She comments that in other exchanges of this type, outside the therapy room, such disclosures usually end in acting on the feelings or closing down the relationship. The therapist and client are not sexually available to each other and this kind of high dare/low care strategy is ideally avoided.

Low care/low dare

This quadrant captures a variety of scenarios where there may be an unethical abuse of power and where there is usually a breakdown of the therapeutic relationship which may be beyond repair. If the relationship is ongoing it may look like the therapist speaks badly of the client and is not doing any work with them as they don't want to lose the income. They don't challenge the client, nor end the work. A stale mate has been drawn. Alternatively it is often when the client announces they are not returning and have been unhappy with the experience for some time or are making a complaint about the therapist. The relationship here is in the fire. The therapist needs to seek consultation with their supervisor and potentially an ethical advisor. These cases can offer a considerable learning if the therapist can bear to reflect deeply.

High dare/high care

Cadence is a therapist working with a female client who has a strong erotic transference to her. Cadence has struggled with feelings of fear, disgust, and dislike of this client as the client has intruded, alluded to desiring a different form of friendship and stalked her on occasion. In supervision we have explored how she might move between the quadrants in her desire to Persecute the client, or Rescue her when she tells her of past hurts. However, Cadence generally manages to head towards the high dare/high care by maintaining a tension of confusion and navigating clear boundaries with the client, which mean disappointment and desire can be explored rather than acted on.

This quadrant is aspirational, and seeks to inspire us to ask questions about the work. This is where our ethical and relational principles are held.

How do we nudge our work towards these and consider the tensions and value in finding the best ways forward through difficult moments? This quadrant is not necessarily about *very* high dare/care, but about maximising the dynamic tension between the two for the best outcome for the client and the work.

The ethical compass is a way to be curious about how the therapeutic dyad might be in an enactment that is impacting the roles and power in the relationship. This can offer some structure as a way of understanding the subsequent ethical disorganisation the therapist may feel and give a direction to unpick the ethical tensions and understand the meaning of the dynamics both historically and in the here and now. It can be used to inform and strengthen the therapist's ethical container when they are working with the magnetic forces inherent in working with sex and sexuality.

Conclusion

In this chapter I discuss two frameworks that can be used to support working with sex and sexuality in psychotherapy practice: exploratory contracts and consent and the ethical compass.

Exploratory contracts are an ongoing process of exquisite ethical attention and negotiation of how to be together, developing a shared and personal ethical code of conduct and consent that is meaningful to both, with the aim of discovering what is lost, unknown, and implicit in the client's world.

The ethical compass offers a frame to explore risk and safety in the work and uses the metaphor of fire to consider the right amount of warmth and heat needed to keep the work creatively alive.

Together these frames can be used to keep the therapeutic/supervisory space open in order to offer an ethical container for erotic confusion, where two subjects can learn through experiences of objectification, excitement, and opportunity with mutual respect and professional integrity.

Bibliography

Barker, M. J. (2019). The conditions of consent. In *Working with Sexuality: Bodies, Desire and Imagination*. Confer. Retrieved from www.confer.uk.com/modules/sexuality/module-sexuality-barker1.html.

Benjamin, J. (1995). *Like Subject, Love Objects: Essays on Recognition and Sexual Difference*. New Haven, CT: Yale University Press.

Bion, W. R. (1967). *Second Thoughts*. London: William Heinemann. [Reprinted London: Karnac Books 1984].

Bordin, E. S. (1979). The generalisability of the psychoanalytic concept of the working alliance. *Psychotherapy: Theory, Research, Practice, Training*, 16(3), 252–260.

Cave, N. (2019). *The Red Hand Files #42*. Retrieved from www.theredhandfiles.com/desire-for-creation/ [Accessed 28.7.2019].

Cooper, M. (2008). *Essential Research Findings in Counselling and Psychotherapy*. London: Sage Publications Ltd.

Cornell, W. F., & Bonds-White, F. (2001). Therapeutic relatedness in transactional analysis: The truth of love or the love of truth. *Transactional Analysis Journal*, 31(1), 71–83.

Davies, J. M. (1994). Love in the afternoon: A relational reconsideration of desire and dread in the countertransference. *Psychoanalytic Dialogues*, 4, 153–170.

Davies, J. M., & Frawley, M. G. (1992). Dissociative processes and transference-countertransference paradigms in the psychoanalytically oriented treatment of adult survivors of childhood sexual abuse. *Psychoanalytic Dialogues*, 2, 5–36.

Duncan, B. L., Miller, S. D., & Sparks, J. A. (2004). *The Heroic Client: A Revolutionary Way to Improve Effectiveness Through Client-Directed, Outcome-Informed Therapy*. San Francisco, CA: Jossey-Bass.

Eusden, S. (2011). Minding the gap: Ethical considerations for therapeutic engagement. *Transactional Analysis Journal*, 41(2), 101–113.

Eusden, S. (2018). The exploratory contract: A mutual collaboration in risk, uncertainty and discovery. In Rotondo, A (2018) (Ed.) *Contratto. Luci e ombre* (Prima edizione) (pp. 97–110). La Vita Felice.

Eusden, S., & Pierini, A. (2015), Exploring contemporary views on therapeutic relating in transactional analysis game theory. *Transactional Analysis Journal*, 45, 128–140.

Freud, S. (1912). The dynamics of transference. In Strachey, J. (1958) (Ed.) *The Standard Edition of the Complete Psychological Works of Sigmund Freud, Volume XII (1911-1913): The Case of Schreber, Papers on Technique and Other Work* (pp. 97-108). London: Hogarth Press and the Institute of Psychoanalysis.

Gabbard, G. O. (1994). On love and lust in erotic transference. *Journal of the American Psychoanalytic Association*, 42(2), 385–386. doi:10.1177/000306519404200203.

Gabbard, G. O. (2017). Sexual boundary violations in psychoanalysis: A 30-year retrospective. *Psychoanalytic Psychology*, 34(2), 151–156. doi:10.1037/pap0000079.

Gabbard, G. O., & Lester, E. P. (1995). *Boundaries and Boundary Violations in Psychoanalysis*. London: American Psychiatric Publishing Inc.

Hirsch, I. (2008). *Coasting in the Countertransference: Conflicts of Self Interest Between Analyst and Patient*. New York: The Analytic Press.

Kahr, B. (2007). *Sex and the Psyche: The Truth About Our Most Secret Fantasies*. London: Penguin Books.

Karpman, S. B. (1968). Fairy tales and script drama analysis. *Transactional Analysis Bulletin*, 7(26), 39–43.

Keith-Spiegel, P. (2014). *Red Flags in Psychotherapy: Stories of Ethics Complaints and Resolutions*. London: Routledge.

Kohlrieser, G. (2012). *Care to Dare: Unleashing Astonishing Potential Through Secure Base Leadership*. San Francisco, CA: Jossey-Bass.

Koocher, G. P., & Keith-Spiegel, P. (2008). *Ethics in Psychology and the Mental Health Professions* (3rd ed.). New York: Oxford University Press.

Little, R. (2018). The management of erotic/sexual countertransference reactions: An exploration of the difficulties and opportunities involved. *Transactional Analysis Journal*, 48(3), 224–241. doi:10.1080/03621537.2018.1471290.

Maroda, K. J. (2002). *Seduction, Surrender, and Transformation: Emotional Engagement in the Analytic Process*. Hillsdale, NJ: Analytic Press.

McGrath, G. (1994). Ethics, boundaries, and contracts: Applying moral principles. *Transactional Analysis Journal*, 24, 6–14.

Novak, E. T. (2015). Are games, enactments, and reenactments similar? No, yes, it depends. *Transactional Analysis Journal*, 45, 117–127.

Pope, K. (2001). Sex between therapists and clients. In J. Worell (Ed.) *Encyclopedia of Women and Gender: Sex Similarities and Differences and the Impact of Society on Gender* (Vol. 2, pp. 955–962). Waltham, MA: Academic Press.

Ringstrom, P. (2010). Meeting Mitchell's challenge: A comparison of relational psychoanalysis and intersubjective systems theory. *Psychoanalytic Dialogues*, 20(2), 196–218.

Schafer, R. (1993). Five readings of Freud's "observations on transference-love". In E. S. Person, A. Hagelin, & P. Fonagy (Eds.) *On Freud's Observations on Transference Love* (pp. 75–95). New Haven, CT: Yale University Press.

Shadbolt, C. (2012). The place of failure and rupture in psychotherapy. *Transactional Analysis Journal*, 42, 5–16.

Sills, C. (2011). The importance of uncertainty. In H. Fowlie, & C. Sills (Eds.) *Relational Transactional Analysis: Principles in Practice* (pp. 129–140). London: Karnac Books.

Stark, M. (1999). *Modes of Therapeutic Action: Enhancement of Knowledge, Provision of Experience, and Engagement in Relationship*. Northvale, NJ: Jason Aronson.

Stern, D. N. (2004). *The Present Moment in Psychotherapy and Everyday Life*. London: Norton.

Stuthridge, J. (2012). Traversing the fault lines: Trauma and enactment. *Transactional Analysis Journal*, 42, 238–251.

Wallin, D. J. (2015). *Attachment in Psychotherapy*. New York: Guildford Press.

3.4 Editor's Summary and reflection on ethical practice and prevention of transgressions

Biljana van Rijn

Introduction

This section further develops the themes addressed previously on working ethically with issues of sexual attraction and sexuality in psychotherapy, and addresses them from the position of looking at the boundaries within different working environments and settings.

While the previous two sections of this book focus on the ways of working with sexuality and sexual attraction in psychotherapy (Part 1) and in supervision (Part 2), Part 3 explores transgressions in clinical work. The authors address this subject in three chapters. In the first chapter (3.1) 'Sexual transgressions and transgressing gender and sexuality', Steven B. Smith reflects on the potential for transgressions arising from the therapist's own beliefs and limitations and stresses the need to remain vigilant and non-defensive about our own values and principles. My chapter (3.2 Firefighting. Managing sexual ruptures and transgressions within counselling and psychotherapy services) explores a potential for transgressions within clinical services and looks for ways to increase awareness within organisational settings. In the final chapter (3.3 An ethical container for erotic confusion), Sue Eusden highlights the importance of what she terms an 'ethical container' that does not curtail exploration and depth in psychotherapy.

Background

All the authors quote some of the psychoanalytic literature on transgressions already visited in other chapters (Celenza, 2017; Gabbard, 2017; Gabbard and Lester, 1995). It is of interest to note that the most informative and sustained body of literature on these issues comes from psychoanalytic practice, while it is far from being sufficiently explored in other approaches to psychotherapy. The other source of literature used by the authors are the professional codes of practice giving guidelines for ethical practice (British Association for Counselling and Psychotherapy, 2018; UKCP, 2009; UKCP, 2017). These two areas of the literature highlight the tension between the apparent clarity of professional boundaries contained in the ethical 'rules' and the ambiguity and complexity of clinical practice where 'the rules' could often be confusing and insufficient.

Research I cited in Chapter 3.2 (Alpert and Steinberg, 2017; Blechner, 2017; Pope and Vetter, 1991) suggests that sexual violations occur in different clinical settings, although most client complaints emerge from within the private therapeutic practice. This is interesting. I don't know whether it means that there are more sexual violations in private practice, or that within organisations they might be more contained and addressed internally, and therefore don't always reach the stage of professional ethical complaints. Whatever the case, alongside the other authors in this section, I also concur with Gabbard (2017) that many violations remain undisclosed and unaddressed by the professional bodies. The limited psychotherapy and research literature on this subject still shows a relatively widespread range of transgressions and abuses that still somehow sit outside of our professional field of vision. In this book we have discussed the importance of a relational context and mutuality in psychotherapy. We have also written about the importance of addressing the unconscious in supervision. We may also need to adopt a wider viewpoint and challenge our professional blindness to sexual transgressions and abuses within our profession. The current literature, and the need for the professional rules that state that sexual exploitation of clients is not acceptable, highlight a need for client protection. Like many other mental health professions, psychotherapists work with vulnerable people within asymmetric power relationships. We all know that violations occur with vulnerable people in these environments, often by people in the positions of trusts, and it is of no surprise that all authors in this section of the book emphasise the importance of client protection and prevention.

Transgressions in therapeutic practice and in services

The authors in this section reflect on different kinds of transgressions, from subtle unconscious infringements and transgressions that could be used for therapeutic growth to clear abuses of power. Emerging from these three chapters, as well as the rest of the book, is a notion that sexuality is ubiquitous in psychotherapy, as it is in all human life. Eusden's statement that it is the task of the therapist to be interested in the client's sexuality, without being interested in them sexually, rings out as a leitmotiv for ethical practice in this area of work.

Awareness

Eusden and Smith focus on the development and the use of personal awareness by the therapist. Smith expands on the material in previous sections (1.4 Michelle Bridgeman: Gender identity and sexual attraction in the therapeutic encounter – a transgender perspective and 2.3 Di Hodgson: Sexual orientation in the supervisory relationship: exploring fears and fantasies when different sexual orientations are present in the client/therapist and/ or supervisory dyad) when he addresses diversity of sexual practices and orientations. Smith, Hodgson, and Bridgeman each recognise the pervasiveness of heteronormative views and values in our society, and how easily they could be communicated in a way that leads to harm. Smith (Chapter 3.1) and Hodgson (Chapter 2.3) give vivid case examples which demonstrate how an enquiry into historical causes for a sexual orientation or preferences could lead to pathologising and labelling in both therapy and supervision. Smith's case vignette of his work with 'Adam' demonstrates how this could be avoided, and how genuine exploration could be achieved through openness. This case vignette is a helpful illustration of the therapist holding theory lightly and abandoning theoretical explanations when they were not helpful to the client. Theories are context and culture bound, and it not surprising that the early 20th century understanding of sexual expression and preference would be outdated in the current cultural context. Prevention and 'beneficence' in the Smith's examples demonstrated therapeutic actions guided by acceptance, rather that theory.

Approaching the subject from an organisational perspective, in my chapter (3.2) I focus on building awareness of some of the more overt transgressions in order to develop protection for clients who engage in therapy is services. I give some of the recognisable examples of the breaking of contact and communication, and ruptures that could lead to the unplanned endings.

Red flags

As we have found throughout this book, the erotic material, sexual attraction, and disturbing transgressions are hidden, sometimes unconscious, and frequently shameful. This makes prevention of abuses and sexual violations challenging and highly complex, as this much cited quotation by Gabbard (2017) well expresses:

> My growing pessimism has emerged from the recognition of the numerous ways that individual clinicians can rationalize why their situation is somehow different from others, the failure to utilize consultation of supervision, and the inability of institutions to see what's in front of their eyes.
>
> (p. 151)

In their chapters the authors attempt to address this from the perspectives of developing the therapists' awareness, knowledge, and receptivity (Smith and Eusdon) as well as the awareness in psychotherapy institutions and training (van Rijn).

Eusden reflects on the need to offer stability and boundaries, while remaining open to exploration. She recognises that attempting to remain safe could lead the therapist to a sterile and rigid way of working which limited depth and therapeutic usefulness. In the area of working with the dynamic of the erotic, the rigidity of the approach could easily lead to ignoring the uncomfortable and the disturbing, and to premature endings with clients. In her chapter, she presents a model she has developed, which she calls an 'ethics compass' with a continuum of a Care/Dare quadrant, which she combines with Transactional Analysis theory (Karpman, 1968) to create an exploratory method for working with enactments. To develop therapeutic containment and safety she also writes about the importance of making exploratory agreements and contract with clients in order to enhance collaboration and protection.

In his case examples Smith models judicious and daring, but informed, use of self-disclosure. If we used Eusden's model for analysis, we could place his example of working with 'Adam' on the quadrant continuum of 'High Care and High Dare'. The example he gives and Eusden's case of 'Cadence' each demonstrate the maintenance of clear boundaries, supporting both the therapist and the client while they engaged in the exploration. However, this type of work can feel destabilising and disturbing for the therapist, and requires personal robustness and support. The red flags in this highly charged experience are personal and require the therapist to be willing and able to use supervision and personal psychotherapy, as we have explored in the previous sections of the book.

I start from the same understanding of the predisposing factors to transgressions as Celenza (1998) and Gabbard and Lester (1995), shared by the other authors in this section. However, in my chapter (3.2), I focus mostly on the service perspectives and discuss approaches for preventing and addressing sexual transgressions. These includes developing an environment in which service managers could become more aware of precursors to transgressions, such as the organisational environment, or personal stressors for the therapists. Overwork, lack of resources, or personal crisis, could all lead to a gradual erosion of boundaries, where a therapist might be tempted to use clients for their own emotional needs. Most therapists can hopefully derive satisfaction and fulfilment in their work. However, in a personal crisis, or during an extended period of stress, a therapist could reach a point where personal contact with clients ends up being the only source of satisfying social contact, or a source of self-esteem. When that latter occurs, it is not hard to rationalise the need for 'saving' a client or providing a 'special relationship', a dynamic frequent in sexual transgressions.

Although we have to accept our inability to see something hidden, and we also need to accept that red flags could be numerous and yet hidden in plain sight. Seeing them requires a willingness to look for them and name them when they occur.

Practice points

Points of good practice in this section of the book are not dissimilar to the previous material and centre on awareness, intention, and boundaries.

Prevention

All three chapters in this section focus on prevention of harm. This is not dissimilar to the rest of the book, and whilst we encourage therapists to engage with the uncomfortable and the hidden, and recognise the importance of sometimes working on a transgressive edge, we do so from the position of developing beneficence in clinical practice. Rules in themselves are not enough for the prevention of harm, but neither is education, professional knowledge, or experience. As psychotherapists, our fitness to practice and levels of personal vulnerability change over time and are affected by different life circumstances and events. Prevention of harm involves using all of our support systems: training, personal therapy and supervision, and maintaining a level of personal humility.

The limited literature in this area suggest that we might need to address issues of sexual boundary violation by developing more professional and training resources and opening more professional discussion.

Containment

Working with the material of the erotic in psychotherapy could be as rich and rewarding, as it could be disturbing and challenging to both the therapist and the client. Containment of this work, alongside the development of personal awareness, seems to be one of the distinguishing features of good practice. When I refer to containment, I link it to the importance of clear boundaries and go back to the Eusden's statement (Chapter 3.2) of being interested in the client's experiences of sexuality, without being sexually interested in them.

When that doesn't happen, and the therapist's sexual interest in the client influences the exploration in therapy, or leads to violations and transgressions, containment and protection need to include the other gatekeepers and professionals, such as supervisors, trainers, and clinical managers. It is important to remember that in those cases both parties require help. Clients need safety, ability to voice their experiences, and attention to their needs. Therapists also need a space to recognise the impact of their actions and reflect on them.

Redress

As we know from research, clients who are most likely to be abused by their therapists are the most vulnerable, and have often had previous traumatic experiences. It is therefore essential that the work with transgressions does not focus only on containment and rehabilitation, but also supports clients in seeking redress.

This is probably another area that is difficult for us as professional community. Psychotherapy is a helping profession. People who come into it have often been motivated by their own early experiences (Bager-Charleson et al., 2010), and wanting to help others. Our training teaches us to develop empathy, and we work with many clients who have been mistreated and abused by others. In our collective psyche, it is not easy to see ourselves or our colleagues as potential abusers. This may be a part of the reluctance to see the abuse in our midst. Supporting the clients in considering and accessing routes for redress, means that we also have to acknowledge our own ability to do harm.

At the end of this summary, I would like to extend my appreciation to the colleagues who have contributed to this book. Their voices, and their willingness to share their practice, their experiences and thinking, models the openness and reflection within a contemporary humanistic-relational psychotherapy and ethical practice. My hope is that many others will join us in the continuing discussion on this theme.

References

Alpert, J. L. & Steinberg, A. (2017) Sexual boundary violations: A century of violations and a time to analyze. *Psychoanalytic Psychology*, 34, 144–150.

Bager-Charleson, S., Chatterjee, S. G., Critchley, P., et al. (2010) *Why Therapists Choose to Become Therapists: A Practice-Based Inquiry*, London, Karnac Books.

Blechner, M. J. (2017) Dissociation among psychoanalysts about sexual boundary violations. In Petrucelli, J. & Schoen, S. (Eds.) *Unknowable, Unspeakable, and Unsprung: Psychoanalytic Perspectives on Truth, Scandal, Secrets, and Lies*, New York, Routledge/Taylor & Francis Group.

British Association for Counselling and Psychotherapy (2018) Ethical Framework for the Counselling Professions. BACP.

Celenza, A. (1998) Precursors to therapist sexual misconduct: Preliminary findings. *Psychoanalytic Psychology*, 15, 378–395.

Celenza, A. (2017) Lessons on or about the couch: What sexual boundary transgressions can teach us about everyday practice. *Psychoanalytic Psychology*, 34, 157–162.

Gabbard, G. O. (2017) Sexual boundary violations in psychoanalysis: A 30-year retrospective. *Psychoanalytic Psychology*, 34, 151–156.

Gabbard, G. O. & Lester, E. P. (1995) *Boundaries and Boundary Violations in Psychoanalysis*, Arlington, VA, American Psychiatric Publishing, Inc.

Karpman, S. (1968) Fairy tales and script drama analysis. *Transactional Analysis Bulletin*, 7, 39–43.

Pope, K. S. & Vetter, V. A. (1991) Prior therapist-patient sexual involvement among patients seen by psychologists. *Psychotherapy: Theory, Research, Practice, Training*, 28, 429–438.

UKCP (2009) UK Council for Psychotherapy, Ethical Principles and Code of Professional Conduct. UKCP.

UKCP (2017) Ethical Principles and Code of Professional Conduct. UKCP.

Index

Note: *Italic* page numbers refer to figures.

Adam (client, case study) 166–170
Adams, M. 92
adolescence sexual awareness 56
Agar, James 22, 57–60, 62–72, 91–93
Alex (client, case study) 22, 28, 35
Alpert, J. L. 180
Angela (client, case study) 65–68, 86–87
anxiety 64
Atlas, G. 60
attitudes 141
Atwood, G.E. 164
authenticity 5
authority 1

Bach, S. 127
Barker, M. 170
Barnett, J. E. 191
Ben (client, case study) 63–64
beneficence 68
Benjamin, H. 77
Benjamin, J. 27, 108, 207
Berne, E. 122
Berry, M. D. 5
Blechner, M. J. 51, 179, 181
Blum, H. B. 39
Bodenheimer, D. 4
Bohart, A. C. 40
Bond, T. 123
Bornstein, K. 78
Boston Change Process Study Group 41
boundary crossings 49
boundary violations 49, 95; sexual transgressions 179–180, 192–193
Boundary Violations Index 52
Bowlby, J. 144
Bradshaw, J. 80
Brandchaft, B. 164

Bridgman, Michelle 91–95, 218
Buber, Martin 130

Cadence (client, case study) 212
Cartesian duality paradigm 39
Cave, N. 196
Celenza, A. 51, 56, 179, 180, 219
Clarkson, P. 6, 51
client's sexual arousal 19
code of ethics 195, 199
Cognitive Behavioural Therapy (CBT) 3, 47
collaboration 187, 190
community-based organisations 181
conceptualisations, sexual feelings: erotic transference 2; psychoanalysis 2–3; sexual dynamics 3–4; transferential *versus* real phenomenon 4–6
consent 207–209
containment 187; *see also* ethical containment
contextual psychotherapy 168
contra-sexuality 169, 170
Cooper, M. 49
Cornell, W. F. 4, 6, 111, 117, 129, 131
co-transference 168; sexual orientation 134–135
counter-transference 107, 167
Cross, M. 25–27
cultural jouissance 72, 73

Daintry, P. 144
Daniel, J. 138
dare/care model 209–210, *211*
David (client, case study) 102–106
Davies, J. M. 106, 111, 200
Davis, P. 5

Deary, V. 130
Dekeyser, M. 40
de-sexualisation 31, 89
Desmond, B. 139, 145–146, 149
DeYoung, P. A. 80
Dhillon-Stevens, H. 27
Dimen, M. 103, 173
dominant discourses 124
DuPont, J. 127

Edi (client, case study) 182–184
embodied countertransference 117, 125–127, 128
embodied relationship 40–41
erotic as sensual experience 55–57
erotic communication 117
erotic conceptualisation: Cartesian duality paradigm 39; embodied relationship 40–41; empathic engagement 40–41; general erotic 39; genital erotic 39; map 41; non-transferential genital relationship 44–49; non-transferential *versus* non-genital 41–44; psychotherapeutic engagement 39; quadrants 41, *42*; transferential and genital 50–52; transferential and non-genital relationship 49–50
erotic confusion 195, 200–201
erotic transference 4, 25, 196; sexual orientation 149
Erskine, R. G. 42, 163
ethical containment: code of ethics 165, 178, 181, 195, 199; consent 207–209; dare/care model 209–210, *211*; development 204; enactments 200; erotic confusion 195, 200–201; erotic transference 196; ethical risks 203; exploratory contracts 204–207; high care/low dare 211; high dare/high care 212–213; high dare/low care 211–212; low care/low dare 212; power dynamics 200; sexual desires 196; sexual transgressions 196–199; shame 202; tensions 203–204; transitional space 203; two-person psychological dynamics 200
ethical practice and prevention: awareness 217–218; containment 220; harm prevention 220; practice points 219; professional codes 216; red flags 218–219; redress 220–221; sextual exploitation 217
ethical risks 203

ethics policy 64
Eusden, Sue 217–219
existential isolation 4
existential sexuality 30
exploratory contracts 204–207

female therapists' experiences: clinical supervision 22; complex clinical issues 32; conflict of roles 28; de-sexualisation 31; embodied knowledge 20; erotic phenomena 21; feminisation 31; gender identities 34; genital sexuality 31; interpersonal dynamics 24; maternal transference 28–29, 31; mentalisation 31; mirroring 31; mutuality and love 29–30; neuro-psychological research 30; power dynamics 24–28; power imbalance 23, 24; professional misjudgement 33; prostitution 32–33; 'real' relationship 21; reciprocal sexual attraction 22, 28; research questions 20–21; self-disclosure 21; societal messages 34; socio-cultural discourses 30; therapists qualities 31; therapist's therapy 30; training 22; unconscious knowledge 20
femininity/feminisation 31, 171
Fenton, Brian 22, 56–72, 91–93
Ferenczi 3, 127
Fisher, H. 52, 69
Flax, M. 27, 34
formative task, supervision 100–101, 153
Foucault, M. 30, 72, 124
Frawley-O'Dea, M. G. 111
Freud, S. 2, 56, 90, 127, 196, 197
Frommer, M. S. 68
Fromm-Reichmann, Frieda 197

Gabbard, G. O. 52, 101, 165–166, 179, 180, 181, 188, 197, 198, 200, 217–219
Gardner, F. 107
gender 1, 94; configuration 24; distinction 73; human sexuality 174; identities 34; rigidity 171; sexual orientation 139
gender identity: abuse 81; behavioural guidelines 79; case studies 84–87; closeness 76; desire 77; familiarity 76; gender spectrum 78; heterosexual 78; homosexuals 77; hormone therapy 79; intimacy 76; male privilege 82–83; power 77; sexual attraction 76, 78–79; sexual manipulation 77;

shame 79–80; supervision 87–88; supportive relationship 76; trans clients 81, 83–84; trans men and trans women 76; trans therapists 81–82, 84; transvestites 77; trusting relationship 76; vulnerability 76, 80–81
gender identity disorder 77, 78
Gerrard, J. 3, 29, 30, 110
Gestalt theory 135
Giovazolias, T. 5
Gornick, L. 25
Graham (client, case study) 84–86, 92
Gutheil, T. 52
Guttman, H. 25

Hauke, G. 40
Hawkins, P. 102, 153
Hedges, F. 30
Hedges, L. 56, 60, 72
Henderson, D. 32
hetero-normative scripting 56
heteronormative sex 208
high care/low dare model 211
high dare/high care model 212–213
high dare/low care model 211–212
Hill, R. 78
Hitchings, Paul 22, 91, 93, 95
Hodgson, D. 113, 153–156, 218
Hollway, W. 20
Hopcke, R. 170
Horney, Karen 197
human sexual development 59
Huysamen, M. 8

Ian (client, case study) 185–186
internal supervisory group 71
interpersonal anxiety 171
interpersonal dynamics 24
intersubjectivity 55, 58, 72, 121
intrapersonal anxiety 171

Jacobs, L. 146
Jacques, G. 139
James, E. 60
Janna (client, case study) 182–184
Jefferson, T. 20
Jennifer (client, case study) 208
Joyce, P. 40, 42, 44
Jung, C. G. 170, 197
Jungian analysis 169

Kahr, B. 167, 172, 195
Kearns, A. 144
Keith-Spiegel, P. 198, 203

Kelvin 211
Kennedy, D. 145
Kirby, V. 45
Kohlrieser, G. 210
Kolarik, M. 26
Kritikos, A. 40

Lemma, A. 33
Lennon, J. 63
lesbian, gay and bisexual (LGB) people 135, 137, 145, 147
Lester, E. P. 26, 180, 219
Loewald, Hans 171–172
linguistic identity 90
Little, R. 57, 198
Lorde, A. 125
Lotterman, J. H. 46
low care/low dare model 212
Lucy 201–202
Lukac-Greenwood, Jasenka 7–8

McCartney, P. 63
McGrath, G. 203, 209–210
McIlwain, D. 51
McNish, H. 56
Mahler, Margaret 197
male privilege 82–83
male sexual desire 26
Mann, D. 39, 45, 48, 56, 69, 70, 73, 89, 110, 139, 179
Maquet, J. 100
Maroda, K. J. 212
Marshall, A. 5
Martin, C. 56
masculinity 171
maternal transference 28–29, 31
Melly, G. 59
mentalisation 31, 90
Michelle (client, case study) 62–63
Milton, M. 5
mind-body dimension 44
mirroring 90
Mitchell, S. A. 129, 171
Mollon, P. 90, 91

Nichols, M. P. 80
non-genital *versus* genital erotic 41
non-maleficence 68
non-transferential genital relationship 44–49; client towards therapist 45–47; clinical vignette 46; management 46; non-verbal communication 45; sexual attraction 44; sexual feelings 46–47; therapist towards client 47–49;

Index 225

transferential elements 45; verbal communication 45
non-transferential *versus* non-genital erotic relationship 41–44
non-transferential *versus* transferential relationship 41
normative task, supervision 101, 153
Novak, E. 131
Nuttall, J. 6

Oedipal anxieties 61
Oedipal experiences 62–63
openness 1, 35
Orbach, S. 116, 119, 125, 129
over-compensation 91
over-identification 91

Parlett, M. 135
Penny, J. 25–27
personal therapy 70
1½ person psychology 65
perversion 173
Pippa 23, 25, 28, 29
Pope, K. S. 179
post-modernism 68, 72
post-Oedipal/adult sexuality 29
power *see individual entries*
power dynamics 1, 57–59, 73, 93–95; cultural norms 27; erotic transference 25; ethical containment 200; gender configuration 24; male dominance 25; male sexual desire 26; pre-Oedipal transference 25; psychotherapeutic relationship 24; relational psychotherapy supervision 124–125; sexual attraction 26; sexual desire 25; sexual dynamics 27; training and clinical support 27–28; vulnerability 24
power imbalance 23, 24; sexual transgressions 162
Praglin, L. 130
pre-Oedipal transference 25
Probyn, E. 124
Proctor, B. 99, 101, 102
prostitution 19, 32–33
psychological contact 40–42, 44
psychological fitness 190–191
psychotherapeutic engagement 39

quantum theories 58

Rank, Otto 197
rationalisations 182
'real' love 69

reciprocal sexual attraction 22, 28
red flags 189, 190, 198, 203, 204, 218–219
reflective process 111–112
relational psychotherapy supervision 1–2, 168; co-transferential components 127–129; cultural prohibitions 123; embodied countertransference 125–127; The Hug 115–121; intersubjectivity 154; Liminal space 130; power 124–125; reflections 121–122; transgressive edge 131
relational supervision 152–154, 157
Renn, P. 71
restorative task, supervision 100, 153
Richards, C. 170
van Rijn, Biljana 6–7
Rodgers, N. 4
Rogerian concept 40
Rogers, N. M. 56
role confusion 1
Rosie (client, case study) 206–207
Russ, H. 25

Sacks, O. 115
Samuels, A. 108
Sarah 23, 29
Sarnat, J. E. 111
Schaverien, J. 25, 108, 109
Scottish Trans Alliance 81
Script Matrix 64
self-assessment 52
self-deception 185, 198
self-differentiation process 73
self-disclosure 5–6, 21, 49, 67, 137, 206
self-esteem 127, 180, 219
self-other dichotomy 163, 174
self-reflection model 1
self-supervision 47
seven-eyed supervisor model 102, 106–107
sexual attraction 1, 26; CBT 2; gender expression 84; gender identity (*see* gender identity); intersubjectivity 21, 68; passive recipient 19; power dynamics 26; reciprocal 22, 93; supervision (*see* supervision); transferential *versus* real phenomenon 4–6
sexual desire 19, 28, 55–57, 91, 167; adult 56; ethical containment 196; male 94; power dynamics 25; reciprocal 93
sexual diversity 139

sexual orientation 1; co-transference 134–135; erotic transference 149; gender 139; Gestalt theory 135; heteronormative structure 146; heterosexual 136; homophobia endures 139; homosexuality 138–139, 142, 145; identity 144–145; LGB people 135, 137, 145, 147; power imbalance 135; *The Psychotherapist* 138; self-disclosures 137; shame 148; societal changes 137; supervisor responsibilities and receptivity 140–144; transferential feelings 148
sexual responsiveness, lack of 22
sexual transgressions: abuse and exploitation 188; *ad hoc* process 163; awareness development 187; boundary violations 179–180, 192–193; client's sexual boundaries 165–166; clinical supervision 182; collaboration 187; containment 187; counselling 180–181; crossing the boundaries 185–187; 'cultural wars' 161; ethical codes 178, 181; ethical containment 196–199; ethical practice and prevention 216–221; harm prevention 189–190; homeostatic mechanisms 164; homosexuality 164; internalised homophobia 164; mutual attraction 182–185; personal 'permissions' 162; personal therapy 177; power imbalance 162; psychological fitness 190–191; psychotherapy modality 162; psychotherapy services 180–181; self-other dichotomy 163; sexual attraction feelings 178; sexual boundary violations 162, 178; shame 182, 184; supervision 177; 'taboos' 162
Shadbolt, C. 131, 153–155
shame 79–80, 90–91; ethical containment 202; sexual orientation 148; sexual transgressions 182, 184
Shaw, D. 127
Shohet, R. 102, 153
Sills, C. 40, 42, 44, 71, 205
Simkin, S. 26–27
Smith-Pickard, P. 5, 29–31, 44, 47
Smith, S. B. 217–219
social media 63
socio-cultural discourses 30

Steinberg, A. 180
Stern, D. B. 164
Stern, D. N. 200
Stolorow, R. D. 164
stress 64
supervision 71–73, 95; counter-transference 107; embodiment 155–156; erotic and sexual dynamics 108; formative 100–101, 153; gender identity 87–88; humility and willingness 157; material psychotherapists 155; normative 101, 153; personal psychotherapy 152; pre-cognitive self-object experiences 110; Proctor's theory 153; reflection 106–107; relational supervision practice 154; relationship dynamics 111–112; restorative 100, 153; seven-eyed model 102; sexual identity 157; socio-political context 156; strategies 157–158; supervisee development 99; supportive relationship 99, 109; training and practice teaching 153; transgressive feelings 101; *see also* relational psychotherapy supervision
supervisory relationship *see* sexual orientation
supportive supervisory relationship 86, 109
Swartz, J. 130

Target, M. 31
therapists qualities 31
therapist's therapy 30
Timothy (client, case study) 171–174
Transactional Analysis theory 219
trans clients 81, 83–84, 91
transference-countertransference interactions 3
transference love 69
transferential and genital erotic relationship: depletion 52; overt boundary violations 51; self-reflective practice 52; 'slippery slope' concept 52; stress 52; supervisory engagement 51–52; vicarious boundary violations 50–51
transferential and non-genital erotic relationship 49–50
transgressive edge 120; relational psychotherapy supervision 131
The Transsexual Phenomenon 77

trans therapists 81–82, 84, 91
two-person psychology 55, 57

United Kingdom Council for Psychotherapy (UKCP) 79, 144, 165

Vetter, V. A. 179
vulnerability 84, 181; gender identity 76, 80–81

Wachtel, P.L 168
Walker, M. 169, 170
Wallin, D. 58
White, J. 27, 34
Winnicott, D. 130
work-life balance 189–190
Worrell, M. 3, 47

Yontef, G. 150